Becoming a Choral Music Teac~~her~~

Becoming a Choral Music Teacher: A Field Experience Workbook, Second Edition is a choral methods textbook that prepares students in Music Education to become middle school and high school choral music teachers. It emphasizes important musical skills, vocal pedagogy, and repertoire suitable for secondary school choirs in order to provide future teachers with the critical experiences to be effective. Focusing equally on rehearsal strategies, auditions, and classroom management, the book is also a "workbook" that requires the students' active learning through participation in fieldwork.

Students learn in a sequential and practical manner, beginning with the study of the middle school voice and progressing to the high school voice, through practice of theory with adolescents, followed by class reflection on common problems and solutions, and then continued practice.

NEW to this Edition

- Updated references to NAfME, and new national and state standards and licensing rules
- More on the needs of Special Learners in the choral classroom
- Latest resources on classroom management theories and practice
- Expanded vocal warm-ups that incorporate body movement and aural skills training
- More on gender issues (including LGBT awareness), sociological impact and meanings of choral singing, and emerging knowledge of multicultural choral music

Becoming a Choral Music Teacher: A Field Experience Workbook, Second Edition fully integrates the choral field experience for hands-on learning and reflection and allows the student to observe and teach the book's principles.

Patrice Madura Ward-Steinman is Professor of Music Education at the Indiana University Jacobs School of Music. She has directed elementary school through university level choirs and currently teaches Choral Methods, Choral Literature, and Vocal Jazz.

Becoming a Choral Music Teacher

A Field Experience Workbook

Second Edition

Patrice Madura Ward-Steinman

Routledge
Taylor & Francis Group

NEW YORK AND LONDON

Second edition published 2018
by Routledge
711 Third Avenue, New York, NY 10017

and by Routledge
2 Park Square, Milton Park, Abingdon, Oxon, OX14 4RN

Routledge is an imprint of the Taylor & Francis Group, an informa business

© 2018 Taylor & Francis

First edition published by Routledge 2009

Library of Congress Cataloging-in-Publication Data
Names: Madura Ward-Steinman, Patrice, author.
Title: Becoming a choral music teacher : a field experience workbook /
Patrice Madura Ward-Steinman.
Description: 2. | New York, NY : Routledge, 2018. | Includes bibliographical references and index.
Identifiers: LCCN 2017029106| ISBN 9781138052994 (hardback) |
ISBN 9781138053007 (pbk.) | ISBN 9781315167411 (ebook)
Subjects: LCSH: Choral singing—Instruction and study.
Classification: LCC MT930 .M33 2018 | DDC 782.5071—dc23
LC record available at https://lccn.loc.gov/2017029106

ISBN: 978-1-138-05299-4 (hbk)
ISBN: 978-1-138-05300-7 (pbk)
ISBN: 978-1-315-16741-1 (ebk)

Typeset in AdobeCaslon
by Keystroke, Neville Lodge, Tettenhall, Wolverhampton

In memory of David, my beloved husband

Contents Summary

Contents

Illustrations

MUSICAL EXAMPLES

Preface to the Second Edition

The world has changed, and so have I, since the first edition of *Becoming a Choral Music Teacher* was published. This second edition reflects these changes, and is more than half new. While the essence of and philosophy behind the first edition have remained intact, I have re-written and updated the entire book. Having taught choral methods from this textbook every year since it was first published in 2009, I became well aware of wordings I needed to clarify, and assignments I wanted to revise. But, most significantly, entirely new topics have been added based on the recommendations of colleagues and reviewers, which include:

- diversity issues in choir, such as gender identity, social identity, and culturally responsive teaching
- LGBTQ implications for choir
- technology for the choir
- National Core Arts Standards
- the contemporary a cappella rage
- expanded information on show choirs, musical theater, madrigal dinners, gospel choirs, and multicultural choral ensembles
- expanded information on improvising, composing, and sight-reading in choir

- performance anxiety concerns
- first year teacher concerns.

I am excited to share this second edition with you! I believe it is a unique, timely, and comprehensive book for preparing future choral music teachers. The following preface to the first edition remains perfectly relevant to the essence and philosophy of this book.

Preface to the First Edition

Frank: "The most indispensable element of this class was field experience. At first, I saw this component as an unnecessary burden. However, I never imagined the professional opportunities that would develop as a result."

Kayla: "I did not realize that in order to gain the respect and attention of the students, I needed to *command* their respect and attention. This aspect of teaching has a lot to do with conductor magnitude, moving around the room, making eye contact, speaking loudly, and giving instructions in '7 words or less.' It really interested me that I could learn so much from just the act of doing."

Whitaker: "Working with the same class for many weeks has allowed me to see the overall progression of a middle school choir class. At the beginning of my observations, the students were just learning the pieces, and by the end they were performing them all the way through. I had never before been with a specific group long enough to see the complete progression."

Rebecca: "Working with the middle school and high school choirs taught me so much about my capabilities as a teacher and future choral director. And in our class I learned so much from others speaking about their experiences in the field. I was highly interested in rehearsal tactics and different teacher models—observing the two different choral directors was in itself a great experience."

Michael: "After taking choral methods and spending almost 50 hours observing and teaching at the middle school and high school, the thing that I feel is most important is having the teaching material and music prepared and memorized. Having the score memorized gave me the flexibility to get up from the piano, walk around and listen to the students sing and pinpoint trouble areas. Having the material for a lesson or score memorized also gave me a strong sense of confidence when teaching and I was able to provide a better teaching experience."

These are the responses from the undergraduate choral music education majors who tested this book in its draft form. I am pleased that what they found most beneficial about the course book were those things that I had thought about for 18 years and were the foundation for this book. Having taught choral methods more than a dozen times with several fine textbooks over the years, and having conducted choirs of all kinds from elementary school through college, I had a clear idea of what I wanted to do differently in this book. My goals were to write a book that:

- gives students the opportunity to explore course content immediately through engaging workbook assignments;
- fully integrates the choral field experience by taking each chapter's content into a secondary choral classroom for hands-on learning and reflection;
- starts with middle school and moves to high school choral teaching to make logical the evolution of the adolescent voice and person;
- immerses each student in extended field experiences with just one or two middle schools and later one or two high schools. These extended placements make it possible for the singers, choral methods students, and public school teachers to develop knowledgeable, trusting, and mentoring relationships, unlike the individual observations and teaching stints that rarely resemble the actual teaching experience;
- allows the student to spend more time observing and teaching the book's principles than reading lengthy and detailed textbook theories;

- impresses upon the choral methods student the importance of strong score preparation, piano and conducting skills; and
- presents comprehensive research findings on effective ways to teach choral music.

These characteristics make this book distinctly different from all of the other secondary choral methods texts, yet, in addition, it covers the essentials of vocal development, auditions, literature, rehearsal planning, classroom management, specialized ensembles, and practical matters. Although teachers may choose to supplement this book with other texts, it can certainly stand alone as the textbook for a choral methods course for undergraduates.

This book is very accessible to the choral methods student, and each chapter includes numerous "brainteaser" assignments from which the instructor may choose. I hope you enjoy and value this new approach to "Becoming a Choral Music Teacher."

To the Instructor

Teaching a student to become a choral music teacher is no easy task, as you know. The complexities of the required skills and knowledge create a challenge for the choral methods instructor. When teaching this course on a yearly basis, I often felt frustrated trying to balance the wealth of knowledge presented in textbooks with applications of that knowledge into tangible skill. Because there is rarely time for both, I chose in this workbook, to 1) simplify the content to the essential points that often get lost in too much narrative, 2) then ask the student to actively explore each chapter's topics through workbook exercises, and 3) finally explore each topic in a real secondary choral rehearsal. These secondary field experiences enable the student to apply the book content in many ways ranging from structured observations and teacher interviews to actual teaching when the choral teacher is amenable. The quotations at the beginning of this section provide evidence of the impact of this approach.

The choral methods instructor will find the book easy to use, with multiple "brainteaser" assignments from which to choose, and extensive resources for further reading. Its approach is realistic and practical, yet supported by the best and most current research in our field. Clear presentations of adolescent vocal ranges, developmental warm-ups, the International Phonetic Alphabet, rehearsal planning and assessment, and repertoire of multiple styles and performance practices are highlighted. Piano and conducting skills are emphasized throughout the book, with sample scores for practice provided.

The organization of field experiences should not be a deterrent to the instructor. Although public school settings are most beneficial, the choral methods student can gain equally valuable experience in private school choral rehearsals, as well as with community groups. Some choral teachers are even willing to mentor more than one undergraduate student. By involving and investing the community of choral teachers in the development of our future choral directors, good will and support for each other's work are enhanced.

To the Student

As you re-read the quotations from my undergraduate choral methods students at the beginning of this section, you will see that this book, *Becoming a Choral Music Teacher*, will actively involve you in the essentials of choral music teaching. It provides numerous projects ("brain-teasers") that you will explore in real choral classrooms with live middle school and high school students. You will explore each topic (adolescent ranges, warm-ups, diction, rehearsal strategies, assessment, repertoire, diverse ensembles, programming concerts, and more) through experience. There is no substitute for experience in learning to become a choral music teacher. I hope you enjoy the learning experiences that I have crafted for you. I have confidence that the knowledge and skills emphasized in this book will serve you well. Enjoy!

Acknowledgments

First and foremost, thanks are due to all of my choral methods students at the Indiana University Jacobs School of Music, past and present, whose nature it is to intelligently question, rather than indiscriminately accept, the words of their professor. While exploring each chapter in conjunction with their field experiences, they often found that "theory" did not match their day to day experiences with secondary choral singers, and provided wonderful insights and suggestions for making this textbook more valuable for future choral teachers. There are too many to name from my 15 years of teaching at IU, but they know who they are!

I am enormously grateful to the following choral music teachers in and near Bloomington, Indiana, who have generously allowed my choral methods students to spend countless hours in their choral classrooms, and selflessly mentored them in the field experience process: Kathy Gorr, Joel Brainard, Sarah Miller, Gwen Witten, Rachel Perkins, Kyle Hanson, and Dan Andersen.

Special thanks are due to the following expert choral music teachers who have visited my choral methods classes to share their specialized knowledge: Patricia Wiehe, Scott Buchanan, Ly Wilder, Brad Gardner, Kyle Barker, and Michael Raunick; to my gospel music informants Raymond Wise and Jeffrey Murdock; and to my own esteemed choral music professor Dr. Jan Harrington.

I would not have the essential practical knowledge upon which to base this book without my own experiences directing middle school, high school, and college choirs. I remember every one of those choirs, and I am grateful for all the singers with whom I have had the opportunity to make music.

My sincerest thanks also go out to the Routledge/Taylor and Francis Group, especially to Constance Ditzel, Senior Editor, Music, whose invitation, steady persistence, and exquisite work are the reasons my dream became a published reality; to her Senior Editorial Assistant, Peter Sheehy; and to the Production Editor, Katie Hemmings. Thanks also go to Kelly-Jane Winter, Fintan Power, Hannah Close, Maggie Lindsey-Jones, Sarah Lindsey-Jones, and Tracey Preece for their copyediting, typesetting, and proofreading. I am also indebted to the anonymous reviewers for their brilliant critiques and suggestions which have made this textbook immeasurably better. Special thanks also go to Nicholas Nickerson for his expert help with editing and creating notation files, and to Nathan Furr for his photography.

And, finally, I am deeply grateful for my family and friends who encouraged me throughout the lengthy writing process, and inspired by the memory of my beloved husband, David Ward-Steinman, who would be (and maybe still is!) cheering me on to the finish, ready to celebrate this achievement.

Patrice Madura Ward-Steinman, D.M.E.
Professor of Music
Jacobs School of Music
Indiana University, Bloomington
May 15, 2017

1

THE CHOIR TEACHER AS COMPREHENSIVE MUSICIAN

Choral music teaching is an honorable profession. While it is time-consuming and work-intensive, there are few careers more rewarding than making music with young people. You probably had a choral music teacher who inspired you to love choral music, to become a better musician, and to consider a career in music. Take time right now to reflect on the qualities of your most inspiring choral teacher, and list them here:

_____

_____

_____

_____

You may have listed some of the following characteristics: passionate, caring, motivating, humorous, organized, and dedicated. As you continue to think about the qualities of effective choral music teachers, consider other musical and teaching skills, and decide how important they are to you.

Essential *musical* characteristics might include knowledge of how the voice develops in middle school and high school singers, excellent piano skills, clear conducting skills, ability to hear errors in individual vocal parts when the whole choir is singing, knowledge of choral music repertory that is effective for secondary school students, how to achieve a beautiful choral tone, arranging skills, and knowledge of music theory and history.

Essential *teaching* characteristics might include the ability to engage and motivate students, classroom management skills, organizational skills, attention to detail, knowledge of short-term and long-term planning, the ability to expertly prepare a choir for contests, and a genuine enthusiasm for helping all students succeed.

The most essential *personal* characteristic is the desire to be a choral music teacher. Someone who loves choral music and the idea of developing that love and appreciation in young people has the right motivation to teach secondary choral music. It will require a commitment of time and hard work, but will be a labor of love. Other personal characteristics include kindness, high energy, a sense of humor, and "people skills" (the ability to work with students, parents, teachers, and staff.)

Take time right now to reflect on the musical, teaching and personal skills identified above (and feel free to add more) that you already possess, as well as those that will need focused attention as you continue to work toward your professional goals. List your strengths and weaknesses.

Strengths   **Weaknesses**

_____   _____

_____   _____

_____   _____

_____   _____

Take another moment to reflect on your most memorable choral experiences and consider what made them so. Think back on those choral performances that were peak experiences for you. What were those choral compositions, and what made them so special? Name the piece(s) that made you feel that way.

_____

_____

_____

_____

Can you put your finger on *why* you felt that wonderful, profound feeling? Was it the occasion, the ensemble, the conductor, the location, the musical composition, or a combination of two or more of those factors? Certainly, music has the power to move humans in extraordinary ways, and some pieces are more powerful than others in providing moving and beautiful experiences that make a difference in our lives. Once we have had such an aesthetic experience through music, we spend our lives seeking those experiences for ourselves and for our students. We can do that best by preparing ourselves as outstanding musicians, educators, and human beings so that we can well execute and express the choral music of masterful composers. Choral music teaching demands a commitment to excellence in order to give students important and rich musical experiences.

THE VOICE TEACHER

As a secondary school choral director, you will be the only voice teacher that the majority of your students will ever have. Therefore, you need to be able to teach them to use their voices in healthy and beautiful ways through vocal warm-ups, appropriately sequenced repertory, awareness of vocal misuse, vocal modeling, and clear explanations. You are encouraged to enroll in a vocal pedagogy course, particularly if it focuses on the adolescent voice. Even if you have taken voice lessons, this does not ensure that you know how to *teach* voice. If your degree does not require or offer such a course, this text will provide multiple ideas and resources to significantly boost your knowledge and skill in this area.

THE ERROR DETECTOR

Although every music major practices error detection in music theory, ear-training, and conducting courses, it is often difficult for the choral methods student to identify specific wrong notes in a choral sound when simultaneously involved in the multi-tasks of conducting, playing the piano, and reading the score. This is where the conductor's preparation is key. With a fully analyzed score and an accurate aural model, the choral teacher has set the stage for hearing and identifying sung errors. One way to practice this aural skill is to sing chorales and other homophonic pieces vertically, from the bottom to top of each chord, focusing especially on the roots and inner parts (Napoles et al., 2016).

THE SIGHT-SINGER

Good sight-reading skills assist the choral teacher in learning scores quickly, but knowledge of the pedagogy of sight-singing is also necessary. Consider how satisfying your choral rehearsals will be as your students become good sight-readers, enabling their music learning to come quickly. No one likes to "pound notes." A sequential approach to teaching sight-singing in the choral rehearsal will be presented in this textbook.

THE MEMORIZER

What are the benefits of memorizing the choral score? In short, it means that the music has been internalized. The more the teacher's and students' eyes are out of the music, the more they can experience and express the music.

THE ARRANGER/COMPOSER/IMPROVISER

The choral music teacher often needs to re-arrange a choral score for the particular voices in the ensemble, arrange the school's theme song for choral voices, or assist students in the creative skills of composition and improvisation. Coursework should have prepared the music education major with these skills, but, if not, they will find that they have enough musical knowledge and resources to explore arranging, composing and improvising on their own or through conference sessions, summer workshops or graduate courses.

THE SCHOLAR

Those music history and theory courses really do matter when the time comes to prepare a choral score for teaching. It is the teacher's responsibility to know the history and theory of every piece in order to effectively teach it. Score analysis also involves searching for information about the piece, the composer, the text, the performance practice, the language, and listening to various recordings. Thorough understanding of the music score will provide rich and meaningful musical experiences for the conductor and the students.

THE MANAGER

A choral music teacher needs to be organized. There are many details that the choral teacher must handle, or delegate to others when possible, for a successful program. These include the choral music curriculum, the budget, the choral library, concert programming, concert dates, concert dress, tours, festivals, parent relations, classroom management, grading, fundraising, and so much more. Many new teachers feel unprepared to control these non-musical demands of their jobs, so numerous organizational procedures are presented in this book to alleviate those concerns.

THE LEADER

Leaders influence others. They improve the lives of others through "vision, trust, teaching, persuasion and character" (Wis, 2007, p. xvii). Your vision is your unique view of how you will make your singers' lives better; your trustworthiness will make your singers feel safe in your choir; your persuasiveness will help singers reach levels of achievement they didn't know they were capable of; and your character will inspire you to use your core values to permeate all that you do and provide you with your life's mission. To learn to develop these leadership qualities in yourself, study *The Conductor as Leader* by Ramona M. Wis.

THE TEACHER

While strong musical skills are a prerequisite to achieving success as a choral teacher, it is the knowledge of effective rehearsal strategies and repertory choices that complete the picture. How does one learn to be a good teacher? Is someone "born" a natural teacher, or can it be taught? Obviously music education professors believe it can be taught, although there is a natural inclination and desire to teach that is vital. Effective teaching strategies fill this textbook.

THE MENTOR

Adolescents participate in choirs not only because they enjoy performing and learning about music, but also for the social aspect—the connection with people. This connection includes the mentorship by the choir teacher. The teacher needs to care not only about music, but also about the students. The choral experience is an emotionally and socially bonding experience, and the choir teacher is the one who provides a safe, structured and healthy environment for adolescents to thrive. Most students will remember their school choral experience forever, so your attitudes toward them, and your enthusiasm for the music, matter!

THE ADVOCATE AND PHILOSOPHER

In some teaching situations you will find yourself comfortably supported by an arts-loving administration, and, if so, keep that job! Other situations are less supportive, and music teachers find themselves in the position of having to lobby and convince those in power that the arts should have a central place in the curriculum. For this reason, it is important that the teacher have a firm belief in the value of choral music education, not only from a personal standpoint (although this will often communicate the most passion) but also on the basis of current research on the value of music study. The National Association for Music Education (NAfME) will continue to publicize new research findings for teachers to use in their advocacy statements for the arts.

THE PIANIST/ACCOMPANIST

Choral conductors who are also strong pianists have a distinct advantage over weaker players because the luxury of having one's own full-time rehearsal accompanist is rare. It is not unusual for vocal music education majors to have beautiful voices but weak piano skills, and they must do everything in their power to rectify this weakness, because the slower they are at the piano, the slower their students will learn. There is only one answer, and that is the discipline of daily piano practice of choral scores (with a metronome), even after the required piano classes and tests (e.g., Piano Proficiency Exam, Upper Divisional Exam) are completed. Any choral score can be used for practice, and you can download them free of charge and legally from the Choral Public Domain Library (www.cpdl.org). A sample of pieces found on CPDL and appropriate for piano practice can be found in Appendix B of this book. However, it is not only the skill to play choral parts that will make your rehearsals run efficiently, but also the ability to accompany vocal warm-ups, complete with modulations to all keys. Your practice should start today.

Warm-Up Skills

The choral director rarely has an accompanist available for all warm-ups, and therefore needs to be able to function at the piano with regard to establishing tonality and key centers. Because warm-ups are regularly transposed up and down chromatically, or by whole tone, the teacher needs to be able to give at least the chord in the new key during the singers' quick breaths between transpositions.

1. Practice playing all major and minor triads, transposing up and down by half and whole step on every fourth beat of the metronome as a starting point. If you are limited by being able to play only one hand at a time, be sure to practice both the right and left hands equally; then move to both hands as soon as possible. Be sure to keep an accurate sense of time with the metronome; if errors in time are made, slow the metronome down to an achievable tempo, and later increase the tempo incrementally.
2. The next step in practice would be to sing the desired warm-up and play the appropriate chord during the breaths between key changes. This should alternate with playing the entire warm-up.

It is important to note, however, that choirs don't need all of the pitches of the warm-ups played all of the time because that practice detracts from their ability to hear themselves, which in turn makes them more dependent on the piano. Once the choir securely knows the warm-up, have the piano only play a chordal accompaniment, or only the transition chord to the new key. The phrase "less is more" often applies to piano accompanying. The pianist is encouraged to play lightly and musically, and particularly on the upright pianos found in many rehearsal rooms which can sound offensively loud due to the strings and soundboard facing the singers.

Score-Reading

The choir director needs to be able to play choral parts at the piano, and therefore this is a skill that needs to be well honed before the student-teaching semester.

1. For 15–30 minutes every day (starting today), practice playing at least two parts of a choral score at the piano; then try singing one line and playing another and then two others, always using a metronome set to a tempo at which you can keep from missing a beat. Slow tempos are perfectly acceptable if the beat is kept

steady, but pausing between beats is not. Keep your eyes on the score, not the keys; cover the keys if you must, because much time is wasted by unnecessarily looking back and forth from the score to the keys. It *is* possible to play the piano without looking at the keys (think Ray Charles, George Shearing and Stevie Wonder!).

2. When that step is achieved (according to an objective source!), repeat it, but play the piano in a vocally expressive way. Shape phrases as a singer would, complete with lifting of the hands at breath marks.

3. When those steps have been achieved, practice three to four parts at the piano, with a steady metronomic tempo. Begin very slowly if necessary, but push yourself to increase the metronome setting incrementally. Remember to play expressively and breathe!

4. Practice all steps above every day with different pieces of choral music.

5. If you are unable to achieve the goal of playing multiple voice parts on the piano, then you must be able to *sing* all vocal parts for all pieces, on solfege or scale degrees, with pitch and rhythmic accuracy. While it may seem preferable for the choristers to hear the pitches modeled by the voice rather than the piano, they also need to hear the way two or more parts sound together. It is also important to know that some school employers choose to hire applicants with piano skills over those without, and have been known to ask applicants to play the piano at the job interview. (Advice: practice!)

Technique

Piano technique exercises train and strengthen the fingers for everything from warm-ups to accompaniments (see Appendix A for scale and arpeggio fingerings). The choral teacher should continue to practice exercises learned in piano lessons, with metronome, including:

1. major and minor scales (two hands, four octaves)
2. major and minor arpeggios (two hands, four octaves), and
3. chord progressions using triads and secondary dominants in major and minor keys (two hands, blocked and broken).

Accompanying

The choir director should be able to play simple accompaniments, but is not necessarily expected to play more elaborate ones unless he or she is a skilled pianist who chooses to conduct from the piano. In most cases, if there are no funds to hire an accompanist, there are piano students available who will enjoy and learn much from the experience of working with a conductor and collaborating with a choir. However, the choral conductor should continue to practice accompaniments for when the need arises.

THE CONDUCTOR

Choral conductors need to have mastered the basic skills of conducting, which include all types of beat patterns, preparatory beats, cut-offs, and fermatas, as well as independence of the left hand, so they can communicate the music to the singers without excessive verbal explanations or distracting gestures. A sequential approach for developing these essential conducting skills is presented below. A Bach chorale is presented at the end of this chapter for practicing these skills.

Beat Patterns

Practice conducting simple songs in various time signatures, such as *Ode to Joy* in 4/4; *America* in 3/4; *Camptown Ladies* in 2/4; *It Came Upon a Midnight Clear* in a slow 6/8; and *When Johnny Comes Marching Home Again* in a quick 6/8. Practice conducting compound meters as well, such as 5/4 in Dave Brubeck's *Take Five*, and *Deck the Halls* in 7/8 by James McKelvy.

Pay close attention to the following points (see Figures 1.1–1.4):

1. confident posture, feet "planted"
2. comfortably low conducting plane
3. clarity of the downbeat
4. bounce each beat on the conducting plane (no dipping below!)
5. left and right positions are truly left and right of the downbeat
6. no left-hand "mirroring" of the beat (lefties should conduct right-handed)
7. use or imagine a baton to find correct palm-down hand position.

Figure 1.1   Proper Conducting Stance, Beat 1

Figure 1.2   Proper Conducting Stance, Beat 2

Figure 1.3   Proper Conducting Stance, Beat 3

Figure 1.4   Proper Conducting Stance, Beat 4

The Left Hand

Use the left hand to cue entrances, shape phrases, show dynamics, turn pages, or reinforce the right hand by emphasizing important musical elements. Practice hand independence by conducting a steady beat in the right hand while the left hand performs other duties, both musical and non-musical (McElheran, 1989). Rather than unnecessary "mirroring" with the left hand, keep it at your side or resting near the front of your body until it is needed.

Figure 1.5   Left Hand Independence

Preparatory Beats

No aspect of conducting technique is more important than a clear preparatory beat. Only one preparatory beat is necessary except in rhythmically difficult entrances or challenging tempo changes. "Multiple preparatory gestures are unnecessary and confusing for ensembles of all ability levels" (Folger, 2012, p. 45).

In your choral methods class, conduct a preparatory beat on all possible beats (for example, as a preparation for beat 1, for beat 2, for beat 3, for beat 4, for beat 5, etc.). Have the class sing a pitch on the desired beat to assess the clarity of your preparatory gesture. Memorize these points:

1. Use only one preparatory beat with no verbal counting.
2. Always inhale (quietly) with the singers on the preparatory beat.
3. Always have eye contact with the singers on the preparatory beat and downbeat.
4. Communicate the desired dynamic, tempo, and expression in your preparatory gesture and facial expression.

Figure 1.6   Preparatory Gesture and Facial Expression

It is also important to practice the preparatory beat to a cut-off, followed by a clean beat and eye contact on the cut-off. This is more effective than the unnecessary movement that goes into curly-cue, finger-tip, or mouth-worded cut-offs (McElheran, 1989).

Off-Beat Cues

A cue or entrance that occurs on an off-beat should not be communicated by subdividing the preparatory beats, despite the temptation to do so. In the case of off-beat cues and entrances, the conductor should give two preparatory beats—the second of which should have a bit more rebound (as in a "hot stove") so that the singers will sing on its off-beat (McElheran, 1989, p. 51). This gesture is sometimes referred to as the "Gesture of Syncopation" (Green and Gibson, 2004, p. 48.) Practice "psychological conducting" (p. 238) with your choral methods class until you can effectively get them to sing on an off-beat without any extra motion besides the right hand's two preparatory beats, the last of which has more bounce. When this is accomplished, experiment with different tempos and dynamic levels. Off-beat entrances occur frequently in music, so opportunities to practice this gesture can be easily found.

Fermatas

The beginning choral conductor often stumbles over fermatas, and needs to gain confidence in executing the three different types of fermatas: no break, short break, long break. The fermata itself is not difficult to conduct; it just requires the conductor to hold the hand (or baton) still as long as desired (McElheran, 1989) or move it slightly while sustaining (Green and Gibson, 2004). It is the end of the fermata that deserves special attention. All three types may be practiced using the Bach chorale (see Musical Example 1.1) at the end of this chapter.

No Break

After holding the fermata at the bottom or bounce level of the beat for the desired length of time, move the hand on to the next beat without a breath. For example, if the fermata falls on beat 2, the conductor should hold the right hand steady on beat 2 for a brief duration, and then move it to beat 3 without a breath. The left hand may be used to indicate no breath (McElheran, 1989).

Semi-Pause and Breathe

The semi-pause fermata is begun identically to the no-break fermata in that it is held still (or slightly moving) at the bounce level of the beat for the desired length of time. Then, however, the conductor must re-beat that beat, as a combined cut-off and preparatory breath to the next beat of entrance. This is the most common type of fermata

(McElheran, 1989), and because the cut-off and preparatory gesture are one and the same, the rhythmic momentum of the musical line continues (Green and Gibson, 2004).

Grand Pause and Start Again

This type of fermata is usually indicated by a caesura (//) and requires a complete cut-off and pause before resuming. Again, the fermata is held at the bottom or bounce level of the beat for as long as desired, followed by a cut-off. Then a preparatory gesture to begin again is given (McElheran, 1989).

Figure 1.7   Conducting from the Piano

Conducting from the Piano

It is not unusual for a secondary school choral teacher to lead the choir from the piano, but this is not ideal from many perspectives: First, the teacher's hands and eyes are occupied with the piano and page turns, and his or her body is partially hidden and limited in movement around the classroom which is not helpful in many middle school and high school behavior environments. Nevertheless, for the teacher who occasionally must or wants to work from the piano, he or she should master the following:

1. Stand while playing the piano and leading the choir.
2. Play the piano with one hand and conduct with the other.
3. Develop preparatory head (and eyebrow) gestures.
4. Keep your eyes on the singers.
5. Be careful not to play so loudly that the singers cannot hear themselves.

BRAINTEASER 1-1: PRACTICING PIANO AND CONDUCTING SKILLS

Practice all the piano and conducting skills described in this chapter, using pieces from your field experience and those found at the end of this chapter and in Appendix B. Prepare to play and conduct at least one middle school and one high school choral piece for your instructor as midterm and final exams, using the Rating Scales for Performance Skills as your practice guide (see Table 1.1).

BRAINTEASER 1-2: SECURING THE FIELD PLACEMENT

Prepare a copy of your semester class and work schedule for your choral methods instructor, so that field experiences at middle schools (for the first half of this semester) and high schools (for the second half of this semester) can be arranged. Know that it is not always possible to find ideal placements, particularly in rural areas where there are few schools, but that there is always much to learn from both good and poor models. Some will request choral methods students with particular skills that the teacher lacks (for example, vocal modeling for high or low voices, or strong piano skills). They are often grateful for your help, and can learn from you as well. Plan to spend approximately two to three hours per week in your field site (depending on your school's field experience requirements), observing at first, but getting actively involved as soon as possible.

Know all of your university's and field site's requirements well in advance of your first field experience. These may include school security issues such as having a government-issued criminal background check or tuberculosis test results on file, as well as behavior guidelines including dress code and cooperating teacher expectations.

Table 1.1 Rating Scales for Midterm and Final Performance Skills

CONDUCTING

CONDUCTOR SKILLS AND STRATEGIES	4.5 = DISTINGUISHED	4 = VERY GOOD	3 = MODERATELY GOOD	2 = NEEDS IMPROVEMENT	1= UNACCEPTABLE
Preparedness					
Beat Patterns					
Left Hand					
Prep. Beats					
Cues					
Cut-Offs					
Fermatas					
Knows Score					
Hears Errors					
Eye Contact					
Modeling					
Speaking					
Expressiveness					
Confidence					
Pacing					
Makes Progress					

PLAYING AND SINGING

	4.5 = DISTINGUISHED	4 = VERY GOOD	3 = MODERATELY GOOD	2 = NEEDS IMPROVEMENT	1= UNACCEPTABLE
Plays 2 parts					
Plays 3 parts					
Plays 4 parts					
Plays 1 part, sings another					
Sings all parts					
Plays M/m chromatic chords					
Plays M/m scales and arpeggios					

Performance Grade:

BRAINTEASER 1-3: ORGANIZING COURSE MATERIALS

Prepare a Choral Resource Notebook. Purchase a three-ring binder, with tabs for organizing topics by textbook chapter titles. Keep all assignments, plus personal reflective writings, in your notebook. Include manuscript paper, a pencil, and any devices needed for video-recording storage.

BRAINTEASER 1-4: WRITING A PHILOSOPHY OF CHORAL MUSIC EDUCATION

Write a detailed summary of all of your experiences in choral music; then express your philosophy of choral music education. Submit to your instructor. Re-read your philosophy statement at the conclusion of this course, and revise it to include your new knowledge, skills, and dispositions.

BRAINTEASER 1-5: ORGANIZING AN ACTION PLAN

In your choral methods class, discuss and list the essential skills and knowledge of an extraordinary choral music teacher. Then consider areas of weakness for the majority of students in your class, and find ways to remedy those areas. Possible remedies follow. Your instructor may decide to spend more time on certain topics than originally planned, such as choral score reading at the piano or vocal pedagogy. Or classmates may commit to practicing or studying together for extra motivation. If your particular strengths and weaknesses are different from most others in the class, decide how you will work to improve them. For example, if your piano skills are not strong, decide if additional private study is in order, or if you should schedule 30 minutes of extra practice per day. Or if you have had very little experience conducting choirs, start now to look for ways to assist the local children's choir or a church choir.

Then, outline an action plan for strengthening your weaker areas, beginning today. Ask your choral methods instructor or other choral directors for advice because they have had to do similar preparations for a choral career. Submit your action plan. Include ways that you will assess your progress, such as keeping a practice record book or scheduling peer observations; add a timeline or schedule for practice and assessments. Expand the following form as necessary. Be specific, realistic, and committed.

A Plan for Action!

Area of Study	Action Plan	Timeline	Assessment

With this action plan in place, you can be confident that you will grow in the musical skills necessary to succeed as a choral music teacher. You will have multiple opportunities to practice and demonstrate these skills throughout this course of study.

Congratulations on pursuing an important profession. May you enjoy the challenges and reap the rewards, whether you are facing your very first class of 60 rowdy middle school "singers" or your final dress rehearsal with your finest high school choir ever! Sit up straight, with a confident conductor's posture, close your eyes, and imagine your ideal choir and their sound.

References

Folger, William M. (October, 2012). The Seven Deadly Sins of Choral Conducting. *Choral Journal*, 53(3), 42–49.

Green, Elizabeth A.H. and Gibson, Mark (2004). *The Modern Conductor*, 7th ed. Upper Saddle River, NJ: Pearson/Prentice Hall.

McElheran, Brock (1989). *Conducting Technique: For Beginners and Professionals*, rev. ed. New York: Oxford University Press.

Napoles, J., Babb, S.L., Bowers, J., Hankle, S., and Zrust, A. (2016). The Effect of Piano Playing on Preservice Teachers' Ability to Detect Errors in a Choral Score. *Journal of Music Teacher Education*, 26(2), 39–49, jmte.sagepub.com, DOI: 10.1177/1057083716639724.

Wis, Ramona M. (2007). *The Conductor as Leader: Principles of Leadership Applied to Life on the Podium*. Chicago, IL: GIA.

Musical Example 1.1   *Nun laßt uns Gott, dem Herren* by J.S. Bach

Nun laßt uns Gott, dem Herren

Aus der Kantate BWV194   Johann Sebastian Bach (1685 - 1750)

2

MIDDLE SCHOOL SINGERS: MANAGING ADOLESCENT VOICES AND BEHAVIOR

One of the biggest challenges of choral music teaching is working with middle school students. Between grades four and nine, students change from children to adolescents, and all at different rates. It is essential to study and understand these changes in order to have a rehearsal and an ensemble that foster positive musical growth.

Puberty refers to the rapid increase in both growth hormones and sex hormones, and this period is accompanied by the physical, psychosocial, emotional, and cognitive changes of early adolescence, usually earlier in girls than in boys (Collins, 1999). A classroom full of hormonally changing students may appear unmanageable and chaotic, and while there may be some truth to the often-heard statement that "some people are born middle school teachers," it is a weak excuse. As committed educators, we owe it to our students to understand them and structure our teaching to maximize the potential of their adolescent energy. And we owe it to ourselves to enter that classroom of adolescents armed with knowledge and understanding, rather than fear of the unknown. Nevertheless, there is no substitute for experience, and so very soon you will be making your own observations of middle school choirs in preparation for your success in years to come.

UNDERSTANDING THE VOICE CHANGE

Consider this scenario: A rehearsal room full of middle school students is assembled and you are excited to begin teaching what you have spent your lifetime learning to master—the music! You decide to ask the newly assembled choir to sing in unison a simple tune that they probably know, *Row, Row, Row Your Boat*. You give them a starting pitch in the key of F major, along with your well-trained conducting preparatory beat, and you hear a vocal sound that disturbs your musically trained ears. You think that perhaps a different key will help them. You try again in the key of C and the results are no better. You think, "How could this be happening when the music is so simple? Something is terribly wrong! I must have chosen the wrong profession!"

The scenario above is not unrealistic. In fact, most music teachers have been there and done that at some point, and some have even changed professions! But do not fear—acquiring knowledge of the adolescent voice through study and practice will prepare you to achieve success with this age group. In the scenario above, the persistent teacher found that unison singing of a song with an octave range was not the way to produce a successful middle school choral sound, due to the varying and often limited ranges of the boys' changing voices.

There are many theories, labels, textbooks, courses, and opinions on the boys' changing voice (see Phillips, 1992). Some of the most important scholars on the topic (and their associated labels for the changing voice) are Duncan McKenzie (the "alto-tenor"), Irvin Cooper (the "cambiata"), Frederick Swanson (the "adolescent bass"), John Cooksey (the "eclectic theory"), Anthony Barresi (the "adolescent voice"), Henry Leck (the "high road"), Sally Herman (the "voice pivoting approach"), Lynn Gackle and Bridget Sweet (the girls' changing voice), and Kenneth Phillips, author of *Teaching Kids to Sing* (1992).

Despite the many theories of the adolescent changing voice, the bottom line is that puberty causes the lengthening, widening, and thickening of the larynx ("voice box") and vocal folds ("vocal cords") along with the growth spurt of the rest of the maturing body. Although both girls and boys have treble ranges of more than a tenth above middle C in the elementary school years, both boys' and girls' vocal ranges begin to lower in the middle school years, and sometimes as early as the fourth grade. Voices are typically unstable from three months to a year, with the peak of voice change considered to be the eighth grade (Fisher, 2014; Sataloff, 2000.) The growth of the larynx from front to back as evidenced by the "Adam's apple," combined with the lengthening and thickening of the vocal folds, causes male voices to drop approximately an octave in pitch at the peak of the change. The female larynx grows in both height and width, and the voice extends both lower and higher by approximately three steps. These sudden growth spurts weaken the laryngeal muscles, allowing excess air into the voice, often resulting in a breathy sound (Sweet, 2016b). Vocal development nears maturity by age 16, making high school choirs much more stable than middle school choirs (Sataloff and Spiegel, 1989).

While sixth grade choirs are made up of mostly unchanged voices, the challenge with the changing voice usually occurs in a classroom of seventh and eighth graders. No two voices seem to change at the same rate or at the same age, although research suggests that boys progress from one predictable stage of lowered voice change to another (Killian, 1999; Thurman, 2012). Most middle school choir teachers find that their singers are a unique group each school year. Some voices may change from soprano to baritone over summer vacation, while others may change little by little throughout the school year (Sataloff and Spiegel, 1989). Some adolescents may experience embarrassing "cracks" when they speak or sing, while others barely notice the gradually changing voice. A demonstration by the American Boy Choir while visiting Indiana University revealed that some boys completely lose their ability to sing except for a few high and low pitches, while others lose their high and low pitches and have only a middle range, and still others continue to sing with ease throughout the change. Some can sing in the alto range at the beginning of the semester, but by the holiday concert can barely sing at all, and by the spring concert can sing a few baritone notes (Leck, 2001). This creates a challenge for the choral teacher when trying to select singable repertoire and when working to balance and teach voice parts in preparation for concerts.

Another challenge for choral directors is understanding LGBTQ vocal concerns, particularly the manipulation of hormones in trans-gender students who are coming out at younger and younger ages (as cited in Palkki, 2016). Middle school transgender male-to-female (M2F) students may take puberty-blocking hormones to keep their vocal ranges high, and transgender F2M students may take testosterone to lower the vocal range. The resulting vocal changes may occur at different ages than those of cisgender (gender-conforming) students, depending on when the hormone treatments begin, and the characteristics and stages of the voice change may differ as well (Ramseyer Miller, 2016). It is recommended that teachers keep students singing in their current vocal range, even if they request the section with which they gender-identify. Adaptations with regard to seating assignment and concert dress can be made to ease their dysphoria, but helping students sing in their healthy vocal range is a choir teacher's responsibility.

An additional challenge is the fear of embarrassment and/or discouragement many adolescents feel when they no longer can sing as easily as they did in the fifth grade, or the avoidance of middle school choir altogether because of the difficulties of their voice change (Sweet, 2015). How do we keep our middle school choirs balanced with high and low voices when this happens, and more importantly how do we keep students interested in high school and lifelong choir singing if they become disenchanted with it during the critical middle school years?

MANAGING THE VOICE CHANGE

Fortunately, there are many practical solutions to these problems. The old-fashioned view that boys should not sing during the voice change is no longer a valid one due to the evolution of knowledge regarding the benefits of training the voice during puberty (Cooksey, 1977). Duncan McKenzie, Frederick Swanson, and Irvin Cooper were pioneers in the development of the "new" view beginning in the middle of the 20th century.

First:

- It is important to listen to the students' voices, individually or in small groups, approximately every six weeks to note any changes in range, quality, and ease of production.
- Octave displacement may be used to limit a song's range or intervals.
- The teacher may have to put arranging skills to work to create parts that the students can sing with ease, even if it is a limited-note vocal ostinato at times.
- The teacher may need to transpose repertoire into keys that work for their students.
- Students should be encouraged to "pivot" to another vocal line when it fits their range best (Dilworth, 2012).

While it may not be convenient to listen to individuals frequently, or to re-arrange compositions and voice parts, especially as the concert date approaches, it is important to keep the students singing comfortably and contributing to the choir's sound.

Second, it may be beneficial to have separate choirs for high and low voices, so that singers can experience their vocal change in the privacy of others who are and will experience the phenomenon, and without the pressure of the possibility of embarrassment. The separate range choirs work best if there are enough treble and changing/changed voices to make a substantial choral sound. Another solution is to bring the two separate choirs (or "sectionals") together for mixed choir repertoire. In order to avoid the assumption of gender-biased groups, they may be called the "Soprano-Alto" and "Tenor-Bass" choirs, or "Treble Chorus" and "Bass-Clef Chorus" (Swanson, 1973), or a clever foreign language translation for high and low voices.

There are also opportunities for students to audition for all-state male/low voice and female/treble choirs. The impact of singing with 100 or more others of the same age and gender with a masterful conductor will leave an indelible impression of the power of singing together. See, for example, the inspiring video *Body, Mind, Spirit, Voice* with Anton Armstrong and André Thomas rehearsing the American Boychoir and the Newark Boys Chorus. Role models like these are vital to middle school singers. It is also important to provide model recordings of diverse choral ensembles (Berman, 2017) such as the Manhattan Girls Chorus, Chanticleer, Vox Femina, Take Six, Anonymous Four, and the San Francisco Gay Men's Chorus.

Lastly, another successful approach is to keep the students singing in their high range throughout the voice change, rather than to pigeon-hole them into a single voice part or label. In the Indianapolis Children's Choir, boys continue to use their high voice (head voice) throughout the voice change in order to keep it. Many boys choose to continue to sing soprano or alto during the voice change, and even after their voice settles into the tenor or baritone range. Warm-ups and vocalises that start in the head voice and move downward, including vocal sighs, are helpful in making the transition throughout the range. Henry Leck's video *The Boy's Changing Voice: Take the High Road* (2001) provides an excellent demonstration for teachers of middle school choirs. Specific warm-ups for the changing voice are presented in the next chapter.

A visual explanation of why unison singing may be challenging for a middle school choir with changing and changed voices is presented in Musical Example 2.1, with half notes indicating the range of each voice part, and quarter notes indicating the tessitura.

Musical Example 2.1   Middle School Vocal Ranges and Tessituras (Phillips, 1992)

Considering only the unchanged (treble) and tenor voices, one can see that the only overlap in unison range is a major sixth from b-flat to g1, but when considering the tessitura (the notes that can be sung easily), the common tones are almost non-existent. Similarly, among the baritone and bass voices there is an overlap of only a minor third (d to f) in range and little overlap of tessitura. Consequently, how many unison common tones can be found among the six voice ranges and tessituras in Musical Example 2.2?

Musical Example 2.2   Middle School Vocal Common Tones

A careful examination of Musical Example 2.2 shows that there are no unison pitches within these six voice parts, which explains the frustrating scenario described at the beginning of this chapter. However, the three lower voice parts have ranges that are similar to the three upper voices, and thus the choir could sing in octaves. But the common range is limited to about a P5, which also illustrates why the octave range of *Row, Row, Row Your Boat* resulted in the undesirable tone found in our scenario. Of course it is important to note that these ranges may vary dramatically based on individual singers and their previous (or lack of) vocal training.

Fortunately, the published repertoire for middle school choirs is becoming increasingly accommodating. Music that is termed "three-part" can usually be sung by everyone, but may necessitate octave displacement. Compositions written for SAB, SACB, and SATB voices are also abundant. We will examine them in a coming chapter.

CLASSROOM MANAGEMENT AND DISCIPLINE

Managing the various vocal issues is only half the challenge with middle school students. Hormonal changes are making everything else change too, from physical size to emotions. Adolescent singers are capable of great expressiveness, enthusiasm, loyalty, and humor (Sweet, 2016a), but may also experience periods of clumsiness, insecurity, independence, self-consciousness, and identity-questioning. Add to these changes the increased diversity seen in many schools, and it becomes clear that middle school choral teachers need to be equipped with knowledge of diverse populations and strategies to keep an orderly environment conducive for learning.

Diversity Awareness

Societal changes in acceptance of diversity are reflected in school policies that protect marginalized populations. Diverse populations include students from various ethnic and cultural backgrounds, students whose first language is not English, students with exceptionalities, students who are homeless and/or poverty-stricken, and those who reject gender norms (note the recommended "people first" language) (Abramo, 2012). Teachers are becoming more and more aware of practical strategies for reaching all of their students. Some of these include greater parental involvement, communication of high expectations, student-centered instruction, familiarity with basic terminology associated with each of these populations, and, of course, equal attention and opportunities given to all students (Larson and Keiper, 2013).

Practically unheard of in the 20th century, the subject of gender identity has entered international public dialogue (see *National Geographic*'s Special Issue: Gender Revolution, 2017). LGBTQQIA (Lesbian, Gay, Bisexual, Transgender, Queer, Questioning, Intersex, and Asexual) is a comprehensive acronym to refer to the possible identities of gender non-conforming students. Although many choral students don't "come out" until high school years or later, others are aware from a young age that they are gender non-conforming.

Choral teachers must be aware of students who may not respond to terms associated with male and female choirs or voice parts, and will need to reword their terminology. A middle school choir teacher wrote:

> I have more students than ever this year that classify their gender as "neutral." In a choir of about 90, I have four girls who consider themselves gender-neutral. When I make comments like, "Ladies only," they look at me sideways like, "I'm not a lady, I'm gender-neutral. If you don't call me by my proper identity then I won't sing." This has posed challenges in multiple classes for me this year, for the first time in my teaching career. The gender classification thing has really exploded within my student community between choir and band. By exploded, I don't mean to exaggerate. I'd say I have 6 gender-neutral students out of 180. But compared to zero, that seems like quite a lot to me. In choir we tend to be very gender-oriented, as opposed to other classes: "OK, this time, just the boys!" or "Ladies only, sing at measure 86," etc . . . When a part of your population doesn't identify as boy or girl, you have to totally reword your common communications, e.g., "OK, all high treble voices, sing at measure 86."

Choral music classrooms are often welcoming environments for students from diverse populations because of the nature of the arts as expressive, enjoyable, inspirational, social, identity-forming, and safe (Ramsey, 2016). These marginalized populations have high rates of homelessness, poverty, depression, and suicide, and are often the victims of bullying. In fact, Elpus and Carter (2016) found that music ensemble and music theater students had a much higher risk of being bullied than non-arts students. Thus, the choral music teacher's assurance of a safe environment is essential. Many put a "Safe Space" sign on their classroom and/or office doors (Paparo, 2016). All teachers need to be aware of and proactive in communicating with the support networks at the school which are now readily available (Berman, 2017).

Day One Strategies

According to Larson and Keiper (2013), "classroom management is a proactive approach to helping students learn" (p. 31). One of the best things a choral music teacher can do to harness the energies of all students in this age group is to make the rehearsal an active and challenging one. By keeping adolescents singing choral music that is expressive of their emotions, the choral classroom can provide an extremely positive environment that can keep them involved in music for a lifetime. Fortunately, the choral teacher who provides structure through rehearsal expectations and routines, and enforces them consistently, fairly, and with appropriate consequences, can enjoy a well-managed choral rehearsal and program. This type of environment is needed for teaching and learning, and we owe it to ourselves and our students to be prepared for middle school behavior management.

The first day of class matters, as illustrated in a most helpful resource for new teachers titled *The First Days of School: How to Be an Effective Teacher* by Harry and Rosemary Wong (1998). The behavior of the students on that first day will be indicative of their behavior throughout the school year. The first day of rehearsal should be carefully planned to provide clear organization and structure to the students. As soon as they enter your classroom:

- Greet the students individually and ask their preferred names and pronouns.
- Address the group as "Singers," and out of sensitivity to gender identity issues it is advisable to refrain from calling them "Ladies and Gentlemen," "Boys and Girls," or even simply "Guys" for both sexes combined.
- Assign each student a seat and a numbered slot in the music folder cabinet.

- Instruct them to be in their seats with music folders and pencils when the bell rings.

When the bell rings at the start of the period, clear expectations should be communicated to the students in the following ways:

- Begin class on time.
- Begin promptly with a physical and vocal warm-up.
- Keep the pace quick.
- Use good eye contact.
- Keep "teacher talk" to a minimum.
- Speak in an adult voice; project!
- Work gradually to calm the body through stretches and breathing, and to train the ears to listen.
- Direct the students to note the rehearsal order on the board.
- Move quickly to the first piece of music, one that engages their minds, bodies, voices, and imaginations.
- Sing small sections of diverse works and make every effort to keep all students engaged in the music in some way.
- When students achieve something musical as a group, congratulate them or thank them for their hard work.
- Ask them to sit quietly.
- Tell them they are dismissed.

Procedures and Rules

Set high standards for behavior. During the first week of class, explain these three management issues:

- procedures
- rules
- consequences.

For example, students need to know the *procedures* of what to do in the following situations (Wong and Wong, 1998):

- if they feel sick
- if they need to use the restroom
- if they have a question
- if a visitor enters the classroom

- if there is a fire drill
- when another person is speaking
- when to be absolutely quiet and when talking is allowed
- when they are dismissed at the end of class, and more.

While procedures illustrate the manner in which the rehearsal will run smoothly, there must also be *rules* which clarify unacceptable behaviors. Rules should be short, clear, and few in number. Although rules are determined by individual teachers, perhaps in discussion with the singers for mutual agreement, two that are highly recommended are: 1. Absolutely NO TALKING when the teacher is talking, and 2. All music-making stops INSTANTLY the teacher gives the established signal (Newell, 2012).

Five unacceptable behaviors are:

- bullying (physical, verbal, social, or cyber) (Elpus and Carter, 2016)
- dishonesty
- defiance
- disruptiveness
- uncooperativeness (Collins, 1999).

The expectations that singers will abide by the rehearsal room procedures and rules need to be organized by the teacher in advance of the beginning of the school year, and may be printed in a choir handbook given to all students, may be written into a contract signed by the students and parents, and/or may be posted in the choir room. In addition, awareness of school-wide behavior policies and national programs can also be useful as preventive measures in the choral classroom, such as the anti-bullying program found at www.stopbullying.gov/educators/confirm_bullying/index.html (Taylor, 2011).

Consequences

When expectations are clearly communicated, as well as consequences for failing to meet those expectations, the stage is set for productivity. However, student misbehavior does occur, and discipline, in terms of consequences of that misbehavior, is the appropriate reaction. The consequences should be clearly described, never enjoyable, never harmful or humiliating, and ultimately boring! They must be enforced firmly, fairly, and consistently (Newell, 2012). They often include several of the following levels, depending upon the seriousness of the infraction:

1. warning to the individual (everyone deserves a second chance)
2. penalty such as demerits toward the class grade
3. detention
4. one-on-one talk with the student outside of class
5. phone call to the student's parents (the teacher should assume a non-threatening tone in order to find support from the parents)
6. dismissal of student to the appropriate administrative office.

It should be mentioned that, even with a carefully executed management plan, some students will act out for reasons that are beyond the teacher's control. At the early signs of this, it would be to the teacher's advantage to speak with the school counselor to see if there is a history of problems with the student. It may be that there are challenges that have nothing to do with you or your class, and may include family, medical, or psychological problems. The school counselor can inform you of effective strategies for working with these individuals.

The following well-known approaches to classroom management have helped many teachers, and are recommended for further study: Behaviorism ("behavior modification"), Canter's Assertive Discipline Model (clear-cut expectations for the classroom), Dreikurs/Albert Model (a democratic approach), Ginott's Model (congruent communication), Glasser's Model (the expectation for high quality work), Jones' Model (non-verbal communication), and Kounin's Model (teacher engagement) (Larson and Keiper, 2013; Scarlett, Ponte, and Singh, 2009).

It can be a challenge to gain and maintain the attention of the singers for a full rehearsal. The middle school choir rehearsal is by its very nature alive with boundless energy that the music teacher is expected to harness into disciplined singing. Engaging the students in the music and as members of a fine ensemble is key to good classroom management. If the teacher finds music that the students enjoy, involves them in constructing the classroom rules and procedures, provides a balance of focused singing with short "wiggle" or humor breaks, and lets them experience success in performance, the students will want to cooperate. While it is human nature to focus on the misbehaving students, it does wonders for the teacher to keep the focus on the music and to express enthusiasm and praise for the behaving ones! Many potentially tense situations can be diffused through positive reinforcement and humor. These suggestions are easier said than done, but are important keys to a well-run and enjoyable rehearsal. Other effective rehearsal strategies are detailed in a later chapter.

BRAINTEASER 2-1: OBSERVING A MIDDLE SCHOOL CHOIR REHEARSAL

At your first middle school field visit, write a reflective observation report regarding the singers' behavior and voices. Notice how the rehearsal is structured. How does the teacher begin and end the rehearsal period? Does the music teacher keep the choir on task through active involvement and a positive approach? How many minutes are spent on music-making, and how many on other important matters, unimportant matters, and behavior control? How much noise does the teacher tolerate? Are you personally comfortable with the behavioral environment? What would you do differently if this was your choir rehearsal? Listen carefully to the voices, and make note of their ranges and qualities. Are the singers making an acceptable sound? What do you like about the sound and what would you like to change?

BRAINTEASER 2-2: INTERVIEWING A MIDDLE SCHOOL CHOIR TEACHER

Contact a middle school choir teacher and request an interview for this assignment. If you want to record the interview, ask permission. You may use the following questions and/or others you have been wondering about. Share the interview results with your choral methods class, and submit the interview transcript to your instructor.

Why did you choose to teach middle school music?
What other teaching and performance experiences have you had?
How long have you taught at this school, and overall?
What do you enjoy most about teaching middle school choir?

Do you have a choir discipline policy? Do you have a copy you could share with me?

What works for you when teaching boys with changing voices?

What advice do you have for me as I prepare for my first choral teaching job?

BRAINTEASER 2-3: APPLYING CLASSROOM MANAGEMENT THEORIES

Study the various classroom management theories presented in this chapter, or others recommended by your instructor, and then select one or more that you would like to apply to your field experience or future choral classroom. Write a three to five page paper explaining the approach and how you would use it in a middle school choral classroom.

BRAINTEASER 2-4: CREATING PROCEDURES, RULES, AND CONSEQUENCES

As a class, discuss and develop a set of middle school choir behavior rules and consequences, and then create a miniature sign for your course notebook as an example to post in your future middle school rehearsal room.

References

Abramo, Joseph (2012). Disability in the Classroom. *Music Educators Journal, 99*(1), 39–45.

Berman, Andrew S. (2017). Creating an LGBTQ-Friendly Music Program. *Teaching Music, 24*(3), 34–39.

Body, Mind, Spirit, Voice (2003, video). Dayton, OH: Lorenz Corporation, the American Boychoir School, and Bolthead Communications Group.

Collins, Don L. (1999). *Teaching Choral Music*, 2nd edition. Upper Saddle River, NJ: Prentice-Hall.

Cooksey, John M. (1977). The Development of a Contemporary, Eclectic Theory for the Training and Cultivation of the Junior High School Male Changing Voice (Part I: Existing Theories.) *Choral Journal, 18*(2), 5–14.

Dilworth, Rollo (2012). Working with Male Adolescent Voices in the Choral Rehearsal: A Survey of Research-Based Strategies. *Choral Journal, 52*(9), 22–33.

Elpus, Kenneth and Carter, B.A. (2016). Bullying Victimization Among Music Ensemble and Theatre Students in the United States. *Journal of Research in Music Education, 64*(3), 322–343.

Fisher, Ryan A. (2014). The Impacts of the Voice Change, Grade Level, and Experience on the Singing Self-Efficacy of Emerging Adolescent Males. *Journal of Research in Music Education, 62*(3), 277–290.

Herman, Sally (1988). *Building a Pyramid of Musicianship.* San Diego, CA: Curtis Music Press.

Killian, Janice (1999). A Description of Vocal Maturation Among Fifth- and Sixth-Grade Boys. *Journal of Research in Music Education, 47*(4), 357–369.

Larson, B.E. and Keiper, T.A. (2013). *Instructional Strategies for Middle and High School,* 2nd ed. New York: Routledge.

Leck, Henry (2001, video). *The Boy's Changing Voice: Take the High Road.* Milwaukee, WI: Hal Leonard.

National Geographic Special Issue: Gender Revolution, January 2017.

Newell, David (2012). *Classroom Management in the Music Room.* San Diego, CA: Kjos.

Palkki, Joshua (2016). My Voice Speaks for Itself: The Experiences of Three Transgender Students in Secondary School Choral Programs. Doctoral Dissertation, Michigan State University, Proquest Number 10141543.

Paparo, Stephen A. (2016). The ABC's of creating an LGBTQ-friendly classroom. *Massachusetts Music Education Journal, 64* (3), 37–39.

Phillips, Kenneth H. (1992). *Teaching Kids to Sing.* New York: Schirmer Books.

Ramsey, Andrea (2016). Adolescents and the *Why* of Choral Music. *Choral Journal, 57*(3), 17–27.

Ramseyer Miller, Jane (2016). Creating Choirs That Welcome Transgender Singers. *Choral Journal, 57*(4), 61–63.

Sataloff, Robert T. (2000). Vocal Aging and Its Medical Implications: What Singing Teachers Should Know, Part I. *Journal of Singing, 57*(1), 29–34.

Sataloff, Robert T. and Spiegel, Joseph R. (1989). The Young Voice. *NATS Journal, 45*(3), 35–37.

Scarlett, W.G., Ponte, I.C., and Singh, J.P. (2009). *Approaches to Behavior and Classroom Management.* Los Angeles. CA: Sage.

Swanson, Frederick J. (1973). *Music Teaching in the Junior High and Middle School.* New York: Appleton-Century-Crofts.

Sweet, Bridget (2015). The Adolescent Female Changing Voice: A Phenomenological Investigation. *Journal of Research in Music Education, 63*(1), 70–88.

Sweet, Bridget (2016a). *Growing Musicians: Teaching Music in Middle School and Beyond.* New York: Oxford.

Sweet, Bridget (2016b). Keeping the Glass Half Full: Teaching Adolescents with a Holistic Perspective. *Choral Journal, 57*(3), 6–15.

Taylor, D.M. (2011). Bullying: What Can Music Teachers Do? *Music Educators Journal, 98*(1), 41–44.

Thurman, Leon (2012). Boys' Changing Voices: What Do We Know Now? *Choral Journal, 52*(9), 8–21.

Wong, Harry K. and Wong, Rosemary T. (1998). *The First Days of School: How to Be an Effective Teacher.* Mountain View, CA: Harry K Wong Publications, Inc. (www.effectiveteaching.com).

3

AUDITIONS AND WARM-UPS FOR MIDDLE SCHOOL CHOIRS

VOCAL RANGES AND THE CHANGING VOICE

As discussed in the previous chapter, several scholars have specified the vocal ranges of middle school singers, but while they agree that there are stages of the voice change, they disagree on the number of stages and on the singable ranges during those stages. To complicate matters, every teacher knows that her or his ensemble is somewhat different from the textbook version; in fact, it differs from year to year. However, a starting point is necessary, and so the ranges found in Musical Example 3.1 are based on a simplified combination of the various theories (Phillips, 1992; Leck and Jordan, 2009), and are presented to aid in auditions, warm-ups, and repertoire selection.

Musical Example 3.1   Middle School Simplified Ranges (for Auditions, Warm-Ups, and Repertoire Selection)

- *Treble* refers to all unchanged voices (girls and boys).
- *Cambiata* refers to boys that are in the first stage of voice change; they may also sing alto or "float" to higher or lower voice parts as necessary (Stockton, 2014).
- *Tenor* refers to those in the second stage of voice change or to newly changed tenors.
- *Baritone* refers to newly changed baritones.

It can be seen that each voice part has the range of approximately a tenth, and the tessitura (the richest and most easily produced pitches) is the middle fifth of each range, except for the trebles who understandably continue to have a larger range and tessitura than the changing voices. Many voices will not have a range of a tenth without significant training and/or a naturally smooth transition through the change. Many boys will experience areas of silence in the voice, called phonation gaps or "blank spots" (Thurman, 2012), where they may be able to hear the pitch but are unable to produce it. Girls will also experience some difficulty in making transitions to their upper and lower registers despite a gradual increase in vocal range at puberty (Gackle, 2006; Sweet, 2016).

AUDITION STRATEGIES AND SECTIONAL SEATING

The audition for middle school part-singing should determine the tessitura of each singer, which includes those pitches that sound easiest and richest by each singer. Because the tessitura is generally the middle fifth of the vocal range, an audition that uses a song with a range of a fifth which can be transposed to different keys works well.

Irvin Cooper and Karl Kuersteiner (1970) developed a large group audition that can place approximately eight singers at a time, which is very efficient when the middle school teacher does not have the luxury of individual audition time. The audition procedure is this:

- Have small groups of students sing the first phrase of *America* ("My country 'tis of thee, sweet land of liberty, of thee I sing") in the key of G, or *Jingle Bells* in the key of F. Give the starting pitch (G for *America*, A for *Jingle Bells*) in octaves above and below middle C, listening carefully to the octave in which each student sings.

- o Ask those who sang the lower octave to temporarily stand together in the Changing Voice category.

- Have the remaining students in the small group sing the same *America* phrase in the key of B-flat (or *Jingle Bells* in A-flat), giving the starting pitch (B-flat for *America*, C for *Jingle Bells*) in the octaves above and below/on middle C:

  - o Place those who sang the higher octave in the Treble I category.
  - o Place those girls who sang the lower octave in Treble II and the boys in the Tenor category. Plan to seat those sections near each other for ease in switching parts as necessary.

- Finally, have the Changing Voice group return to sing the *America* phrase in the key of C (or *Jingle Bells* in B-flat). Give the starting pitch (C for *America*, D for *Jingle Bells*), near middle C and the octave below.

  - o Place those who sing the upper octave in the Cambiata or Alto category. Plan to seat them near the Tenors.
  - o Place those who sing the lower octave in the Baritone part.

This audition can be done quickly in small groups while the other students in the class are completing the top portion of the Audition Form (see Table 3.1), requiring name, age, gender-identity, and previous music experience. The small groups are less inhibited when they have the opportunity to sing with others during the audition, and they often enjoy having a label assigned to their vocal range. Within the first class meeting, you can determine all voice parts, and by the second meeting you can have seats assigned and music in their assigned folders. This "quick and dirty" audition process works well for getting started with an ensemble quickly, but does not preclude regular checking of the voices as they continually mature and change. You may use the Audition Form to record range and quality changes over time, as well as other musical characteristics, such as sight-reading, pitch memory, intonation, and use of the head voice.

As soon as you have time, each singer must be auditioned individually not only to get a thorough check of the voice range and tessitura, but also to assess musical aptitude, including pitch and rhythm memory, sight-reading, and tone quality within a ten-minute time frame. Range and tessitura can be assessed by having the student sing a descending five-note pattern (or major scale, if able) on *oo*, *ee*, or *ah* or solfege

Table 3.1 Audition Form for Middle School Choir

Name: _____

Age: _____ Gender-Identity: _____ Current Voice Part: _____

Previous Choir and/or Instrumental Experience: _____
_____
_____

Range and Tessitura: (Notate on the staff below, add clef signs)

_____
_____
_____
_____
_____

_____
_____
_____
_____
_____

Voice Part Designation: (Circle one based on ranges/tessituras presented in this chapter)

      Unchanged Treble I or II

      Cambiata (or Alto)

      Tenor

      Baritone

Describe Tone Quality: _____

Rate Rhythmic Memory:	1	2	3	4	5
Rate Pitch Memory:	1	2	3	4	5
Rate Sight-Reading:	1	2	3	4	5

Rating Scale: 1 = All Incorrect, 2 = Mostly Incorrect, 3 = About Half Correct, 4 = Mostly Correct, 5 = All Correct

*For the "quick and dirty" group audition, notate the tessitura and circle the Voice Part Designation based on the key and octave in which *America* or *Jingle Bells* was sung.

syllables, starting on a pitch near their speaking voice to instill confidence. Repeat several times, ascending and descending by half steps.

After a simple stepwise, quarter note pattern, progress to one that includes some skips (chord tones) and eighth notes, transposing by step, higher and lower. In order to identify volume capabilities, ask the student to accent the first three notes of Musical Example 3.2, maintaining a *forte* dynamic throughout. Transpose to identify the top and bottom of the student's range (Lamb, 1988).

Musical Example 3.2   *Forte* Audition Exercise

Sight-singing is a valuable audition tool only if the singer has had some previous musical experience, and even then a very simple melody of repeated tones, steps, and skips, combined with simple rhythms of quarter notes and eighth notes, is sufficient under the stress of an audition (see Musical Examples 3.3 and 3.4). Without previous musical experience, laborious testing for sight-singing ability is a waste of audition time.

Musical Example 3.3   Sight-Singing Example for Trebles/Tenors

Musical Example 3.4   Sight-Singing Example for Cambiatas/Baritones

Musical memory tests are useful tools because they are indicative of musical potential—if someone has good musical "ears." Tests should include simple pitch matching in their range, as well as three or four short (four- or eight-beat) rhythms and melodies to imitate, progressing

from very simple to more complex (see Musical Examples 3.5 and 3.6). You may use the following examples which are transposed to the comfortable tessituras of each voice part (key of G for trebles and tenors, and key of C for cambiatas and baritones).

Musical Example 3.5   Musical Memory Examples for Trebles/Tenors

Musical Example 3.6   Musical Memory Examples for Cambiatas/Baritones

Regarding sectional seating, it is beneficial to seat the singers with changing voices near other sections so that they may choose to sing higher or lower parts as their vocal ranges develop. It is recommended to rotate the Treble I and Treble II singers, so that they learn to sing high and low with healthy vocal production (Bowers, 2008).

BRAINTEASER 3-1: AUDITIONING MIDDLE SCHOOL SINGERS

Individually or in teams of two, arrange to conduct (or assist with) auditions at your local middle school, or with other middle school children. Make every effort to include some changing or changed voices in your audition experience. Depending on the music teacher's preference, administer either the "quick and dirty" group audition as described in this chapter, or the ten-minute individual audition to assess the range, tessitura, sight-reading, musical memory, and voice part of at least two students. If the choral director wants you to include specific sight-reading and/or ear-training examples in the audition, ask for a copy to share with your choral methods class, as well as any other audition procedures. Prepare the necessary number of audition forms (see Table 3.1) in advance of your visit. If possible, administer auditions on two sequential dates, and record in your course notebook your reflections of the experience after each audition.

Audition procedure:

- Greet students warmly.
- Have a short conversation to help them feel at ease and to hear the pitch of their speaking voices. The speaking voice is generally two to three half steps above the lowest singable pitch, which will help you determine not only if the voice is unchanged or changing, but also the range and voice part to assign (Killian, 1999).
- Position the student so that the keyboard is not visible to eliminate "fear" of high notes.
- If working in teams of two, one choral methods student may sit at the piano and the other stand (modeling good singer's posture); either or both students may take brief notes on the Audition Form.
- At first you may find it difficult to complete each individual voice check in ten minutes, but work quickly to achieve that goal (resist the urge to "teach" the student during the ten-minute time frame).
- Share your experience with your choral methods class. Submit audition forms (with names deleted for privacy) to your instructor.

EFFECTIVE WARM-UPS

The warm-up period of the rehearsal is an important one, not only to get the students mentally and musically focused, but also to assist in the development of the voice. Most students have no voice teacher other than their choir director in their entire lives, and one of the music teacher's main responsibilities is to teach proper and healthy use of the voice.

Essential things to consider as you create warm-ups for your middle school choir are the known characteristics of the developing adolescent voice, which include a lack of control and difficulty with:

- agility
- articulation
- large intervals
- dynamics
- register change
- clarity of tone.

Girls tend to sound breathy at this stage, and boys may sound husky. These vocal challenges can be minimized by the choral teacher who has the knowledge to help the young singers navigate through their vocal changes.

One of the critical aspects of a warm-up session is to stay aware of the ranges of the singers, and avoid forcing students too high or too low when they are uncomfortable. Watch for signs of vocal strain, which include lifting of the chin to reach high pitches, tension in the upper body, or a grimace on the face. As Henry Leck stated in a conference session, "70% of what you hear is what you see," indicating that you can see vocal tension in the body. If you have not memorized the ranges of the middle school choir as described earlier, stop now to do that. Notate them again, find them on the piano, sing them, and internalize them visually, aurally and kinesthetically.

There are a multitude of vocal warm-up books available for choral teachers, and Ken Phillips' (1992) vocal technique curriculum is especially useful because of its clear structure, objectives, guidelines for achieving the objectives, and assessment. He presents an instructional sequence for the middle school choral program, and provides 30 warm-ups per school year that teach five main aspects of singing: Respiration, Phonation, Resonance, Diction, and Expression.

Respiration exercises teach:

- posture development
- breathing motion
- breath management.

Phonation exercises teach:

- lower and upper adjustment
- lower and upper coordination.

Resonance exercises teach:

- vocal resonance and coordination
- uniform vowel colors.

Diction exercises teach:

- vocal tract freedom
- word pronunciation
- consonant articulation.

Expression exercises teach:

- phrasing
- dynamics
- tempo
- agility.

Phillips' (1992) octave designations will be used to label pitches throughout this book.

Musical Example 3.7   Octave Designations

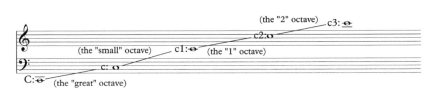

Another clear and concise vocal skill building curriculum designed for use in secondary choral rehearsals is James Jordan's *The Choral Warm-Up* (2005). He presents the following sequence for teaching that is "non-negotiable . . . and must be taught in that order in every warm-up . . . each time" (p. 29):

1. Relaxation
2. Body awareness and alignment

3. Relaxation of the vocal tract
4. Creating space
5. Breathing
6. Exhalation and inhalation
7. Support
8. Resonance
9. Vowels
10. Register consistency.

He identified the following additional vocal principles as essential, but does not specify a schedule for teaching them:

- Dynamics
- Crescendo/Decrescendo
- Range extension
- Leaps
- Legato
- Staccato
- Martellato
- Diction.

These two vocal pedagogy curricula (Phillips, 1992; Jordan, 2005) are valuable because they provide comprehensive and sequential approaches to developing healthy adolescent singers. What follows is a merging of these two pedagogies in an attempt to provide the aspiring choral teacher with a solid base upon which to build warm-ups, with additional suggestions gleaned from other authors' works. For example, Dan Andersen's (2017) *Warm-Ups for Changing Voices* is especially useful because it provides warm-ups with specific key, range, and direction guidelines that are differentiated by grade level (sixth, seventh, and eighth grades) and gender.

Preparing the Body for Singing

None of the warm-ups in this category involve phonation or vocalization, and in fact silence should be nurtured.

- Begin with stretches and/or shoulder massages to relax the body.
- Insist on alignment of the hips, head, pelvis, shoulders, knees, and feet (Jordan, 2005).

Posture development exercises include (Phillips, 1992):

- spinal stretches
- shoulder rolls
- neck relaxation
- knee flexes
- side stretches
- shrugs
- head nods and shakes
- facial expressions
- heel marches
- torso twists
- shoulder flexes
- neck stretches
- model posturing
- diving board spring position
- sitting tall
- standing tall.

Breathing motion (respiration) exercises include:

- abdominal breathing on the floor
- filling up with air like a balloon
- slowly sipping air as through a straw
- quickly gasping for a quick breath
- breathing as in a deep yawn
- breath suspension.

For breath management exercises, changing voice expert Dan Andersen advocates:

- inhaling for two beats and exhaling on a hiss for 12 beats
- then inhaling for two beats and exhaling on a hiss for 16 beats.

Students enjoy the competition of who can exhale the longest.
Henry Leck and Flossie Jordan (2009) use:

- four-beat echoed rhythm patterns with consonants *s*, *sh*, and *f*
- rhythms of known songs with consonants *s*, *sh*, and *f*,

and stress that inhalation should be quiet, and that both inhalation and exhalation should be accompanied by a feeling of the spine lengthening.

Phonation

Many adolescents speak in their low voice and need help finding their high singing voice. One of the best phonation exercises is the sigh or descending glissando from very high to low on the vowel sound *oo*. It is essential that the lips be rounded, the soft palate slightly raised as in a yawn, and the jaw slightly lowered (Jordan, 2005). Keep the sound light and show the direction of the glissando with the hand. This can be done once or twice every rehearsal.

The feeling of breath support combined with phonation is sometimes called "singing on the breath." Having students use circular hand motions to represent the spinning energy, or an extended pointed finger to represent the "drive" of the breath-supported sound, can make a difference between a weak and a vital sound (Jordan, 2005).

Other phonation exercises include:

- shouting "Hey!" as if someone just grabbed your money and is running away with it
- lip trills on siren sounds
- light, pulsing belly laughs in both the lower speaking range and midvoice registers
- soundscapes: vocal exploration, such as storm sounds (see Agrell and Ward-Steinman, 2014).

Resonance

Middle school singers can begin to discover vocal resonance through the following procedure:

- Students hum the pitch g1 or a1 (above middle C), except for changed baritones who will hum one octave lower
  - o with lips closed but slightly protruded, and
  - o with teeth slightly parted until a tingle in the lips is felt.
- Keeping that feeling, students drop the jaw approximately one finger's width and open up to an *oo*.

- The teacher models the desired choral tone, which should be rather light and unforced.
- Students then sing the *ee* vowel

  o lips remain slightly rounded, and
  o the tip of the tongue touches the bottom front teeth (Jordan, 2005).
  o The jaw remains the same as for the *oo* vowel.

- There should be much space in the mouth for proper resonance, resulting in "maximum sound with minimal effort" (Collins, 1999, p. 217).
- Visual imagery can be very effective, so asking the singers to feel as if they have a golf ball or the Astrodome in their mouth can create the optimal resonant space for singing.

Registration

Once the high voice is found and placed, adolescents can practice and become aware of going between their high and low registers. As in the previous exercise, have the students sing g1 or a1 (baritones an octave lower), with vowels *oo* and *ee*, keeping the same lip, tongue, and jaw positions, and do the following:

- Sing descending legato five-note patterns.
- Sing descending legato triads.

Then sing descending five-note patterns with lip trills. To assist in smoothing out the register break, ask the lower voices to open the throat and push more air as they feel the approaching break. Instruct students to sing as they are able—to drop out when uncomfortable but to join back in as soon as possible.

To help singers learn to feel the difference in singing in their upper (head voice), middle (combined) and lower (chest voice) registers:

- Move the previous exercises to c2, with changed voices an octave lower, and
- then to c1 (middle C), with changed voices an octave lower.
- You may add the *d*, *n*, and *v* consonants to the *oo*, *ee*, and *ah* vowels in the previous exercises (Jordan, 2005). It is important

to achieve unification on these three basic vowel anchors before moving on to others. The first two (*oo* and *ee*) require similarly rounded lips, relatively high placement of the tongue, and relatively closed jaw position, while the third (*ah*) is the most open, with a lowered tongue and jaw.

- If singers are able, expand to an octave arpeggio exercise, beginning in the head voice on c2, slurring each two notes: 8 – 5, 5 – 3, 3 – 1; you may add new vowels, such as *eh* and *oh*. Descend chromatically (White and White, 2001).

Listen carefully for students who struggle with matching pitch and finding their different registers. With practice, the voices will become easier to manage, so it is important for the teacher to remain encouraging, patient, and resourceful. Two important strategies are to keep them singing in their head voices despite the voice change, and if all else fails, find the pitches they *can* sing, match *those*, and begin to work outward from there. They *will* hear the difference between those matched and unmatched pitches.

Agility and Expression

Staccato, marcato, rapid tempos, and dynamic control are some of the middle school vocal challenges, especially for changing and changed voices. The following guidelines are particularly helpful:

- Sing patterns no wider than the interval of a fifth, descending from the head voice (keeping above middle C for changing voices) (Phillips, 1992). Create your own patterns using different phrasing, articulations, tempos, and dynamics, as well as repeated notes and skips. Create space in the mouth that allows the sound to resonate. Ascend and descend. Add arm motions. Examples can be found (with accompaniment) in Leck and Jordan's book (2009) and come to life in Leck's video *Take the High Road* (2001). Imagine the sound spinning forward toward the cheekbones and forehead, using hand gestures to reinforce the spinning and energized tone (Jordan, 2005).
- Sing 16th note passages of ascending and descending five-note patterns on the alphabet letters (see Andersen, 2017).

Because there are few common tones among the various ranges in the middle school choir, once warm-ups leave the head voice area, it is essential to keep in mind the common notes among the ranges. Commit them to memory.

Range Extension

As treble voices mature, they develop an expanded range and need to use it in order to keep it flexible (Gackle, 2006). For all singers, it is important to warm up the entire range, paying special attention to taking the head voice quality down into the chest voice range, rather than vice versa. Most students will be afraid of their rarely used head voice until its use becomes a regular routine in choir. This is essential to good voice production and good choral tone, even if the sound is very light and breathy at the start. Good posture, good breath support, good vowel unification with a dropped jaw, and dynamic exercises will improve the tone dramatically with time and instruction.

- For ascending range extension vocalises, chord tones sung on open vowels (e.g., *oh* and *ah*), taken at fast tempos, are best.
- For descending range extension vocalises, stepwise exercises sung on resonant vowels (e.g., *ee*), taken at slow tempos, are best (Jordan, 2005).

Diction

Diction warm-ups help to make choral text intelligible. They also teach the production of pure and uniform vowels which make beautiful choral tone possible, and clean and crisp consonants which provide rhythmic impetus. Put more artistically, the soul of choral singing is in the vowels, but the passion is in the consonants. Put more technically, vowels are sung "on the breath" with the vocal cords in vibration, while consonants obstruct the breath stream, either partially or fully, and the vocal cords may or may not be in vibration (Moriarty, 1975).

At the middle school level, diction warm-ups should utilize the following consonants, according to Jordan (2005):

- *d* (point the tongue toward the ridge of the upper teeth)
- *n* (useful for building legato)
- *v* (useful for building resonance and controlled airstream).

Phillips (1992) presents a developmental curriculum based on two aspects of diction: word pronunciation and consonant articulation. The sequence to achieve intelligible word pronunciations is:

- Tongue Twisters
- Final Consonants (emphasized and interpolated *uh*)
- Hissing Sibilants (*s, sh, c*)
- The Three Rs (American, flipped, and soft)
- Short Songs (such as the traditional "Pop Song")
- IPA Studies.

The sequence for consonant articulation is:

- Voiceless Plosives *(p, t, k, ch)*
- Voiced Plosives (*b, d, g, j*)
- Voiceless Sibilants (*f, s, th, sh*)
- Tuned Continuants (*m, n*)
- Voiced Continuants (*v, z, th, zh*)
- Aspirates (voiceless *h*, voiced *wh*) (Phillips, 1992).

The hierarchy for teaching uniform vowel colors is often determined by the needs of a particular choir, but Phillips (1992) recommends the following vowel sounds and their IPA (International Phonetic Alphabet) symbols:

- *oo* [u], *oh* [ɔ], *ah* [a], *eh* [ɛ], *ee* [i].

These are the pure vowel sounds that are needed to sing solfege syllables, as well as Latin texts. While experts agree that these vowels should be practiced before the others, they differ regarding the order in which these five vowels should be presented. Other recommended orders from which you may choose are these:

- *ee* [i], *eh* [ɛ], *ah* [a], *oh* [ɔ], *oo* [u]
- *ah* [a], *eh* [ɛ], *ee* [i], *oh* [ɔ], *oo* [u].

Create warm-ups that sustain each vowel for two to four beats to assure a unified sound. Once mastered, progress to unifying the first vowel of diphthongs (e.g., "I like my bike" and "Oh No! Don't Go!")

(Phillips, p. 293). The first vowel sound of a diphthong should receive 95% of the duration, while the vanishing vowel receives only 5%. Have the students perform hand or arm motions that reinforce the desired vowel sound (Leck and Jordan, 2009).

Many music education curricula are too full to include a course in diction, yet it is one of the most important aspects of choral singing. Even the youngest choristers can be taught to sing beautiful uniform vowels which make the difference between a fine choir and a mediocre one. Therefore, attention to diction principles and the IPA symbols are necessary. What follows are guidelines for learning to sing the basic vowel sounds.

- Practice singing the *lip* vowel [u] (as in *noon*) with rounded and projected lips ("fish mouth") and a slightly dropped jaw.
- When forming *tongue* vowels, practice singing:
  o [ɔ] (as in *Domine*), with lips rounded, making sure the sound doesn't become the diphthong [ɔu]
  o [a] (as in *father*), keeping the jaw relaxed, with the bottom of the upper teeth showing (as if biting into an apple)
  o [ɛ] (as in *met*), with lips unrounded, making sure the sound doesn't become the diphthong [ɛi]
  o [i] (as in *meet*), keeping the lips rounded.
- Form the mouth position for the vowel during inhalation before singing.
- Sing five-note descending patterns for each vowel, beginning on c2 and not descending below middle C.
- Sing five-note patterns on enjoyable combinations of vowels such as *doo-bee-doo-bee-doo*.
- Sing four-part harmonic progressions on pure vowels (see Musical Example 3.8) (Phillips, 1992, p. 290).

Musical Example 3.8   Vowels Exercise

oo - oh - ah - eh - ee

Tongue twisters are very effective in improving choral diction. Try "Double Bubble Gum," as seen in Musical Example 3.9, using increasing tempos and minor tonality for extra challenge and fun.

Musical Example 3.9   Diction Exercise

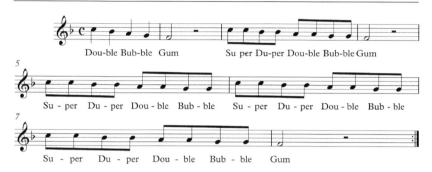

"Red Leather Yellow Leather" (see Musical Example 3.10) is another challenging tongue twister that can be adapted to fit a number of five-note patterns.

Musical Example 3.10   Diction Exercise

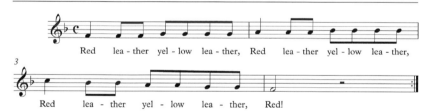

Warm-ups should occur at every rehearsal because they teach the students how to sing well. By keeping the pace quick, the entire warm-up sequence can be accomplished within ten minutes. Adding movement will keep the students engaged, and is highly recommended. Jordan's (2005) *The Choral Warm-Up* includes several chapters detailing physical gestures and kinesthetic exercises to reinforce vocal principles. And while a predictable warm-up sequence is often beneficial, it can also cause students to "tune out," so find exercises that make students think and be attentive. One such example from a collection of *Lame Brain Games* asks students to sing a major scale on solfege, but to only snap (not sing) on *fa* and *la* (Herrington and Miller, 2000). There are many published warm-up books for adolescents that are easy to use, but it is most important that you know what you want to accomplish in your warm-up period, why it is important, and how to best carry it out.

BRAINTEASER 3-2: CREATING MIDDLE SCHOOL WARM-UPS

Create a middle school warm-up sequence, completing the Middle School Warm-Ups form below for the vocal concepts you will teach. Script actual verbal instructions that you want to remember to say, and add clef signs to the five-line staves provided. Review middle school vocal ranges. In order to avoid waning attention spans, don't spend too much time on any one warm-up. Present this draft to your instructor and/or classmates for feedback.

BRAINTEASER 3-3: OBSERVING MIDDLE SCHOOL WARM-UPS

Notate the warm-ups observed at your local middle school. Identify the apparent objective of each and if you think it was achieved. Include what worked and why, and what you might do differently. Submit to your instructor.

BRAINTEASER 3-4: CONDUCTING MIDDLE SCHOOL WARM-UPS

After revising your warm-ups created in Brainteaser 3-2, conduct them in a local middle school. You may team-teach with another choral methods student who will serve as your accompanist, and vice versa. Note the following keys to success:

- Memorize your warm-ups.
- Time your warm-up sequence carefully.
- Be energetic and keep your eyes on the students.
- Move quickly from one warm-up to the next.
- Include singer movement, such as shaping phrases with the arms or stepping to the beat.
- Keep your own "teacher talk" to a minimum.
- Keep vocal ranges in mind.
- Check student posture throughout the warm-up.
- Have high expectations for your ideal sound, and demand it.

Assignment requirements:

1. Video-record your warm-up sequence in the field.
2. Watch the recording and evaluate your teaching for five strengths and five areas of needed improvement.
3. Submit your video-recording, written warm-ups and self-evaluation to your instructor.
4. Watch peers' video-recordings in your choral methods class. Discuss what you have learned, and compile a list of the best vocal warm-ups for middle school choirs. Make copies for everyone in the class to place in their choral teaching resource notebooks.

Proceed to conduct warm-ups at every opportunity, always with specific goals and ranges in mind; and practice conducting from the piano as well as with an accompanist. Both are necessary skills.

Middle School Warm-Ups

Relaxation and Alignment:

_____

_____

_____

_____

_____

Minutes:

Respiration:

_____

_____

_____

_____

_____

Minutes:

Phonation:

_____

_____

_____

_____

_____

Vowel/Syllable:

Range and Direction:

Minutes:

Resonance:

_____

_____

_____

_____

_____

Vowel/Syllable:

Range and Direction:

Minutes:

Registration:

_____

_____

_____

_____

_____

Vowel/Syllable:

Range and Direction:

Minutes:

Agility and Expression:

_____

_____

_____

_____

_____

Vowel/Syllable:

Range and Direction:

Minutes:

Range Extension:

_____

_____

_____

_____

_____

Vowel/Syllable:

Range and Direction:

Minutes:

Diction:

_____

_____

_____

_____

_____

Vowel/Syllable:

Range and Direction:

Minutes:

References

Agrell, J. and Ward-Steinman, P.M. (2014). *Vocal Improvisation Games for Singers and Choral Groups*. Chicago, IL: GIA.

Andersen, Dan (2017). *Warm-Ups for Changing Voices: Building Healthy Middle School Voices*. Milwaukee, WI: Hal Leonard.

Bowers, Judy (2008). The Middle School Choral Program, in Holt, M. and Jordan, J., *The School Choral Program: Philosophy, Planning, Organizing, and Teaching*. Chicago, IL: GIA.

Collins, Don L. (1999). *Teaching Choral Music*, 2nd ed. Upper Saddle River, NJ: Prentice Hall.

Cooper, Irvin and Kuersteiner, Karl O. (1970). *Teaching Junior High School Music*, 2nd ed. Boston, MA: Allyn and Bacon.

Gackle, Lynne (November, 2006). Finding Ophelia's Voice: The Female Voice During Adolescence. *Choral Journal, 37*(5), 29–37.

Herrington, Judith and Miller, Clayton (2000). *Lame Brain Games*. Milwaukee, WI: Hal Leonard.

Jordan, James (2005). *The Choral Warm-Up: Method, Procedures, Planning, and Core Vocal Exercises*. Chicago, IL: GIA.

Killian, Janice (1999). A Description of Vocal Maturation Among Fifth- and Sixth-Grade Boys. *Journal of Research in Music Education, 47*(4), 357–369.

Lamb, Gordon (1988). *Choral Techniques*. Dubuque, IA: Wm. C. Brown.

Leck, Henry (2001, video). *The Boy's Changing Voice: Take the High Road*. Milwaukee, WI: Hal Leonard.

Leck, Henry and Jordan, Flossie (2009). *Creating Artistry Through Choral Excellence*. Milwaukee, WI: Hal Leonard.

Moriarty, John (1975). *Diction: Italian, Latin, French, German . . . The Sounds and 81 Exercises for Singing Them*. Boston, MA: E.C. Schirmer.

Phillips, Kenneth H. (1992). *Teaching Kids to Sing*. New York: Schirmer.

Stockton, Phillip (October, 2014). Classifying Adolescent Male Voices. *Choral Journal, 55*(3), 85–87.

Sweet, Bridget (2016). Keeping the Glass Half Full: Teaching Adolescents with a Holistic Perspective. *Choral Journal, 57*(3), 6–15.

Thurman, Leon (2012). Boys' Changing Voices: What Do We Know Now? *Choral Journal, 52*(9), 8–21.

White, C.D. and White, D.K. (May, 2001). Commonsense Training for Changing Male Voices. *Music Educators Journal, 87*(6), 39–43, 53.

4

REPERTOIRE FOR MIDDLE SCHOOL CHOIRS

SELECTION CRITERIA

When selecting music for middle school choirs, essential considerations include:

- appropriate vocal ranges and tessituras
- vocal development objectives
- music learning objectives
- appropriate texts
- "quality" music.

"Quality" is an elusive term that means that it is worth learning. Aim for high quality music and the rewards will be so much greater than from music of little value. Quality music is available for all ages in all styles. Although the term is difficult to define, it is generally assumed that if something lasts, it has value. Trite music becomes boring with repeated rehearsal. Music that continues to uncover layers of meaning, musical or otherwise, is worth learning.

REPERTOIRE RESOURCES

There are numerous resources that can aid the choral director in finding literature that meets the five essential criteria, the first being state-approved music lists for contests. For example, in Indiana, the Indiana State School Music Association (www.issma.net) publishes a yearly list of required and recommended choral compositions, graded by difficulty level and voicing, ranging from junior level 3 (for the beginning middle school choir) to senior level 1 (for the most advanced high school choir). Here, and in other states' contest lists, the choir director will find repertory that is approved and appropriate for the middle school choir.

The two major professional organizations that serve as resources for choral music educators are the National Association for Music Education (NAfME) and the American Choral Directors Association (ACDA) (see Appendixes D and E). Their annual conferences feature "reading sessions" of middle school choral repertoire and concerts performed by outstanding middle school choirs. Both organizations also publish helpful articles and books on the topic of repertoire. One such book provides a complete list of pieces that were performed by middle school choirs at ACDA regional and national conventions between 1960 and 2000 (Schmidt, 2002). The pieces that have been performed multiple times over the years obviously work, and are excellent indicators of "quality" music for middle school choirs. In addition, choral music publishers regularly send out promotional recordings featuring new choral music for middle school. You will no doubt be able to find good literature for your choirs through conferences, concerts, and recordings. Other outstanding middle school choral repertoire resources are listed below:

Middle School Choral Repertoire Resources

Abrahams, Frank and Head, Paul D. (2011). *Teaching Music Through Performance in Middle School Choir*. Chicago, IL: GIA.

Buchanan, Heather J. and Mehaffey, Matthew W. (2005). *Teaching Music Through Performance in Choir: Volume I*. Chicago, IL: GIA.

Butler, Abby and Lind, Vicki (2005). Renaissance Repertoire for Middle School Choirs. *Choral Journal, 46*(1), 37–41.

Collins, Drew (2012). Using Repertoire to Teach Vocal Pedagogy in All-Male Changing Voice Choirs. *Choral Journal, 52*(9), 34–41.

Hower, Eileen (2006). Designing a New Paradigm for Selecting Music for the Middle School Choir. *Choral Journal, 47*(5), 62–74.

Indiana State School Music Association Required List Download for Organizational Events: www.issma.net/required.php.

Lucas, Mark (2012). Real Men Sing ... Choral Repertoire. *Choral Journal, 52*(9), 42–48.

Phillips, Kenneth H. (2004). *Directing the Choral Music Program*. New York: Oxford University Press. (See Appendix C: List of Recommended Choral Repertory for Junior High Choirs, pages 392–402.)

Reames, Rebecca R. and Warren, Matthew (November, 2006). Recommended Literature: Middle-Level Mixed Choirs. *Choral Journal, 47*(5), 76–88.

Schmidt, Sandefur (2002). *Music Performed at American Choral Directors Association Conventions, 1960–2000*. Lawton, OK: ACDA Monograph 12. (See Junior High or Middle School Choir, pages 203–209.)

Sharp, Tim (2004). Choral Music and Print-on-Demand. *Choral Journal, 44*(8), 19–23.

Shelton Jr., Tom T. (2016). Repertoire and the Compositional Process: A Conversation with Composers of Junior High/Middle School Repertoire. *Choral Journal, 57*(3), 28–38.

REPERTOIRE VOICINGS

Because of the variety of unchanged, changing and changed voices in middle school choirs, you will encounter literature in the following voicings:

- SA and SSA (for treble voices)
- two-part and three-part (for treble and/or changing voices)
- SAB (often too low for most boys, but works well for some groups)
- SACB (often an excellent choice; the "C" stands for Cambiata or Changing Voice)
- SATB (for a mature and advanced middle school choir).

It is best to select music written for the ranges and tessituras of your particular choir. Music designated as "three-part" can work well with any middle school chorus, as long as the teacher carefully places the students on the part that they are able to sing as they negotiate the voice change. It doesn't matter who sings part 1, 2, or 3, as long as the part fits the singer's range and tessitura. A fine three-part arrangement is *Yonder Come Day* by Judith Cook Tucker, in which the vocal ranges are very small and fit the changing voice well. The piece is simple without being trite, and relies on an authentic Georgia Sea Island song as its theme with repetitive text. The theme is sung in unison once, then repeated with a simple upper harmony part with the range of a minor third, and then repeated again adding a lower ostinato part with the range of a fourth. The arranger suggests that this a cappella piece be transposed to any key for ease in singing. Claps, steps, and chant add to its appeal.

Freedom Is Coming by Henry Leck is similar in its number of parts, simplicity of range, and musical demands, and is based on an attractive and authentic non-Western song. As in *Yonder Come Day*, it allows all singers to contribute vocally and musically, and thus have a quality choral music experience, despite limited musical knowledge and vocal ability. Many similarly effective pieces can be found on state-approved lists for beginning middle school choirs. It should be noted that sacred pieces with Latin texts may also be found among the simpler literature lists, and are important and accessible for this age group because they teach the five pure vowels that are essential to beautiful singing.

As middle school singers mature into stronger musicians, the level of difficulty of the music can be increased. However, the teacher must continue to be attentive to the vocal range limitations that many singers may be experiencing even while their musicianship is expanding. It is essential to seek music with accessible ranges to enable all to experience success in the singing experience. The music studied can become increasingly complex, involving three to four parts and more challenging melodies, rhythms, tempos, harmonies, forms, styles, languages, and even tone quality for some world music.

A favorite example is *South African Suite* for three-part voices (also available for four-part and SAB), arranged by Henry Leck. The vocal ranges are perfect for the changing voice (see Musical Example 4.1), and the African music is authentic and stimulating. The addition of the African language is a unique learning experience for the singers, and the pure vowels are the same as in Latin and are therefore easy to learn. The three pieces of the suite, *Tshotsholoza*, *Siyahamba*, and *Gabi Gabi*, can be performed by singers of all ages, but fortunately fit the

Musical Example 4.1 Ranges for *Siyahamba* by Henry Leck

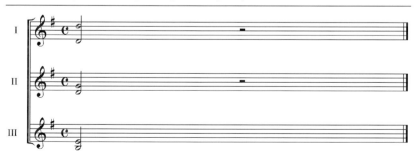

adolescent voice extremely well. It has been recorded by the Indianapolis Children's Choir.

Separate high and low voice choirs in middle school can perform SSA and TTB pieces. For example, a beautiful treble arrangement of the famous Finnish folk song *Who Can Sail? (Vem kan segla förutan vind?)* by Carl-Bertil Agnestig provides moderate musical challenges, moderately large ranges (see Musical Example 4.2), minor tonality, some chromaticism, and the option of singing in English or Swedish. *Who Can Sail?* has been recorded by the Glen Ellyn Children's Chorus.

Musical Example 4.2   Ranges for *Who Can Sail?* by Carl-Bertil Agnestig

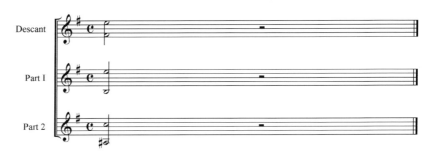

Likewise, André Thomas' TTB arrangement of the spiritual *Good News!* emphasizes careful tuning of three-part chords contrasting with independent unison tenor and bass lines. It also teaches dynamics and breath control, and features the gradually expanding ranges of the adolescent boys (see Musical Example 4.3).

Musical Example 4.3   Ranges for *Good News!* by André Thomas

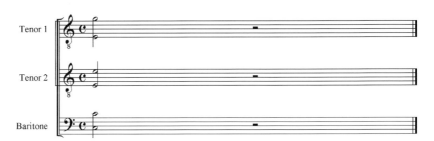

SATB music can be carefully chosen for the more advanced middle school mixed choir, and André Thomas created a model arrangement in *Keep Your Lamps!* The characteristics of this piece can be used as a

guide in selecting repertoire for the middle school mixed choir: It is written in the comfortable tessitura of the four voice parts (see Musical Example 4.4), is based on a spiritual that is rhythmically attractive for this age group, includes an interesting accompaniment of three conga drums, features syncopation which is accessible due to effective repetition, includes a vocal solo, requires good consonant diction and placement, and uses a large dynamic range.

Musical Example 4.4   Ranges for *Keep Your Lamps!* by André Thomas

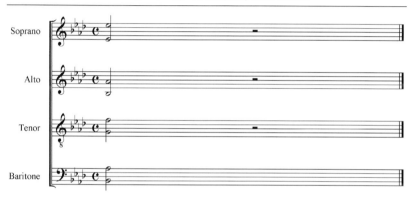

GRADED CHORAL REPERTOIRE

Most middle schools will offer at least one beginning chorus that is open to any student regardless of musical experience, and another more advanced ensemble. To find literature that differentiates between beginning and more advanced music, choral teachers can look to their state's recommended literature list, or to other graded resources. Examples include *Teaching Music Through Performance in Middle School Choir* (Abrahams and Head, 2011), and *Teaching Music Through Performance in Choir* (Buchanan and Mehaffey, 2005) where specific musical criteria (vocal, tonal, and rhythmic) are sequentially outlined and used to grade the literature on a scale from 1 to 5. The level 1 and 2 pieces may be used with beginning and advanced middle school ensembles.

Level 1 criteria include:

- simple, short, conjunct, and comfortable vocal lines
- major and minor tonalities with no chromaticism or modulations
- basic rhythms.

Level 2 criteria include:

- basic challenges in phrase length, range, diction, and disjunct melodic lines
- brief chromaticism, modulations, modal passages, and dissonances
- brief rhythmic challenges.

The following "starter-list" of recommended pieces is based on these criteria.

SELECTED REPERTOIRE

Beginning Middle School Choirs: High Voices

All the Pretty Little Horses (2-part)	arr. Earlene Rentz
For the Beauty of the Earth (SA)	John Rutter
Freedom Is Coming (3-part)	Nyberg, arr. H. Leck
Hashivenu (unison or 3-part)	arr. Doreen Rao
Jubilate Deo (2-part canon)	Praetorius/arr. D. Rao
O Music (3-part canon)	Mason/arr. P. Liebergen
Old Abram Brown (SSAA)	Benjamin Britten
South African Suite (SSA)	arr. Henry Leck
Yonder Come Day (SSA)	Judith Tucker

Beginning Middle School Choirs: Low Voices

Aura Lee (TB)	arr. Emily Crocker
The Holly and the Ivy (CCB)	arr. Don Collins
Kyrie (TB)	Ruth Schram
Loch Lomond (TB)	arr. Earlene Rentz
New River Train (TB)	Donald Moore
Set Me as a Seal upon Your Heart (TB)	Laura Farnell
Simple Gifts (TB)	Aaron Copland
This Train (TTB)	arr. Roger Emerson

Beginning Middle School Choirs: Mixed Voices

Be Thou My Vision (SATB)	arr. Alice Parker
For the Beauty of the Earth (2-part)	John Rutter

The May Night (SATB)	Brahms, arr. A. Frackenpohl
No Greater Gift (SAB)	Ruth Schram
River in Judea (SAB)	arr. John Leavitt
The River Sleeps Beneath the Sky (3-part)	Mary Lynn Lightfoot
South African Suite (SAB)	arr. Henry Leck
The Tiger (3-part)	Sherri Porterfield

Advanced Middle School Choirs: High Voices

Dance on My Heart (SSA)	Allan Koepke
Fire (SSA)	Mary Goetze
I'm Goin' Up a Yonder (4-part)	Walter Hawkins
Savory, Sage, Rosemary and Thyme (SSAA)	Donald Patriquin
Scarborough Fair (SSA)	Mary Goetze
Simple Gifts (2-part)	Copland, arr. I. Fine
The Snow, Op. 26, No. 1 (SSA)	Edward Elgar
Three Choral Pieces (SSA)	Jean Berger
Who Can Sail? (3-part)	Carl-Bertil Agnestig

Advanced Middle School Choirs: Low Voices

Amor Vittoriso (TBB)	Gastoldi, arr. R. Leininger
Climbin' up the Mountain (TTBB)	arr. Henry Smith
Good News! (TTB)	arr. André Thomas
Let Us Now Praise Famous Men (TB)	Gerald Finzi
My Bonnie (TTBB)	arr. A. Parker and R. Shaw
Poor Man Lazrus (TTBB)	arr. Jester Hairston
The Sailor's Song (TTB)	Patti DeWitt
Sometimes I Feel Like a Motherless Child (TTBB)	arr. Nina Gilbert
Till the Walls Come Down (TTB)	Lon Beery
Vive l'amour (TTBB)	arr. Terry Barham

Advanced Middle School Choirs: Mixed Voices

Can You Hear (SAB)	J. Papoulis and F. Nunez
Cantar! (SAB or SATB)	Jay Althouse
Cantate Domino (SATB)	Giuseppe Pitoni
Chester (SATB)	William Billings
Come in from the Firefly Darkness (3-part)	Amy Bernon

Die Nachtigall, Op. 59, No. 4 (SATB)	Felix Mendelssohn
Der Tanz (SATB)	Franz Schubert
El Grillo (SATB)	Josquin Desprez
Fa Una Canzona (SATB)	Orazio Vecchi
A Festive Alleluia (3-part)	Mary Lynn Lightfoot
Hush! Somebody's Callin' My Name (SAB/SATB)	arr. Brazeal Dennard
I Got a Robe (SATB)	arr. Moses Hogan
Jasmine Flower (SATB)	arr. Jing Ling-Tam
Keep Your Lamps! (SATB)	arr. André Thomas
Now Is the Month of Maying (3-part)	Morley, arr. R. Robinson
O Bone Jesu (SATB)	G. P. Palestrina
Prayer of the Children (SAB)	K. Bestor. arr. M. Hayes
Psallite (SAB, SATB)	Michael Praetorius
Rock-a My Soul (3-part)	arr. Kirby Shaw
Soldier Boy (SATB)	John Rutter
Steal Away (SATB)	arr. Ruth Schram
Three Madrigals (SATB)	Emma Lou Diemer
The Turtle Dove (3-part)	Linda Spevacek
Wiegenlied (SATB)	Brahms, arr. S. Porterfield

SCORE ANALYSIS AND PREPARATION

After the choral teacher has selected music based upon the five essential criteria outlined at the beginning of this chapter, he or she must thoroughly study and prepare each score for teaching and conducting. The following procedure assures a comprehensive understanding of each piece:

- Notate the range and tessitura of each voice part.
- Note the key, tempo, style, texture, and language.
- Analyze the form of the piece, marking the score with letters.
- Note the harmonic structure of the piece, marking modulations and/or unusual progressions.
- Determine where breaths should be taken and place breath marks in the score where not obvious.
- Write out the IPA symbol for every vowel sound in every syllable.
- Mark primary (1), secondary (2), and unstressed (3) syllables based on a combination of natural word stress, metric stress, and phrase considerations.

- Provide a literal translation for each word if not in English.
- Give some background on the composer and the purpose for which the piece was written.
- List the "teachable moments" of the piece that will enhance student learning.
- Sing through all vocal parts, circling in pencil any melodic or rhythmic errors that you make (your students will certainly make those too).
- Listen to various recordings of the piece.
- Practice the accompaniment.
- Practice conducting the piece in front of a mirror, working on challenging conducting gestures (preparatory beats, cues, expressive markings, cut-offs, etc.).
- Memorize the score; then conduct it in front of a mirror from memory, complete with important gestures.

COPYRIGHT LAW AND PHOTOCOPYING MUSIC

Many future choral music educators see little harm in photocopying choral music for their choirs because they have witnessed it done so often. While few teachers ever get fined or sued for abusing the copyright law, it can and does happen. And even if it never happens to you, it is your responsibility as a teacher and artist to respect the rights of composers and arrangers, and to teach your students to do so as well. If you don't teach them, perhaps no one ever will.

The U.S. Copyright Law was designed to encourage artists to create new works by protecting those works. Composers and arrangers deserve to be paid for their musical publications. Consider the fact that when someone copies music, they are stealing from the artist. Ignorance or a small music budget is no excuse to break the law.

Here are a few relevant aspects of the law:

- The copyright law *does* permit copying music in the emergency of an imminent concert date, but it also requires that the same music be purchased regardless of whether it is needed after the performance or not.
- The law prohibits purchasing music but then making copies to preserve the original scores—scores are considered "consumable" and therefore by law should be replaced when no longer usable.

- The often used phrase that the music is for "educational use" does not permit photocopying more than 10% of a complete work for study purposes.
- Out-of-print music may not be freely photocopied. The publisher of the work must be contacted for permission to copy the work.
- Compositions or arrangements with an expired copyright or that never had a copyright are considered "public domain" (PD) and are free to use.

However, establishing if a piece is public domain is not a simple task due to updates of the copyright law. The simplest explanation is that most copyrights expire no less than 75 years after they were granted. Exceptions to that rule are those copyrights granted between 1950 and 1964 that were not renewed, so they would be free to use today. Currently, a teacher can generally presume that a work copyrighted less than 95 years ago is still covered by the law. See www. nafme. org/my-classroom/united-states-copyright-law-a-guide-for-music-educators/ or simply go to www.namfe.org and search for the term "copyright."

Penalties for infringement of the copyright law include basic fines from $750 to $30,000, but if the court determines willfulness to photo-copy for commercial advantage, that penalty can be a $250,000 fine and/or five years' imprisonment. The complete copyright law and its implications are available online at www.copyright.gov.

VIRTUAL CHORAL MUSIC LIBRARIES

The good news is that technology advances have made it possible to access digital files of choral music legally through the Internet. Commercial music publishers often require a credit card transaction, but the speed at which these transactions take place eliminates the need for emergency photocopying, or for waiting for permission to copy out-of-print pieces, as the music is available almost instantaneously (Sharp, 2004). Public domain choral scores are now available for downloading from numerous websites provided by both commercial and non-commercial sources.

Online Choral Library Resources

The Choral Public Domain Library (CPDL) (www.cpdl.org) provides more than 25,000 choral compositions that are available to download, edit, print, and copy free of charge.

Musica is a free resource for ACDA members that currently has over 170,000 scores from 30,000 composers described, with 300,000 multimedia links. If not an ACDA member, you can still access the Musica Virtual Choral Library (www.musicanet.org/en/index.php).

Vigilance, however, is advised with digital downloading of choral music. The role of the choral director as scholar is critical when identifying appropriate editions of available scores. Due to the ease of procuring free downloadable music, it is also easy to access inaccurate scores or poor editions. The burden is on the choral conductor to make scholarly decisions regarding the scores that best reflect the intentions of the composer and appropriate performance practice (Sharp, 2004).

BRAINTEASER 4-1: ATTENDING CHORAL MUSIC CONFERENCES

Register for a state, regional, or national NAfME or ACDA conference this term, and attend two sessions, a choral music reading session geared for middle school teachers and a middle school choir concert. Write a three-page paper on each, listing details of the repertory and your assessment of each piece's appropriateness for middle school singers.

BRAINTEASER 4-2: ANALYZING AND MARKING THE CHORAL SCORE

Select at least one piece for a middle school choir that has changing or changed voices. This may come from your middle school field experience, or be chosen by your instructor. Complete a detailed score analysis and mark the score as indicated in this chapter. Submit your analysis with a copy of the score attached. Be prepared to conduct your choral methods class for practice (provide scores).

BRAINTEASER 4-3: SEARCHING FOR MIDDLE SCHOOL CHORAL MUSIC

Explore some of the repertoire resources identified in this chapter, and make a list of ten pieces for middle school choir that you would like to teach and conduct. Identify the title, composer/arranger, voicing, accompaniment, and publisher.

References

Abrahams, Frank and Head, Paul D. (2011). *Teaching Music Through Performance in Middle School Choir*. Chicago, IL: GIA.

Buchanan, Heather J. and Mehaffey, Matthew W. (2005). *Teaching Music Through Performance in Choir: Volume I*. Chicago, IL: GIA.

Butler, Abby and Lind, Vicki (2005). Renaissance Repertoire for Middle School Choirs. *Choral Journal, 46*(1), 37–41.

Collins, Drew (2012). Using Repertoire to Teach Vocal Pedagogy in All-Male Changing Voice Choirs. *Choral Journal, 52*(9), 34–41.

Hower, Eileen (2006). Designing a New Paradigm for Selecting Music for the Middle School Choir. *Choral Journal, 47*(5), 62–74.

Indiana State School Music Association Required List Download for Organizational Events: www.issma.net/required.php.

Lucas, Mark (2012). Real Men Sing ... Choral Repertoire. *Choral Journal, 52*(9), 42–48.

Phillips, Kenneth H. (2004). *Directing the Choral Music Program*. New York: Oxford University Press.

Reames, Rebecca R. and Warren, Matthew (November, 2006). Recommended Literature: Middle-Level Mixed Choirs. *Choral Journal, 47*(5), 76–88.

Schmidt, Sandefur (2002). *Music Performed at American Choral Directors Association Conventions, 1960–2000*. Lawton, OK: ACDA Monograph 12.

Sharp, Tim (2004). Choral Music and Print-on-Demand. *Choral Journal, 44*(8), 19–23.

Shelton Jr., Tom T. (2016). Repertoire and the Compositional Process: A Conversation with Composers of Junior High/Middle School Repertoire. *Choral Journal, 57*(3), 28–38.

5

RECRUITING AND PLANNING FOR MIDDLE SCHOOL CHOIRS

RECRUITING SINGERS

New teachers are expected to build and develop their choral program, which requires the ability to recruit new students into the ensembles. While there will always be a core of students that enrolls because of past choral experiences or family musical values, the choral teacher needs to "pound the pavement" until the reputation of the program naturally attracts students to join. There are a number of strategies that can help with recruiting students into your ensembles.

Pounding the Pavement

- The guidance counselor at the school can be most helpful in suggesting appropriate students whose abilities and schedules are conducive to choir participation.
- The drama teacher, local piano teachers, and church choir directors will know of students with musical interest, and should be contacted for names of those students.
- Your school colleagues will support your program if you support theirs. Make an effort to attend various academic and sports events at the school, and you will find the support to be reciprocated.
- The elementary feeder school is a primary source of interested students. If fifth graders have a positive choral experience, they are likely to choose choir when they move to the middle school. Invite them to the middle school to hear all of the choirs; then audition them during fifth grade and let them all pass the audition.

- Send a letter to parents/guardians explaining the benefits of choral participation and asking them to encourage their children to enroll.
- Give small prizes to students who recruit additional members into your ensemble.
- Plan and advertise an annual choir trip to perform at state solo and ensemble events.
- Provide annual opportunities for your students to audition for all-state honor choirs hosted by NAfME and ACDA.
- Create scholarship opportunities for students whose participation in choir might be limited due to finances.
- Offer a specialized ensemble, such as a contemporary a cappella group or gospel choir, and have them perform for students during lunch.
- Have your choir perform at local arts, community, and education organizations for increased visibility.
- Get out of your choir room, and personally invite students who you see at lunch and in the hallways to join the choir.
- Make it known that your choir room is a "safe space" for all students.
- Offer single-gender ensembles or separate choirs for high and low voices (Carp, 2004).
- Host an end-of-year choir awards luncheon.
- Organize a curriculum arts "wheel" where non-choir students rotate into a choir class for six to eight weeks. This experience inspires many to enroll in choir as an elective (Hinkley, 1992).

Nothing Succeeds Like Success

The simplest answer to the question of how to recruit and retain is the old adage that "nothing succeeds like success." If a choral program has a reputation for the inclusion of diverse types of students, exciting tours and successful performances, banquets, and awards, and basic word of mouth regarding the "enjoyment" and "pride" quotients, students will want to be part of that scene. Yet, achieving that level of success doesn't happen overnight. It may take a couple of years of experience for the teacher to win over the students with his or her vision, especially if following in the footsteps of a beloved teacher. But energy, passion, love, dedication, humor, and organization will win. None of these characteristics can be underestimated when it comes to growing a successful choral program.

Brainstorm about other ways to recruit new members, and list them here:

_____

_____

_____

NATIONAL MUSIC STANDARDS

What exactly should a middle school student be able to do musically? How well should we expect them to read music? Should they participate in select ensembles such as vocal jazz, madrigals, world music, or show choir during the middle school years? What is the best age to learn to improvise? When should ear-training start? Should middle school students compose? These are just some of the many questions you may have when preparing for a middle school choir, and, fortunately, there are many resources that provide guidance in answering these questions.

National Standards for Arts Education

First, the *National Standards for Arts Education* (1994), although now obsolete, provided useful and concrete recommendations for specific skills and knowledge that all middle school choir students should achieve:

1. Sing choral literature of diverse genres and cultures, with a difficulty level of 3 on a scale of 1 to 6, using good breath control throughout their singing ranges, including some songs performed from memory.
2. Perform instrumental music of diverse genres and cultures, with a difficulty level of 2 on a scale of 1 to 6, accurately and independently.
3. Improvise simple rhythmic and melodic variations in pentatonic and major keys, keeping a consistent style, meter, and tonality.
4. Arrange and compose short pieces for voices, demonstrating how the elements of music are used to achieve unity and variety, tension and release, and balance.
5. Sight-read music with a difficulty level of 2 on a scale of 1 to 6, and read and notate whole, half, quarter, eighth, sixteenth, and dotted notes and rests, in 2/4, 3/4, 4/4, 6/8, 3/8, and 2/2 meters.

6. Use appropriate terminology to describe aural examples of music from diverse genres and cultures.
7. Develop and apply criteria for evaluating the quality and effectiveness of music performances and compositions.
8. Compare choral works with other artworks and describe how they are used to transform similar events, scenes, emotions, or ideas.
9. Compare musical characteristics, functions, and conditions in several cultures of the world.

National Core Arts Standards

The *National Standards for Arts Education* (1994) have been replaced by the voluntary National Core Arts Standards (2014, www.national artsstandards.org/content/conceptual-framework), which contrast in several ways. The National Coalition for Core Arts Standards (NCCAS) emphasize music literacy, with a greater emphasis on creativity than the national content standards provided. The overarching structure of the NCCAS involves three artistic processes: *Creating*, *Performing*, and *Responding*, rather than the nine content standards. The three artistic processes are divided into 13 developmental stages (see below), and each stage is aligned with a descriptive rubric that can be used to rate student understanding from Novice (#1) to Advanced (#5).

National Core Arts Standards (2014)

Creating:
Imagine—Plan and Make—Evaluate and Refine—Present

Performing:
Select—Analyze—Interpret—Rehearse, Evaluate and Refine—Present

Responding:
Select—Analyze—Interpret—Evaluate

There are no specific National Core Arts Standards (2014) for middle school choral music, but there are general ensemble standards (www.nafme.org/my-classroom/standards/core-music-standards/)

which can assist the middle school choir (and high school) director in structuring the curriculum. These include:

- *Creating*
  - o Imagine: Generate musical ideas for various purposes and contexts.
  - o Plan and Make: Select and develop musical ideas for defined purposes and contexts.
  - o Evaluate and Refine: Evaluate and refine selected musical ideas to create musical works that meet appropriate criteria.
  - o Present: Share creative musical works that convey intent, demonstrate craftsmanship, and exhibit originality.

- *Performing*
  - o Select: Select varied musical works to present based on interest, knowledge, technical skill, and context.
  - o Analyze: Analyze the structure and context of varied musical works and their implications for performance.
  - o Interpret: Develop personal interpretations that consider creators' intent.
  - o Rehearse, Evaluate, and Refine: Evaluate and refine personal and ensemble performances, individually or in collaboration with others.
  - o Present: Perform expressively, with appropriate interpretation and technical accuracy, and in a manner appropriate to the audience and context.

- *Responding*
  - o Select: Choose music appropriate for specific purposes and contexts.
  - o Analyze: Analyze how the structure and context of varied musical works inform the response.
  - o Interpret: Support an interpretation of a musical work that reflects the creators'/performers' expressive intent.
  - o Evaluate: Support personal evaluation of musical works and performances based on analysis, interpretation, and established criteria.

New teachers will need to become familiar with the standards of the states in which they become employed so that they can determine their choral curriculum goals. Many state music standards were based on the nine national content standards (1994) and have yet to be revised/ updated.

It may be helpful to consider a similarity between the National Core Arts Standards (2014) and the *National Standards for Arts Education* (1994). The nine national content standards are general, and can easily be applied to one of the three artistic processes of *Creating, Performing,* or *Responding.* For example, national standards #1 (singing alone and with others), #2 (performing on instruments alone and with others), and #5 (reading, notating, and interpreting music) are *Performing* standards; #3 (improvising music) and #4 (composing music) are *Creating* standards; and #6 (listening to, analyzing, and describing music), #7 (evaluating music and music performances), #8 (under-standing relationships between music and other disciplines), and #9 (understanding music in relation to history and culture) are *Responding* standards.

LONG-TERM CURRICULUM PLANNING

Choral methods students will think of interesting ways to address the various standards when planning to teach choral music, but will also grapple with how to accomplish a comprehensive curriculum during the middle school years. Fortunately, most middle schools will offer two to three choirs—at least one beginning choir and one advanced choir, or two beginning single-range (high and low) choirs and one advanced choir—through which students may progress and deepen their musical knowledge and skills. The beginning chorus(es) should be open to all students and they should be taught music fundamentals and good vocal technique, so that they may advance to the next level of choir which provides more challenging musical experiences and knowledge (*Opportunity-to-Learn Standards for Music Instruction*, 1994).

Curricular Units

Thinking large, the teacher whose state's music standards resemble the nine national content standards (1994) might create a three-year curriculum with different units for the various standards. For example, as seen in Table 5.1, during the fall semester the sixth grade chorus would prepare and sing a world music concert complete with costumes

Table 5.1 Curriculum Unit Example

	6TH GRADE	7TH GRADE	8TH GRADE MIXED
September	Standards 1 and 5	Standards 1 and 5	Standards 1 and 5
October	Standards 1, 5, 8, 9	Standards 1, 2, 5, 9	Standards 1, 5, 6, 9
November	Standards 1, 5, 8, 9	Standards 1, 2, 5, 9	Standards 1, 5, 6, 9
December	Standards 1, 5, 8, 9	Standards 1, 2, 5, 9	Standards 1, 5, 6, 9
January	Standards 1, 5, 7	Standards 1, 5, 7	Standards 1, 5, 7
February	Standards 1, 5, 8, 9	Standards 1, 4, 5, 6	Standards 1, 5, 6, 9
March	Standards 1, 5, 8, 9	Standards 1, 4, 5, 6	Standards 1, 3, 5, 6
April	Standards 1, 5, 8, 9	Standards 1, 4, 5, 6	Standards 1, 3, 5, 6
May	Standards 1, 5, 8, 9	Standards 1, 4, 5, 6	Standards 1, 3, 5, 6
June	Standards 1, 5, 7, 8	Standards 1, 4, 5, 7	Standards 1, 3, 5, 6, 7

All Year:	Singing/Reading	Singing/Reading	Singing/Reading
Fall Semester:	World Music	Gospel/Instruments	Classical Listening
Fall Semester:	Cultural Connections	History and Culture	Classical History
Spring Semester:	Classical Repertoire	Composition	Vocal Jazz History
Spring Semester:	History/Language	Listening/Analyzing	Vocal Improvisation
Post-Concerts:	Performance Eval.	Performance Eval.	Performance Eval.

and artwork, the seventh grade chorus would study and perform gospel music with instrumental accompaniment, and the eighth grade mixed chorus would focus on classical music singing, listening, and history; then in the spring semester the sixth graders might engage in a classical music unit that integrates history and language classes, the seventh graders would engage in a composition unit and perform their own compositions, and the eighth graders would study and perform a vocal jazz unit, including improvisation. Singing, reading, and evaluating their own concerts would be a regular part of the choral curriculum for all grades. If the school did not have a large enough choral program to accommodate such a structure, the units or themes could rotate so that every student in choir for all three years would experience a comprehensive music education.

Music Literacy

One of the most important skills to be developed throughout the middle school choral curriculum is music reading, and it must be practiced regularly. A study of nationwide sight-singing requirements of choral festivals revealed the alarming results that only 17 of the 50 United States required sight-singing for middle school students, and only eight states included the sight-reading score in the overall festival rating (Norris, 2004).

More encouraging results were found in other studies. For example, 93% of Florida middle school choral teachers taught sight-singing, and almost half did at every rehearsal (Kuehne, 2007); and directors of contest-winning middle school choirs in Indiana taught sight-singing daily, with most using moveable *do* solfege, Curwen hand signs, rhythmic counting, and regular testing (Madura, 2016). Other approaches can work well too, but only if they are practiced regularly (Demorest, 2003). Materials for teaching sight-singing are readily available, including those listed in the Resources below. A sequential guide to teaching sight-singing can be found in Chapter 9.

Resources

A comprehensive and sequential choral curriculum can be a challenge to plan because of the different standards, skills, knowledge, and music to teach. Various choral curriculum guides have been published, and future teachers should become familiar with them and make informed decisions about their own choral curriculum.

Curriculum Resources for Middle School Choir

Beck, A., Surmani, K.F., and Lewis, B. (2005). *Sing at First Sight: Foundations in Choral Sight-Singing*. Van Nuys, CA: Alfred.

Crocker, Emily and Leavitt, John (2005). *Essential Sight-Singing*. Milwaukee, WI: Hal Leonard.

Experiencing Choral Music (2008). New York: Glencoe/McGraw-Hill.

Madura, Patrice D. (1999). *Getting Started with Vocal Improvisation*. Lanham, MD: R&L Education/National Association for Music Education (NAfME).

Teaching Choral Music: A Course of Study (2006). Lanham, MD: R&L Education/National Association for Music Education (NAfME).

Telfer, Nancy (2006). *Successful Performing*. San Diego, CA: Kjos.

Xiques, David J. (2014). *Solfege and Sonority: Teaching Music Reading in the Choral Classroom*. New York: Oxford.

BRAINTEASER 5-1: CREATING A MIDDLE SCHOOL CHORAL CURRICULUM

In small groups, study the various choral curriculum series; then design a middle school choral curriculum in table format, divided by ensemble type or grade levels. Indicate national or state standards to be addressed through the choral experience, as seen in Table 5.2 on page 82. You may eliminate or add to the skills, concepts, and content areas provided, as long as you can defend your reasons. You may expand the table to any size you wish, or re-create your own visual approach to curriculum.

BRAINTEASER 5-2: APPLYING THE NATIONAL OR STATE STANDARDS

Refer to the National Core Arts Standards or your state's standards for the middle school choral ensemble, and examine your analyzed choral score from the previous chapter to identify those standards that could potentially be integrated into the teaching of that piece. Sketch the following details:

Title of piece:_____

Composer: _____

Publisher: _____Voicing: _____

Grade level: _____

Specific standards: _____

_____

_____

_____

State a selected standard as an important "objective" of one rehearsal (What will students know and/or be able to do as a result of this lesson?):

_____

_____

_____

State how you will assess whether the students have achieved the objective(s) (How will students demonstrate their learning?): _____

_____

_____

_____

Table 5.2 Middle School Curriculum Framework

MIDDLE SCHOOL BEGINNING CHORUS CURRICULUM

	SING/ PERFORM	INSTRUMENT/ PERFORM	IMPROV/ CREATE	COMP/ CREATE	READ/ PERFORM	LISTEN/ RESPOND	EVAL/ RESPOND	INTEGRATE/ RESPOND	HIST/CULT/ RESPOND
SEPT									
OCT									
NOV									
DEC									
JAN									
FEB									
MAR									
APR									
MAY									
JUNE									

MIDDLE SCHOOL ADVANCED MIXED CHOIR CURRICULUM

	SING/ PERFORM	INSTRUMENT/ PERFORM	IMPROV/ CREATE	COMP/ CREATE	READ/ PERFORM	LISTEN/ RESPOND	EVAL/ RESPOND	INTEGRATE/ RESPOND	HIST/CULT/ RESPOND
SEPT									
OCT									
NOV									
DEC									
JAN									
FEB									
MAR									
APR									
MAY									
JUNE									

LESSON PLANNING

Instructional Objectives

Every plan should begin with a statement of the specific instructional objective to be accomplished by the end of the lesson, and end with a specific assessment task. The objective states what the student will learn and the assessment states what the student will do to demonstrate that learning. In fact, these two statements in a lesson plan should be nearly identical.

Sequenced Activities

But how do we get from a learning objective to evidence of learning accomplished? The teacher must organize the lesson by analyzing and breaking down the task into its smallest components, beginning with what is known/familiar to the student and progressing to the unknown (the objective of the lesson), keeping a common thread from step to step. A memorable illustration of this concept is the path from HATE to LOVE, by changing one thread (letter) at a time:

HATE

RATE

ROTE

ROVE

LOVE

In other words, the teacher "backwards plans" in which she or he begins planning with the end goal (the objective) in mind, and then outlines the teaching strategies necessary to move from the choir students' current abilities and knowledge to the new skill or knowledge (Wilson, 2016).

Sample linking strategies to work toward the objective of learning to sing a section of a composition using expressive word stress might be: 1) Sing a vocal warm-up in the key or tonality of the section of music to be learned; 2) perform a call-and-response activity in which the choir echoes the teacher's modeling of challenging melodic patterns in the music to be learned; 3) have the choir sight-read the section of the music prepared in the above steps, using solfege and Curwen hand signs; 4) have the choir repeat that section on the syllable *doo* for a uniform vowel sound; 5) speak that section on text; 6) sing that section on text; 7) analyze the important words and add word stresses to that section. In all likelihood, these seven steps would take more than one rehearsal to accomplish, as all music is learned over multiple rehearsals. Yet the common thread from step to step is evident.

The key to effective lesson planning is to make each step toward the instructional objective achievable and satisfying. The lesson should create a "need to know" in the student by triggering interest and motivation. The motivation may be extrinsic, such as a friendly competition to see which section can sing a melody correctly first, or intrinsic, where the teacher provides a model performance that the student would like to emulate. The students' attention spans must also be taken into consideration. One rough guideline is to keep an activity going for as many minutes as the students' age in years; thus, if the middle school student is 11 to 14 years old, no single piece, improvising lesson, sight-reading activity, or listening lesson should last for more than 11 to 14 minutes for optimum attention.

Modes of Instruction

The lesson plan should include various modes of instruction for actively engaging all students, including:

- Kinesthetic
- Visual
- Aural
- Tactile
- Cognitive
- Emotional.

The teacher should also make use of the following strategies in every lesson:

- Modeling
- Questioning
- Practice
- Formative and Summative Assessment.

Adaptations for Special Learners

Keep in mind that the choir teacher may need to modify instruction for students with disabilities. The instructional pace may need to be slowed down, sheet music and other teaching materials may need to be enlarged, and different colors may be used (Hammel and Hourigan, 2011). The teacher may white-out or highlight a student's vocal part in a four-part choral score to keep attention focused, or seat the student next to a strong and helpful singer (Guthe, 2017.) A student with a visual impairment may benefit from music Braille (learn the basics at www/brl.org/index.html and how to translate notation into Braille at http://delysid.org/freedots.html), or from recordings of his or her individual vocal parts (Abramo, 2012). No matter what the disability, it is important to consider alternate instructional and assessment strategies to accurately measure what students know and can do musically, and to ask for help when needed. The following valuable resources for teaching students with hearing impairments, autism, and many other disabilities are recommended for study.

Music Education Resources for Special Learners

Abramo, Joseph (2012). Disability in the Classroom: Current Trends and Impacts on Music Education. *Music Educators Journal, 99*(1), 39–45.

Adamek, M.S. and Darrow, A. (2010). *Music in Special Education,* 2nd ed. Silver Spring, MD: The American Music Therapy Association.

Hammel, A.M. and Hourigan, R.M. (2011). *Teaching Music to Students with Special Needs: A Label-Free Approach.* New York: Oxford.

Sobol, E.S. (2017). *An Attitude and Approach for Teaching Music to Special Learners,* 2nd ed. Lanham, MD: R&L Education/National Association for Music Education (NAfME).

Ultimately, a lesson plan is just that—a plan. Often the day's circumstances require that the teacher be flexible and alter the plan on the spot. Sometimes the plan just doesn't work, and it is necessary to re-think it for the next rehearsal. It is not appropriate to strictly follow a lesson plan that is clearly not working! It is most important to be present in the moment with the singers, and adjust accordingly.

BRAINTEASER 5-3: WRITING A MIDDLE SCHOOL REHEARSAL PLAN

Using your analyzed score, write a lesson plan using the format in Table 5.3 based on one national or state standard, and one very specific "instructional objective" (Wesolowski, 2015, p. 41), making note of the timings for each step. The acronym SMART can assist in remembering the essential parts of an instructional objective: Specific, Measurable, Appropriate, Realistic, and Time Limited. Carefully reflect upon the many teaching strategies suggested in this chapter. Include various modes of instruction such as verbal, aural, visual, kinesthetic, modeling, questioning, reflecting, practice, and of course, singing. Use the following rehearsal plan as a model for your work.

Sample Rehearsal Plan

Grade Level and Name of Choir: Beginning Middle School Choir

National Standard: National Standard #3B: Improvising Melodies, Variations and Accompaniments: "Students improvise … simple rhythmic and melodic variations on given pentatonic melodies."

State Standard: Indiana State Standard #6.3.1-2: Improvising Melodies, Variations and Accompaniments: "Improvise call and response conversations in vocal and rhythmic warm-ups; improvise sung melodies to a steady beat over an established accompaniment."

Instructional Objective: At the conclusion of the lesson, the middle school choir member will demonstrate the ability to improvise rhythms and melodies by clapping and singing two-bar call-and-response patterns in measures 21–24 of *Chatter with the Angels*.

Materials Needed: *Chatter with the Angels*, arr. Charles Collins, Boosey and Hawkes (two-part treble); metronome.

Previous Lesson(s): The singers learned the melody to *Chatter with the Angels*, as written in measures 5–20; they can sing pentatonic solfege syllables.

Motivating Opening or Script: Announce that you are going to play a recording of Bobby McFerrin improvising, and that at the end you will ask them if they can define what improvisation is. Play the recording. "Can someone please raise your hand and tell me what the word 'improvise' means?" (e.g., "make up the music as you go along").

Procedure: (14 minutes)

Step 1: "Please sit up straight, and be ready to take a good breath and be ready to sing in measure 5 after the piano introduction."

- Review singing *Chatter with the Angels* in measures 5–20. (2 minutes)
- *Anticipated problems*: lazy consonants, lack of support.
- *Possible solutions*: Ask for crisp consonants and four-measure phrases.

Step 2: Direct the students to the improvisation instructions in measure 21.

- All clap the rhythm to the melody of the song.
- Practice Call and Response: Teacher claps two-bar patterns from the song and asks the choir to imitate exactly, and then asks individuals to change the response ("improvise") a little. (Alternatively, they may use "found sounds" or percussion instruments.) (4 minutes)
- *Anticipated problems*: too many beats; too much contrast.
- *Possible solutions*: Practice with class counting beats aloud; practice keeping the original melodic rhythm in mind.

Step 3: "Let's try to improvise with solfege this time!"

- Review singing the G-flat pentatonic scale on solfege (*do re mi so la do*).
- While playing the chordal accompaniment, the teacher sings a simple two-bar call on solfege and asks the choir to imitate it exactly, and then asks individuals to change the response ("improvise") a little. (5 minutes)
- *Anticipated problems*: Pitch inaccuracy; solfege inaccuracy.
- *Possible solutions*: hand signs, repetitive practice.

Step 4: Choir sings from the beginning through measure 24, repeating measures 21–24 with rhythmic and/or melodic improvisations, until each individual has had the opportunity to improvise for two measures. (3 minutes)

Summative Assessment: The middle school choir member will demonstrate the ability to improvise rhythms and melodies by clapping and singing two-bar call-and-response patterns in measures 21–24 of *Chatter with the Angels*.

Extension: After a review of this lesson, singers will improvise pentatonic variations, adding the creative elements of lyrics, dynamics, silence, and varied tone color in two- and four-bar phrases.

Table 5.3 Rehearsal Plan

Grade level and name of choir:

National and/or state standard(s) addressed:

Instructional objective:

Materials needed, including title, composer, publisher, and voicing:

Previous knowledge, if relevant:

Motivating opening or script: (minutes)

Step 1: (min.)

Step 2: (min.)

Step 3: (min.)

Step 4: (min.)

Step 5: (min.)
Etc.

Summative assessment:

Possible extension:

ASSESSMENT AND GRADING

Assessment informs the teacher of what the students learned. Teachers sometimes feel that they taught a great lesson, later to find out that students didn't remember important details. With assessment built into every lesson plan, the teacher can check learning, and if it is found to be inadequate, the teacher needs to take responsibility. It is easy to blame the students for being "inattentive" or "undisciplined" but the truth of the matter is that a good teacher *teaches*. And she or he *learns* to teach by exploring strategies until the students "get it."

What percentage of students should "get it" before the teacher moves on to new material? 25%? 50%? 75%? 90%? A good guideline is that at least 75% of the students should be ready to move on when the teacher does. With repetition, reinforcement, and extra challenges, it is possible to help the 25% catch up, and to provide an extra boost for the gifted.

One of the least pleasant jobs of any teacher is assigning grades. It is human nature to want to encourage students to continue to participate in choir. Yet at the same time, school administrators often want music teachers to be more discriminating in their assessment of their students, rather than assigning an A to everyone who participates. A grade is meant to inform the student and parents of achievement and progress, and to provide feedback on strengths and areas in need of improvement. Some feel that measured skills are less important than the overall music experience, yet others believe that choir grades must be reflective of actual achievement if music is to be considered an academic and rigorous core part of education.

The teacher must decide on the components and their associated percentages of the choir grade, and how those components will be assessed. For example, if memorization of music is a portion of the grade, how will the teacher test each student to be sure that the grade given is appropriate? If sight-singing is important, how much of the course grade will be based on it, and how will the teacher assess it? When a parent wants to know why a student earned a B rather than an A, the teacher needs to have kept accurate records and be able to give specific instances where points were deducted from the course grade. As you can imagine, a grading system can be difficult to implement during a busy rehearsal. Some teachers are masters of effective point systems and others are not quite organized enough to use an elaborate grading method. But every teacher needs a systematic method for reliable and valid assessment.

Music teachers record growth and achievement in various ways. Some follow assessment models, such as closed tasks, open tasks, performance tasks, informal assessments, and self-assessments (Fox, 2016), and use a variety of assessment tools, such as rubrics, performance checklists, rating scales, written assignments, portfolios of student work, and self-assessments (for examples see Wesolowski, 2014, 2015).

Rubrics are especially useful tools for assessment, and teachers are familiar with them because they are typically used in ensemble festival ratings. They enable ratings of specific aspects of performance (tone quality, intonation, rhythmic accuracy, etc.) through clear descriptors of each level of achievement. For example, the description of a "beginning" level *tone quality* might be "breathy" and "unsupported," while the description of an "advanced" level would be "vibrant" and "projecting." The rubric can be used to assess the whole choir, a smaller group, or the individual. The descriptors help teachers and adjudicators provide objective assessment, but they also provide students and parents with clear indicators of what is required to achieve higher levels of performance. For any skill measured, the teacher can easily indicate the appropriate category, such as Beginning, Basic, Proficient, or Advanced. A sample rubric can be seen in Table 5.4.

Table 5.4 Sample Rubric for Sight-Singing Assessment

BEGINNING	BASIC	PROFICIENT	ADVANCED
No sense of pulse	Inconsistent pulse/beat	Consistent pulse/beat	Strong pulse/beat
Missed 7+ rhythms	Missed 3–6 rhythms	Missed 1–2 rhythms	Missed no rhythms
Lacks a tonal center	Developing tonal center	Stable tonal center	Strong tonal center
Missed 7+ pitches	Missed 3–6 pitches	Missed 1–2 pitches	Missed no pitches

FINAL THOUGHTS ON MIDDLE SCHOOL TEACHING

Now that you have studied the middle school changing voice, have conducted auditions and warm-ups, analyzed and learned appropriate repertoire, and planned curriculum and lesson plans, you are ready to conduct your own rehearsals. Always keep in mind that a teacher's positive attitude and high expectations contribute to a positive and interesting experience for the choir members. Not surprisingly, a teacher's negative and discouraging attitude contributes to negative behavior and performance (Wentzel, 2002).

A fascinating study found that middle school choir students who were asked to practice deep breathing and silently repeat the words "bold," "confident," and "free" before a performance achieved significantly improved performances, dynamics, expression, and timing, suggesting that middle school students are capable of high levels of expressive performance skill when encouraged by a positive teacher (Broomhead et al., 2012).

These final thoughts are offered as inspiration for effective and enjoyable rehearsals:

- Be yourself.
- Be enthusiastic.
- Care about your students.
- Call students by their preferred name.
- Focus on the well-behaving singers.
- Insist on good posture.
- Insist that students watch the conductor.
- Insist on good choral tone and intonation.
- Know and love the music.
- Have your students sight-sing every day.
- Have the singers stand sometimes, sit sometimes, and move frequently.
- Talk less, model more.
- Talk less, make more music.
- Don't work just for notes—listen for entrances, cut-offs, intonation, phrasing, dynamics, diction, vowels, and word stress.
- Make some beautiful music at every rehearsal and bring the students' attention to that beauty when it occurs.

BRAINTEASER 5-4: CREATING A RUBRIC

Create a rubric for the assessment stage of the lesson plan you just created in Brainteaser 5-3.

BRAINTEASER 5-5: CREATING A GRADING PLAN

Request a copy of your local middle school choir teacher's grading system, and share it with the choral methods class. Discuss the pros and cons of the various approaches, and then create one for your future choir. Specify grade percentages for important skills, knowledge, and participation.

BRAINTEASER 5-6: OBSERVING THE MIDDLE SCHOOL CHORAL REHEARSAL

Observe a middle school choral rehearsal to analyze the teacher's instructional objectives, strategies used to achieve those objectives, and ways achievement of the objectives was assessed. Does it match the model presented in this chapter? If not, how is it different?

References

Abramo, Joseph (2012). Disability in the Classroom: Current Trends and Impacts on Music Education. *Music Educators Journal, 99*(1), 39–45.

Adamek, M.S. and Darrow, A. (2010). *Music in Special Education*, 2nd ed. Silver Spring, MD: The American Music Therapy Association.

Beck, A., Surmani, K.F., and Lewis, B. (2005). *Sing at First Sight: Foundations in Choral Sight-Singing*. Van Nuys, CA: Alfred.

Broomhead, P., Skidmore, J.B., Eggett, D.L., and Mills, M.M. (2012). The Effects of a Positive Mindset Trigger Word Pre-performance Routine on the Expressive Performance of Junior High Age Singers. *Journal of Research in Music Education, 60*(1), 62–80.

Carp, Randi S. (2004). Single Gender Choral Ensembles, Attitudes and Practices: A Survey of Southern California High School Choir Directors. USC Doctoral Dissertation, UMI 3145167.

Crocker, Emily and Leavitt, John (2005). *Essential Sight-Singing*. Milwaukee, WI: Hal Leonard.

Demorest, Steven M. (2003). *Building Choral Excellence: Teaching Sight-Singing in the Choral Rehearsal*. New York: Oxford University Press.

Experiencing Choral Music (2008). New York: Glencoe/McGraw-Hill.

Fox, Derrick (2016). Assessment in the Choral Rehearsal. *Teaching Music, 24*(2), 28–31.

Guthe, Emily (2017). The Choral Process: Enhancing the Success of Students with Disabilities within the Choral Structure. *Choral Journal, 57*(10), 51–55.

Hammel, A.M. and Hourigan, R.M. (2011). *Teaching Music to Students with Special Needs: A Label-Free Approach*. New York: Oxford University Press.

Hinkley, June (February, 1992). Blocks, Wheels, and Teams: Building a Middle School Schedule. *Music Educators Journal, 78*(6), 26–30.

Kuehne, Jane M. (2007). A Survey of Sight-Singing Instructional Practices in Florida Middle-School Choral Programs. *Journal of Research in Music Education, 55*(2), 115–128.

Madura, Patrice D. (1999). *Getting Started with Vocal Improvisation.* Lanham, MD: R&L Education/National Association for Music Education (NAfME).

Madura, Patrice (2016). A Descriptive Study of Award-Winning Secondary School Music Teachers in Indiana. *ICDA Notations, 38*(1), 14–15.

National Standards for Arts Education (1994). Lanham, MD: R&L Education/National Association for Music Education (NAfME).

Norris, Charles E. (Spring, 2004). A Nationwide Overview of Sight-Singing Requirements of Large-Group Choral Festivals. *Journal of Research in Music Education, 52*(1), 16–28.

Opportunity-to-Learn Standards for Music Instruction (1994). Lanham, MD: R&L Education/National Association for Music Education (NAfME).

Sobol, E.S. (2017). *An Attitude and Approach for Teaching Music to Special Learners,* 2nd ed. Lanham, MD: R&L Education/National Association for Music Education (NAfME).

Teaching Choral Music: A Course of Study (2006). Lanham, MD: R&L Education/National Association for Music Education (NAfME).

Telfer, Nancy (2006). *Successful Performing.* San Diego, CA: Kjos.

Wentzel, Kathryn R. (2002). Are Effective Teachers Like Good Parents? *Child Development, 73*(1), 287–301.

Wesolowski, Brian C. (2014). Documenting Student Learning in Music Performance: A Framework. *Music Educators Journal, 101*(1), 77–85.

Wesolowski, Brian C. (2015). Tracking Student Achievement in Music Performance: Developing Student Learning Objectives for Growth Model Assessments. *Music Educators Journal, 102*(1), 39–55.

Wilson, Roland (June 24, 2016). Chopping up the Score: Effective Lesson Planning for the Secondary Choral Director. www.nafme.org.

Xiques, David J. (2014). *Solfege and Sonority: Teaching Music Reading in the Choral Classroom.* New York: Oxford University Press.

6

HIGH SCHOOL SINGERS: HEARING THEIR VOICES

The teaching of singing continues to be an integral part of the choral curriculum throughout high school. Although many high school chorus members have had previous choir experience, there will be students who are new to the choral program or whose choral experience did not provide adequate voice instruction. You must remember that you will be the only voice teacher most of the students will ever have.

Although both young men's and women's voices continue to mature throughout the high school years, they are more settled than in the middle school years, and the traditional classifications of SATB can be used. An exception would be a ninth grade male ensemble with both unchanged and changing voices, necessitating SCB or SACB or other voice classifications.

VOCAL RANGES

Although every textbook will present a slightly different set of ranges for high school SATB voice parts, and every choir will have singers in various stages of vocal development, the following ranges and tessituras for SSAATTBB should be committed to memory for ease in auditions, warm-ups, and repertoire selection (Phillips, 1992). Looking closely at Musical Example 6.1, it can be seen that each voice part has an approximate range of a twelfth and a tessitura made up of the middle fifth of the range. This will aid in memorization.

To identify the ranges for the *beginning* SATB group, conflate the S1 and S2 parts (from Musical Example 6.1) to include only the shared notes between them; and do the same for the A1 and A2, T1

Musical Example 6.1   High School SSAATTBB Ranges and Tessituras

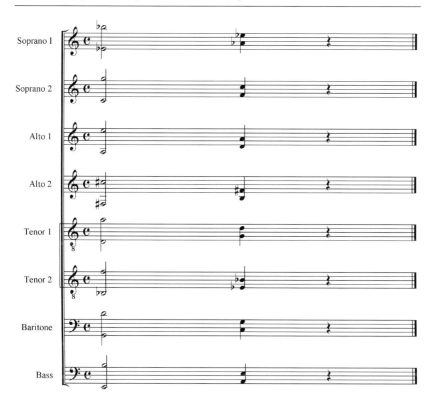

and T2, and B1 and B2 parts. See the resulting range of a tenth and tessitura of a third in Musical Example 6.2. These limited ranges and tessituras are very conservative and generalized, but will assist in selecting accessible repertoire for novice high school singers.

Musical Example 6.2   High School SATB Ranges and Tessituras (Beginning)

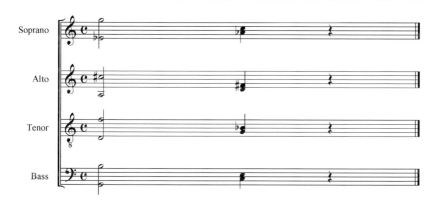

For the *advanced* SATB group, simply combine all the pitches of the S1 and S2, A1 and A2, T1 and T2, and B1 and B2 ranges and tessituras from Musical Example 6.1. Each vocal part indicated in Musical Example 6.3 ranges from the lowest note of part 2 to the highest note of part 1. These wider ranges reflect the vocal development of experienced high school singers and assist in selecting challenging repertoire.

Musical Example 6.3   High School SATB Ranges and Tessituras (Advanced)

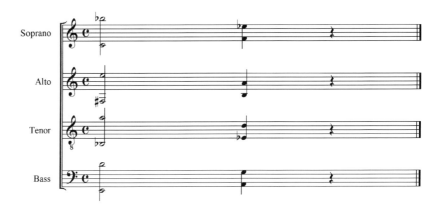

AUDITIONS

The choral audition has two main purposes: to determine choir membership and to place singers in sections. While auditioning can be nerve-wracking for many students, it is important for them to know that audition experience actually improves one's ability to audition successfully (Fuller, 1989). The preparation for and pressure of the first audition make the second one a little easier, and so on, similar to athletes who perform better under the pressure of a championship game when they have had that experience previously.

There is no simple "quick and dirty" audition procedure for high school choirs as there was for middle school choirs. Auditions can be quite varied in the high school because of the different types of groups—there is often a non-select ensemble, a treble or low voice group, a middle-level mixed ensemble, an advanced mixed ensemble, and at least one specialized group such as a vocal jazz ensemble or show choir. But no matter what type of choir, the choral director will want to hear each student for proper choir and section placement.

Auditions for the various groups may include some or all of the following criteria (Crabb, 2002):

- vocal range and tessitura
- tone quality
- intonation
- sight-singing skill
- pitch and rhythm memory
- blend
- controllable vibrato
- flexibility of tone
- diction
- dynamics
- breath management
- theory knowledge
- improvisation skill
- solo potential
- dance ability
- attitude
- schedule availability
- reliability
- past musical experience
- enthusiasm for choral music.

Audition Procedures

The choir director needs to announce the auditions, post a sign-up schedule for students at 10- or 15-minute intervals (outside of class time if possible), and distribute audition forms. Part I of the form requests demographic information to be completed by the student and brought to the audition, and Part II is for the instructor to complete during the audition. The audition form found in Table 6.1 can be adapted to fit any type of audition.

When the student enters the room, greet him or her by name in a warm and friendly manner to help ease the tension that comes with any audition. Make short conversation about the student's information on the form in order to hear the pitch of the speaking voice. Position the student so that he or she cannot see the piano keys to alleviate any fears of singing "too high." Move quickly to five-note descending vocalises that are easy to sing, and then move to those that reveal the extremes of the student's range, all the while taking notes on the student's range, tessitura, tone quality, and intonation.

Table 6.1 High School Choir Audition Form

Students: Please complete Part I of this form, and bring to your audition.

Part I:

Name: Date:

Year in school:

Choir experience:

Private music study:

Current class and work schedule:

Hobbies:

Contact information:

Do not write below this line

Part II:

Range and Tessitura

_____

_____

_____

_____

_____

Tone Quality:	1	2	3	4	5
Intonation:	1	2	3	4	5
Sight-Singing:	1	2	3	4	5
Tonal/Rhythmic Memory:	1	2	3	4	5
Solo Ability:	1	2	3	4	5
Other:	1	2	3	4	5
Other:	1	2	3	4	5

Voice Part Assigned: _____

Choir Assigned: _____

Comments: _____

_____

_____

_____

Tessitura

It is essential to find the student's tessitura (best sounding, easiest to produce pitches) as quickly as possible, and if this is difficult to hear, one approach is to have the student sing the first phrase of *America* ("My Country 'Tis of Thee, Sweet Land of Liberty, of Thee I Sing") in at least two different keys (G and C), to see if the voice sounds better in the soprano/tenor tessitura (key of G) or the alto/bass tessitura (key of C).

Voice Timbre

Listening for the following timbres in conjunction with range and tessitura can help determine voice classification (Phillips, 1992).

- Soprano I: Light and pure
- Soprano II: Full; common voice type at this age
- Alto I: Similar quality to soprano II, but a bit lower
- Alto II: Full and rich; rare at this age
- Tenor I: Light and lyric; the last voice to develop
- Tenor II: Fuller than Tenor I
- Baritone: Full; common voice classification at this age
- Bass: Heavy and dark; rare at this age.

Pitch and Rhythmic Memory

A test of tonal memory can predict choral achievement (Mowrer, 1996). Tonal imitation exercises require no previous formal music training, and can provide vital information on how well the student can remember melodies. Two or three short examples (four or eight beats in length) sequenced from extremely simple to more challenging such as those in Musical Example 6.4 work well. A student's performance can be rated quickly on a five-point scale, with "1" indicating that no notes were correct, "2" indicating that only one or two notes were correct, "3"—about half of the notes were correct, "4"—most notes were correct, and "5"—a perfect performance.

Musical Example 6.4   Melodic Imitation Exercises

Sight-Singing

Sight-reading examples should also be sequenced from simple to more challenging in order to determine proper choir placement. However, if a singer cannot sight-sing at all, do not belabor the point by asking him or her to sing all examples. Two key aspects to keep in mind are that 1) sight-reading material for an audition should be several levels simpler than the actual music to be performed, and 2) sight-reading material should be placed in an appropriate key for the student's range to provide the opportunity to succeed. In the next examples, the same melody is notated in different keys and clefs to illustrate this point.

Musical Example 6.5   Beginning Sight-Singing Example

Musical Example 6.6 Advanced Sight-Singing Example

Solo

You may also want the students to sing a solo of their choice, ranging from "Happy Birthday" to an art song, or an improvisation of a scat solo to the blues. However, with only ten minutes, the teacher has to be extremely organized and efficient, which takes practice.

CHOIR SEATING

Once you have finished auditioning, you can determine the best seating arrangement for your singers. There are many ways that choral sections can be arranged to sit, and the choral director must experiment to find the best sounding arrangement of voices. Some directors place the bass and alto sections in the back row, with the sopranos in front of the basses for optimal tuning.

B A

S T

Other directors place the low voices in the middle, particularly if there are noticeably fewer of them in the ensemble.

S B T A

If the tenor voices are few in number, they may be placed in the middle with the basses in the back row.

B

S   T   A

Generally, sectional seating is preferred for polyphonic pieces, but mixed quartets are often preferable for homophonic pieces for better intonation.

SATB   SATB   SATB   SATB   SATB   SATB

SATB   SATB   SATB   SATB   SATB   SATB

Regarding sectional seating, Brenda Smith and Robert Sataloff, in their book *Choral Pedagogy* (2006), suggest that, within each section, singers with dark, more fundamental tones should be placed between lighter voices, and strong singers should be placed behind the other singers in each section. Charlene Archibeque (1977) seats two strong readers next to two weaker readers so that the strong ones reinforce each other and help the ones to the side. It is also desirable to give singers some physical space between them for optimal hearing. Singers and audiences tend to prefer the choir's overall sound when singers are given more acoustical space around one another (Daugherty, 1999; Ekholm, 2000). The choral teacher will need to experiment with different placements to find the best sound, and may occasionally change seating arrangements to give the singers a fresh sonic experience.

VALUES AND CHALLENGES

The high school choral program has different challenges for the teacher than the middle school program. The rapid hormone changes and the accompanying turmoil are less pronounced during the high school years, and the voices are beginning to settle into their new, adult ranges. SATB music can generally be used, and most students enrolled in choir are there because they want to be. This no doubt sounds as if high school teaching is easier than middle school teaching. This may be true, but as we learn, every level has its challenges.

Age Proximity

One challenge is that first year teachers are somewhat close in age to senior high school students. The age proximity often causes the high school students to test the authority of the young teacher, and the teacher to lack confidence asserting that authority with older (and often larger!) students. New teachers must firmly and consistently enforce classroom procedures, rules, and consequences to establish clear student behavior expectations.

A related issue is the infatuation that some high school students may feel toward a dynamic and caring music teacher who is close in age. It is the teacher who must be aware of and refrain from any behavior that could potentially be misunderstood by a student as mutual admiration, or by a parent or staff member as questionable. One major safeguard is to avoid being alone with any student, ever. The loss of a teaching license for life is the usual result of inappropriate teacher–student behavior, and that is always a tragedy after all the years devoted to the professional goal of becoming a music teacher.

Recruiting and Retaining Singers

Another potential challenge is attracting enough singers, especially low voices, to the choral program. Students have many options for curricular and extra-curricular activities in high school, and time conflicts naturally arise between choir and other commitments. If there is a strong choral feeder program at the middle school and especially if a relationship has been established between the middle and high school programs to assist in recruiting to the next level, then the high school director is fortunate. Without that, it can take patience and a few years to establish a strong and valued choral program comprising multiple levels of choral ensembles with balanced vocal parts.

The high school choral director needs to be an active recruiter for the choral program, especially in the early years. There are many students who wouldn't consider joining choir without an invitation from the teacher or from other students. It is important to consider some of the reasons high school students may choose not to join or stay in the choir (Tipps, 2003), and to approach recruitment with these reasons in mind:

- time conflicts
- friends not involved in music
- music not considered important to adulthood
- vocal insecurity

- inability to read music
- stage fright
- dislike of classical music.

The suggestions given in the previous chapter for recruiting middle school singers are applicable to the high school level as well (contacting the guidance counselor, drama teacher, local piano teachers, church choir directors, and parents; providing financial aid to students who otherwise would not be able to participate; giving small rewards to singers who recruit new members; and offering single-range choirs). Other recruitment strategies (Horne, 2007) include:

- inviting local elementary school or middle school students to perform with the top high school choir at a school basketball game or other event
- visiting the middle school frequently to conduct warm-ups or sectionals
- posting flyers about choir auditions, including descriptions of the different choirs, an invitation to everyone to audition, and information on when, where, and how to audition
- starting a "choir club" for any students who were ever in choir
- advertising choir as a "safe" zone for all students
- advertising choir trips, tours, festivals, and contests
- presenting innovative and special performances for peers and parents
- presenting choral role models that inspire students to join.

There will always be students whose priority it is to join the choir, and these tend to be students who have had the following experiences:

- previous positive school music experiences
- previous private instrumental instruction, particularly the piano
- parents and peers who value and participate in music (Siebenaler, 2006).

In fact, these are the same singers who often enjoy a lifelong commit-ment to music and continue to sing in choirs as adults (Bell, 2004; Darrough, 1990). This long-term commitment is the goal of every music teacher—to plant a seed, nurture it, and watch it blossom during the school years so that singers will have rich and satisfying musical lives. Thus, the music teacher would be wise to actively invite and welcome *all* students into the choral program and place them in the most appropriate choir for their skills, abilities, and interests. These musical experiences may provide the only opportunities for students to develop the skills, knowledge, and attitudes that will allow them to participate in meaningful music experiences during their lifetime.

A startling result of the National Assessment of Educational Progress (NAEP) was that only 35% of eighth graders were able to sing *America* with tonal accuracy, and less than 25% sang with an appropriate tone quality (Jellison, menc.org/documents/onlinepublica tions/vision2020/HowCanAllPeopleContinue.pdf). Thus, there is much work to be done by high school choral music teachers to help our nation's and our world's people to learn to sing, and it begins with effective recruiting into our choral ensembles.

Performance Anxiety

Performance anxiety, also known as stage fright, is a common experience for many choral singers, and undoubtedly a reason why some students resist joining choir. Ryan and Andrews (2009) found that 57% of choir members felt moderately anxious during at least half of their choral performances. This was particularly a problem for singers with few years of choral experience. Factors that increased anxiety for choral singers were difficult music, memorization of music, the importance of a particular performance, and the conductor. Especially notable was that 59% reported that the conductor made "a lot, even all, of the difference" (p. 115) in their level of anxiety. The conductor's anxiety was the major contributor to communicating anxiety to the singers. Conductors' awareness of the impact of their behavior on the choristers' anxiety may help to diminish this debilitating condition.

Choral singers with performance anxiety reported using a variety of coping strategies, including meditation, exercise, prayer, deep breathing, yoga, self-help books, extra practice, quiet time, Alexander technique, prescription drugs, over-the-counter drugs, alcohol, and psychotherapy (Ryan and Andrews, 2009.) Clearly, the choral teacher has to take responsibility for the singers' sense of readiness for performance.

Mindfulness scholar Frank Diaz (2017) recommends this "4–7–8" technique and teaches it to ensembles to calm them before a perfor-mance: Breathe in through the nose for 4 counts, hold for 7 counts, and exhale through the mouth for 8 counts. Repeat four to five times.

When finished, breathe normally, noticing the sensation of air as it enters your nostrils for two to three minutes. Then, with eyes closed, allow the sounds in the room to enter your awareness, without fixating on any of them, for two to three minutes.

Performance psychologist Noa Kageyama (2017) developed a comprehensive course at the Juilliard School to overcome music performance anxiety, and it is also available online at www.bulletproof musician.com. In *Beyond Practicing*, he provides practical steps, videos, workbooks, illustrations, research, and assessments to guide musicians in achieving the seven psychological skills of top performers: energy, preparation, confidence, courage, concentration, focus, and resilience. These seven psychological skills can be subdivided as follows: Energy (optimal energy, performance energy, and audition energy); Preparation (ability to learn, practice habits, and memorizing music); Confidence (self-talk, expectancy, and mental rehearsal); Courage (confronting fear, building courage, and confronting failure); Concentration (accessing alpha, building stamina, and concentrating on command); Focus (getting present, getting mentally quiet, and focusing past distractions); and Resilience (recovering from mistakes, and becoming mentally tough.) Choral teachers who are serious about overcoming their own performance anxiety and/or that of their singers will benefit greatly from this course of study and, as a result, eliminate students' fears of joining and staying in choir.

Gender Identity

Gender identity is a complex and fluid issue that is becoming more and more noticeable in choral classrooms, and therefore has implications for recruiting and retaining singers in our ensembles (Palkki, 2016). *Gender-diverse* adolescents often prefer clothing, mannerisms, and voice pitch from other than their birth sex, but have not planned to medically transition from one gender to another, while *transgender* adolescents consistently pursue a cross-gender identity because they are very uncomfortable ("dysphoric") with their birth-assigned gender. Choral directors need to be aware of and respect both groups of students for practical reasons such as assigning voice parts, sectional seating, concert dress, and rehearsal language.

One of the choral teacher's main responsibilities is to guide the healthy development of the adolescent singing voice, as discussed throughout this book. Gender-diverse and transgender singers often have different needs than the cisgender students (those whose gender identity matches their birth sex). For example, gender-diverse students may identify with and want to sing in a choir section that does not match their actual vocal range. In these cases, the teacher may allow the students to sit near, and dress like, their preferred gender, while helping them to sing in the section that doesn't harm their voice. On the other hand, transgender students often take hormones, particularly testosterone ("T"), and need the teacher's help with monitoring their vocal range changes. Not unlike adolescent boys with changing voices, transgender men (female-to-male, or F2M) will need voice testing every few months to assure that they are singing in the choir section that matches their vocal development.

Individual voice lessons are often very helpful and encouraging to transgender students who are in the beginning stages of hormone treatment (Steele, 2016). Each voice is unique, and lessons incorporating the middle school changing voice warm-ups found in Chapter 3 will help the singer adjust to and transition into the new voice, and into the choir. During the early transition, students will often have a limited range, and will need to be encouraged to sing whatever pitches they are able in the choir's warm-ups, exercises, and repertoire. If the singer reveals when he started taking "T," the teacher can anticipate 6–12 months from that date for the voice to settle (Ramseyer Miller, 2016, AD@GALAChoruses.org).

The following suggestions, as identified by the U.S. Departments of Education and Justice, Joshua Palkki (2017), and GALA Choruses, are important for secondary choral teachers to know and do, in order to provide a welcoming and safe rehearsal environment.

- Teachers should introduce themselves and ask students for their chosen pronouns on the first day of class or in the audition (e.g., "Hi! I'm Dr. Madura and I use she/her/hers pronouns. Please introduce yourself. Share your name, your pronouns, and your favorite song.").
- Teachers should ask students what name they prefer to be called on the first day of class, even if different from school records.
- Consider whether ensembles such as the "Women's Choir" might include a trans woman who sings an octave lower, or whether the ensemble should be renamed.

- Consider seating transgender students on the edge of a section where they will feel comfortable vocally and socially.
- Consider changing from the traditional choir uniform of dresses and tuxedos to a more gender-neutral concert attire.
- Refer to choir sections by their names (SATB) rather than by gender.
- Don't make assumptions about a transgender person's sexual orientation (e.g., a trans man may or may not be gay).
- Be respectful of confidentiality.
- Confront disrespectful attitudes.

Become informed about resources for all of your LGBT students, and provide a safe and supportive learning environment for them. They are at risk for harassment, suicide, homelessness, family rejection, and harsh disciplinary action. The statistics are alarming (Indiana GSANetwork.org). For example, 58% of LGBT students feel unsafe at school, 30% of LGBT youth have been physically abused by a family member, 40% of youth experiencing homelessness identify as LGBT, and 25% of trans youth have attempted suicide. The teacher can make the choral ensemble one of the safest places for LGBT high school students to belong. Just a few of many helpful websites are www.GenderNexus.org, www.webetrees.org, www.GALAChoruses. org, www.apa.org/pi/lgbt/aspx, http://familyproject.sfsu.edu, and http://community.pflag.org.

Social Identity

A sense of belonging to a group is key to healthy adolescent social identity development. Choir is a team-like organization where individual and collaborative responsibilities contribute to the sense of belonging. In one study, high school singers reported that the more time they spent together, the smaller the ensemble, and the more intense the rehearsals and performances, the stronger they identified as a team (Parker, 2014). Their social identity developed through feelings of accomplishment and pride in individual daily work and successful performances, although they considered "cliques" and "egos" detrimental to team identity. Students felt that belonging to choir had helped them become more outgoing and more at peace with themselves. Importantly, Parker suggested that this "identity-defining process of choral participation may act protectively to aid adolescents as they enter new and more challenging stages of development" (p. 30).

Social identity development is a process, however, and it may take time for a new choir member to adjust to a particular choir's expectations. "Singing here I feel trapped and oppressed in one voice," expressed one singer who was first encouraged to sing in her head voice when she joined an urban community choir (Becker and Goffi-Fynn, 2016, p. 9). She wanted to "sing out" and "strong with meaning" (p. 15) as she did in her gospel choir. Her gospel singing voice was deeply tied to her sense of personal and social identity. Fortunately, her new choir director not only taught her the value of being able to sing in her head voice, but nurtured her (and all the singers') "esteem and agency" by regularly inviting and honoring their repertoire preferences, solo performance readiness, and opinions about the chorus and singing experience through questionnaires and interviews. When singers understand that their voices (both literally and metaphorically) matter and contribute to the choir, they feel individually and socially empowered and engaged.

Culturally Responsive Teaching

Culturally Responsive Teaching (CRT) refers to student-centered teaching in which the cultural knowledge and performance styles of diverse students are used as conduits to make learning more appropriate and effective for them (Gay, 2000). The term "culture" has been interpreted broadly, to include the following: age, gender, sexual orientation, socio-economic status, ethnicity, religion, disability, culture, educational background, geographic/regional background, and language. The purpose of CRT is to eliminate negative stereotypes and micro-aggressions through understanding (Columbus State Community College website, Columbus, OH).

The more a teacher can learn about the students' cultural values, traditions, learning styles, and communication styles, the better. Thus, preservice teachers should seek opportunities for field experiences in urban settings to deepen their understanding of the urban context. Experiences singing popular music, gospel music, and world music also help prepare them for urban choral teaching (Shaw, 2015, 2016). The goal of providing a safe and inclusive learning environment for all students in our choirs is a complex one that will require continued learning and commitment.

BRAINTEASER 6-1: OBSERVING HIGH SCHOOL CHOIRS

Observe a beginning and an advanced high school choral ensemble, and compare and contrast the number of voice parts, the vocal ranges, and the choral tone between the two ensembles. Prepare to discuss in your choral methods class.

BRAINTEASER 6-2: AUDITIONING HIGH SCHOOL VOICES

Ask the local high school teacher if you may practice auditioning a couple of students for ten minutes each. Individually, or in teams of two, audition at least two students following the procedures outlined in this chapter and completing the High School Audition Form found in Table 6.1. Prepare the necessary number of audition forms in advance of your visit. Discuss your results with your choral methods class, and submit the completed forms to your instructor.

BRAINTEASER 6-3: EXPLORING SINGER PLACEMENT

In your field experience or in your choral methods class, rehearse a composition and experiment with different placements of singers as suggested above. Listen carefully and discuss what arrangements you preferred and why.

BRAINTEASER 6-4: RECRUITING SINGERS

Study all of the values and challenges presented in this chapter, and compose detailed strategies that you will use to encourage and recruit students to join your high school choir. If possible, interview a few high school students and ask them why they decided to join and stay in the choral program.

BRAINTEASER 6-5: INTERVIEWING A HIGH SCHOOL MUSIC TEACHER

Ask a high school music teacher if you may interview him or her. You may use the questions below, or prepare others that you have been wondering about.

Why did you choose to teach high school music?

What other teaching and performance experiences have you had?

How long have you taught at this school, and overall?

What do you enjoy most about teaching high school choir?

What are the biggest challenges of teaching high school choir?

Do you have to recruit singers for your program? If so, how?

Do you have a school-wide and/or choir discipline policy?

What percentage of your overall program has boys with unchanged voices?

What advice do you have for me as I prepare for my choral teaching career?

How can I assist you during my time here at your school?

References

Archibeque, Charlene (August, 1997). A Choral Director's Rehearsal Checkup. *Choral Journal, 38*(1), 33–34.

Becker, Nicole and Goffi-Fynn, Jeanne (2016). Discovering Voices: Expanding Students' Musical and Vocal Ideals in an Urban Community Children's Choir. *Choral Journal, 56*(7), 8–19.

Bell, Cindy L. (2004). Update on Community Choirs and Singing in the United States. *International Journal of Research in Choral Singing, 2*(1), 39–52.

Crabb, R. Paul (2002). Choral Audition Procedures of Six Well Known Conductors: Webb, Noble, Bruffy, Carrington, Ehly, and Warland. *Choral Journal, 42*(9), 35–58.

Darrough, Galen Paul (1990). Older Adult Participants in Selected Retirement Community Choruses. DMA Doctoral Dissertation, Arizona State University, AAT 9101869.

Daugherty, James F. (1999). Spacing, Formation, and Choral Sound: Preferences and Perceptions of Auditors and Choristers. *Journal of Research in Music Education, 47*(3), 224–238.

Diaz, Frank M. (April 21, 2017). Personal Interview.

Ekholm, Elizabeth (2000). The Effect of Singing Mode and Seating Arrangement on Choral Blend and Overall Choral Sound. *Journal of Research in Music Education, 48*(2), 123–135.

Fuller, Charles Lee (1989). Factors Related to Success at All-Region and All-State Choir Auditions in Texas. DMA Doctoral Dissertation, Arizona State University, DA 9005981.

Gay, Geneva (2000). *Culturally Responsive Teaching: Theory, Research, and Practice.* New York: Teachers College Press.

Horne, Camilla Joy (2007). Recruitment, Participation and Retention of African Americans in High School Choral Ensembles. Doctoral Dissertation, University of Minnesota, AAT 3279675.

Jellison, Judith A. (n.d.). How Can All People Continue to Be Involved in Meaningful Music Participation? menc.org/documents/onlinepublications/vision2020/HowCanAllPeopleContinue.pdf.

Kageyama, Noa (2017). *Beyond Practicing*, 2nd ed. New York: The Bulletproof Musician.

Mowrer, Tony A. (1996). Tonal Memory as an Audition Factor for Choral Ensembles. PhD Doctoral Dissertation, Temple University, DA9632078.

Palkki, Joshua (2016). My Voice Speaks for Itself: The Experiences of Three Transgender Students in Secondary School Choral Programs. PhD Dissertation, Michigan State University, ProQuest Number 10141543.

Palkki, Joshua (June/July, 2017). Inclusivity in Action: Transgender Students in the Choral Classroom. *Choral Journal, 57*(11), 20.

Parker, Elizabeth Cassidy (2014). The Process of Social Identity Development in Adolescent High School Choral Singers: A Grounded Theory. *Journal of Research in Music Education, 62*(1), 18–32.

Phillips, Kenneth H. (1992). *Teaching Kids to Sing.* New York: Schirmer Books.

Ramseyer Miller, Jane (2016). Creating Choirs That Welcome Transgender Singers, *Choral Journal, 57*(4), 61–63.

Ryan, Charlene and Andrews, Nicholle (2009). An Investigation into the Choral Singer's Experience of Music Performance Anxiety. *Journal of Research in Music Education, 57*(2), 108–126.

Shaw, Julia T. (2015). "Knowing Their World": Urban Choral Music Educators' Knowledge of Context. *Journal of Research in Music Education, 63*(2), 198–223.

Shaw, Julia T. (2016). "The Music I Was Meant to Sing": Adolescent Choral Students' Perceptions of Culturally Responsive Pedagogy. *Journal of Research in Music Education, 64*(1), 45–70.

Siebenaler, Dennis James (September, 2006). Factors That Predict Participation in Choral Music for High-School Students. *Research and Issues in Music Education, 4*(1), 1–9.

Smith, Brenda and Sataloff, Robert T. (2006). *Choral Pedagogy*, 2nd ed. San Diego, CA: Plural Publishing.

Steele, Danielle (2016). Training the Transgender Singer. *INform: A Quarterly Publication from the Indiana Music Education Association and Foundation, 71*(2), 13–16.

Tipps, James W. (2003). A Preliminary Study of Factors That Limited Secondary School Choral Involvement. *International Journal of Research in Choral Singing, 1*(1), 22–28.

7

WARM-UPS FOR HIGH SCHOOL CHOIRS

Every choir director knows numerous warm-ups from years of choir experience. Therefore, the preparation of warm-ups for choral rehearsals should be simple, right? And isn't it acceptable to skip warm-ups altogether in favor of getting right to the rehearsal of the music of the day? The answer to both questions is "No," for two main reasons.

First, warm-ups are important for all singers, trained or not, because they help focus the voice, body, and mind away from all of the speaking, mental preoccupation, and physical stresses of the day. And, in addition, *all* muscles should be warmed up before and cooled down after exercise, and these include the many muscles involved in singing, such as the chest and neck muscles (Smith and Sataloff, 2006). Second, it bears repeating that, for most high school chorus members, the choir director is the only voice teacher they will ever have. Therefore, to prepare the choir for singing each day, and to teach students how to sing well for a lifetime, a curriculum for voice building needs to be followed.

Teaching Kids to Sing (Phillips, 1992) and *The Choral Warm-Up* (Jordan, 2005) provide sequential and comprehensive vocal warm-ups for high school students, which are built upon the foundation learned in middle school. There are many other fine choral warm-ups books, and while they may not be organized with sequential lessons, they provide a rich array of warm-ups that may be used to achieve the vocal development goals provided here.

In teaching vocal technique to high school students, have them review the middle school warm-ups described in Chapter 3. Then follow the high school vocal curriculum presented here (Phillips, 1992). Vocal warm-up exercises will address the following concepts:

- Relaxation and Respiration
- Phonation and Registration
- Resonance
- Diction
- Expression
- Range Extension and Agility
- Articulation
- Intonation.

RELAXATION AND RESPIRATION

Begin with the foundational alignment, relaxation and respiration exercises as described in Chapter 3. When those are reviewed and achieved, add new *Posture* exercises.

Grades 9–10:

- Practice weight distribution, keeping knees and hips loose.
- Stretch the sternum, shoulders, and neck to keep them loose.
- Balance an imaginary cake on each shoulder, or basket of fruit on the head (Ehmann and Haasemann, 1981).

Grades 11–12, add:

- energized, buoyant posture
- stepping
- conducting.

Add new *Breathing Motion* exercises.

Grades 9–10:

- First exhale air as if blowing out the candles on a cake, then
- practice silent inhalation through the nose,
- suspend the breath "without any sensation of holding it" (Miller, 1996, p. 31), and
- exhale silently while holding the sternum and rib cage high (Smith and Sataloff, 2006).

Grades 11–12:

- Do rhythmic breathing while mock-rowing.
- Inhale while whispering "one" and exhale while whispering "two."
- Breathe the "Tired Dog Pant" (slow and quiet rhythmic breathing).
- Breathe the "Hot Dog Pant" (light and quick breathing) (Phillips, 1992, p. 207).

Add new *Breath Management* exercises.

Grades 9–10, exhale strongly on non-vocal puffs and aspirates in the following ways:

- as on a mirror to fog it,
- as on eyeglasses to clean them (Phillips, 1992), or
- as if blowing the fuzz off of dandelions (Ehmann and Haasemann, 1981).

Grades 11–12:

- Breathe pulsed echo patterns.
- Breathe as in a "Slow Leak."
- Perform "Lip Trills."
- Be aware of rib control (Phillips, 1992, p. 215).

PHONATION AND REGISTRATION

After reviewing the middle school phonation (sound-producing) exercises in Chapter 3, add voiced abdominally supported sounds.

Grades 9–10:

- the belly laugh
- light laughs in the upper register
- singing with laughing syllables ("ho," "hee," etc.) in the middle register, moving the pattern chromatically down and then up (see Musical Example 7.1) (Ehmann and Haasemann, 1981)
- Include rising inflection sounds such as "a-choo" and "a-ha!" to coordinate the upper and lower registers (Phillips, 1992).

Musical Example 7.1   Pitched Laughing Syllables for Phonation

- Continue the use of the sigh (on an *oo* or *ah* vowel) from the high voice downward, making the *passaggio* (transitional areas between registers) smooth. This can be used in all rehearsals because the sigh relaxes the larynx and the entire body, and it uses the singer's entire range (Walders, 2005).

Grades 11–12, add:

- short glissandos between the high and middle voice, and the middle and low voice, upward and downward, with no audible break between registers
- long glissandos from high to low and vice versa, with no audible break between registers
- singing the same pitch repeatedly, alternating registers (Austin, 2008).

Ehmann and Haasemann (1981) emphasize the importance of integrating the registers through vowel modification, which "unites the registers and the resonators" (p. 37) by allowing different overtones to color the tone. For example, they recommend the umlaut (*ü* is produced by rounding the lips in an *oo* formation while singing *ee*) because it results in both a low larynx and a high placement, enriching the resonance of the tone and uniting the quality over the interval of an octave. Practice Musical Example 7.2 first on *u* and then on *ü*.

Musical Example 7.2   Consistency of Registers Exercise

RESONANCE

To achieve a resonant ringing sound, practice the six middle school warm-ups in Chapter 3, and then add the following.

Grades 9–10:

- five-note descending patterns focusing on *vv* leading to *oo*, keeping the vowel vertical and the throat and tongue free from tension
- glissandos of a fifth or octave, and scales, on a hum (Ehmann and Haasemann, 1981).

Grades 11–12:

- Begin on g1 (*sol*) on the umlaut or other resonant syllable,
- pulse and sustain on a *ti-ti-ti-ti ta-a* rhythm pattern, and
- then move to c2 (high *do*) and c1 (low *do*) (see Musical Example 7.3).
- Repeat that pattern, ascending a P4 by half steps.
- Repeat the original exercise again, descending a P5 by half steps.

Musical Example 7.3   Resonance Exercise

Mo mo mo mo mo   Mo mo mo mo mo   Mo mo mo mo mo

DICTION

Following the foundational diction warm-ups, advanced diction goals include *Vocal Tract Freedom, Word Pronunciation,* and *Consonant Articulation.*

Grades 9–10:

- Practice sighs and inner smiles for vocal tract freedom.
- Practice warm-ups with hissing sibilants (*s, sh, c*) followed by a cut-off with a sudden dropped jaw.
- Practice warm-ups with voiceless sibilants (*f, s, th, sh*) (Phillips, 1992).
- Create tongue twisters to focus on these consonants.

Grades 11–12, *Vocal Tract Freedom* exercises focus on:

- singing the five primary vowels with attention to the tip of the tongue touching the lower front teeth, and

- general facial and tongue relaxation (see Musical Example 7.4) (Ehmann and Haaseman, 1981).
- "Always breathe in the shape of the initial vowel . . . Stay on the vowel sound as long as possible . . . Almost all vowels are tall vowels—space between the molars" (Copley, 2012, p. 9).

Musical Example 7.4   Vocal Tract Freedom Exercise

Word Pronunciation exercises include attention to:

- the Three Rs (the American R as in "run," sung very quickly; the flipped R as in "spirit;" and the soft R as in "arm," keeping the tongue forward)
- pronunciation études as found in many warm-up books
- IPA studies (see Appendix C).

Consonant Articulation exercises include (Phillips, 1992):

- tuned continuants (*m, n*)

    o   Sing "mee, meh, mah, moh, moo" on a single pitch.
    o   Emphasize and elongate the *m* before each beat.

- voiced continuants (*v, z, th, zh*): Have the singers echo rhythm patterns which exaggerate these.
- aspirates (voiceless *h* and voiced *wh*, pronounced *hw*)

    o   Have students echo rhythm patterns that exaggerate these.
    o   Practice this phrase: "Why, when, where and how?"

- "Consonants are almost always short and ahead of the beat" (Copley, 2012, p. 9).

EXPRESSION

Review the middle school expression exercises and then add the following.

Grades 9–10:

- catch breaths and staggered breathing
- *accelerando* and *ritardando* control exercises
- arpeggios on *oo* and *ah* (Phillips, 1992).

Advanced goals for expression focus on *Phrasing* and *Dynamics*.

Grades 11–12 (*Phrasing*):

- analysis of word and syllable emphases, marking a "1" (primary stress), "2" (secondary stress), or "3" (unstressed) over each syllable determined by considerations of:

  o   important words
  o   metric stress, and
  o   phrase flow (see Appendix C)

- conducting phrases
- physically moving and feeling the support needed to create forward motion, as in moving a pointing finger forward throughout a phrase, or drawing imaginary arcs in the air for phrases.

Grades 11–12 (*Dynamics*):

- supported crescendo and decrescendo
- sudden dynamics changes
- *messa di voce* (a crescendo followed by a decrescendo on one sustained pitch) (Phillips, 1992).

Musical Example 7.5   *Messa di Voce* Exercise

RANGE EXPANSION AND VELOCITY

- Arpeggiate chords, always beginning with the vowel [u] (or preceded with a consonant such as l[u], c[u], and f[u]) and later moving to other primary vowels,

- keeping a relaxed jaw, open throat and low larynx, and
- singing lightly and quickly.
- Repeat with legato articulation (Ehmann and Haasemann, 1981).

ARTICULATION

Although choral ensembles routinely sing legato and staccato exercises, Austin (2008) recommends that they practice *sostenuto* and *portamento* exercises first. In fact, ever since the 18th century, the sustained tone has been a fundamental practice in strengthening the muscles of the vocal mechanism and improving vocal volume and tone, and recent studies have reaffirmed the importance of this practice. Because singing sustained tones is a slow, simple, and potentially uninteresting warm-up, the role of a moving harmonic progression accompaniment becomes important to helping the high school singers feel and shape the phrase. Cottrell (2015) suggests this basic accompaniment used in the *Marchesi Vocal Method*: I-IV-I progression on beats 1, 3, and 1, followed by the dominant of the next semitone when the singer breathes.

Sostenuto is practiced as follows:

- Begin in the low chest voice register.
- Sing a major (or other mode) ascending and descending scale over 32 measures, vocally sustaining each pitch for three to five beats (over a more active accompaniment).
- Sing on *ah*, *oh*, or *oo* at a *mezzo forte* to *forte* dynamic level.
- Repeat, ascending by step, for an octave.

Musical Example 7.6   *Sostenuto* Exercise

Portamento is practiced as follows:

- Begin in the low chest voice register.
- Sing a major (or other mode) ascending and descending scale over 14 measures, sliding from *do* to *re*, *re* to *mi*, etc., "with a continuity of tone that . . . is evenly distributed from the first to the second note" (p. 59).
- Sing on *ah* at a *mezzo forte* to *forte* dynamic level.

Musical Example 7.7   *Portamento* Exercise

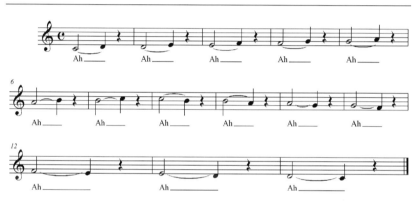

Legato exercises should achieve the same continuity and vibrancy of tone that the *portamento* exercises achieve, with the vocal folds in an almost constant state of phonation, but without sliding from pitch to pitch. The same exercises may be used, or other legato exercises, focusing on the following vowels:

- Unification of the five primary vowels:

  o *oo* [u]
  o *oh* [ɔ]
  o *ah* [a]
  o *eh* [ɛ]
  o *ee* [i]

- Unification of the short vowels:

  o [U] as in "book"
  o [I] as in "sit"
  o [æ] as in "sat"
  o [ʌ] as in "up"

- Unification of diphthongs:

  o [ai] as in "kite"
  o [ɛi] as in "great"
  o [ou] as in "go"
  o [au] as in "round"
  o [ɔi] as in "noise"
  o [iu] as in "music"

- Uniform vowels, a dropped jaw, vertical space, and steady breath support will greatly enhance legato singing.
- Melismatic singing (on one syllable) extends from legato practice and should be performed lightly, with abdominal pulsing but not with an added "h."

Staccato articulation requires vocal coordination which can be achieved by:

- singing lightly on [u] and [a] vowels in low to high arpeggios or on simple familiar songs
- singing "ho-ho" choruses (any known piece may have "ho-ho" lyrics substituted), with the staccato produced at the larynx while the breath flow remains constant (Austin, 2008)
- preceding vowels with a *d* to assist in a breath-supported staccato (Ehmann and Haasemann, 1981).

INTONATION

- Practice and memorize a tuning pitch such as A440; use a tuning fork.
- Sing an ascending D major scale on solfege in unison. Then sing it in canon every two beats, with sopranos starting, followed by altos, then tenors, and then basses. Each part holds its high D (stagger breathe) until all parts arrive on that pitch.
- Sing an ascending D major scale on solfege. Have the sopranos hold high D (*do*), while the other voices descend the scale, with altos holding B (*la*), tenors holding G (*fa*), and basses holding E (*re*). Then all but sopranos resolve down a step to *do, mi, so, do.* Repeat by half steps upward (Leck, 2009).

- Sing a chromatic scale ascending (*do di re ri mi fa fi so si la li ti do*) and descending (*do ti te la le so se fa mi me re ra do*); alternatively, sing the scale to the words "Mary had a little lamb its fleece was white as snow; ev'rywhere that Mary went the lamb was sure to go" (Archibeque, 1987).
- Sing a whole-tone scale on solfege (*do re mi fi si te do*) or with the words "She sells sea shells by the shore. She can't sell them anymore" (Archibeque, 1987).
- Sing major and minor ascending and descending intervals by interval name.
- Build three- and/or four-note chords from the bottom up on solfege, both melodically and harmonically.
- Move high and low voices outward from a unison by half step to a minor sixth, as in Musical Example 7.8 (Phillips, 1992).
- Tune up with canons, hymns, and chorales.

Musical Example 7.8   Intonation Exercise

Oo

For advanced study of in-tune choral singing practices, the book *Choral Intonation* by Per-Gunnar Alldahl (2008) is strongly recommended.

SUMMARY

Vocal warm-ups within the choral rehearsal serve not only to prepare the voice, mind, and body for the rehearsal, but to teach proper and healthy vocal technique. It should be pointed out that there are differing views on the teaching of vocal technique and choral tone, even among experts. For example, choral directors usually prefer a more blended tone, while private voice teachers tend to prefer a more soloistic sound (Ekholm, 2000). Even choral directors may differ greatly in their concept of the ideal choral tone. Preferential variations in vibrato rate, timbre, resonance, dynamics, blend, balance, and diction are often due to choral directors' own teachers and mentors who were influenced by different historical choral schools of thought (Swan, 1988.) International choirs also have distinctive choral sounds.

One is not necessarily better than another, except to the ears of each individual conductor.

So, it is only natural that you, as conductor, have and continue to develop your own concept of an ideal choral tone, based on the views of your teachers and your own experiences. You may want to use warm-ups from previous choral rehearsals because of familiarity, but familiarity alone can result in a haphazard approach to vocal development. You are urged to think carefully through the vocal objectives of the high school warm-up sequence presented here, because it provides a solid structure for a vocal curriculum.

VOCAL HEALTH

Finally, it is important to address vocal health. Resources include the Voice Care Network (www.voicecarenetwork.org) and the Voice Foundation (www.voicefoundation.org).

In addition, the following guidelines from *Prescriptions for Choral Excellence* (Emmons and Chase, 2006) are helpful. They may be edited to post in your rehearsal room.

- Avoid throat clearing.
- Drink no more than two cups of caffeinated drinks per day.
- Drink no more than one glass of acidic juice per day.
- Drink copious amounts of plain water.
- Avoid smoke, smoking, and excessive use of alcohol.
- Do not scream or yell unless it is an emergency.
- Avoid talking in loud settings.
- Keep environmental humidity at approximately 40%.
- Keep your immune system strong by getting enough sleep.
- When others around you are sick, wash your hands often.
- At the first sign of a cold, try zinc lozenges; if it worsens, take ibuprofen or acetaminophen (not aspirin); go to rehearsal!

BRAINTEASER 7-1: OBSERVING HIGH SCHOOL WARM-UPS

Observe choral warm-ups at your local high school, and notate those warm-ups, including their goals. Discuss those warm-ups you found valuable.

BRAINTEASER 7-2: CREATING HIGH SCHOOL WARM-UPS

Create a ten-minute high school warm-up plan, using the format below. Begin with a short alignment and respiration sequence, and then teach a few of the vocal development concepts sequentially. Refer to the exercises in this book, as well as to others recommended by your instructor. Add any script to assist you in remembering how to explain a concept, and submit the plan to your instructor or choral methods peers for feedback.

BRAINTEASER 7-3: CONDUCTING AND SELF-EVALUATING HIGH SCHOOL WARM-UPS

After revising your warm-ups created in Brainteaser 7-2, conduct them in a local high school.

Keys to success:

- Memorize your warm-ups.
- Time your warm-up sequence carefully.
- Know each part's vocal range and do not exceed it by more than a minor third.
- Include physical movement.
- Be energetic.
- Connect with and respond to your ensemble.
- Keep your own "teacher talk" to a minimum.
- Have high expectations and listen carefully (and urge the singers to listen) to make sure a unified ensemble sound is being achieved.

Assignment requirements:

1. Video-record your warm-up sequence in the field.
2. Watch the recording and evaluate your teaching for five strengths and five areas of needed improvement.
3. Submit your video-recording, written warm-ups, and self-evaluation to your instructor.
4. Watch peers' recordings in your choral methods class. Discuss what you have learned, and compile a list of the best vocal warm-ups for high school choirs. Make copies for everyone in the class to place in their choral teaching resource notebooks.
5. Continue to conduct warm-ups at every opportunity.

High School Warm-Up Plan

Relaxation and Respiration:

_____

_____

_____

_____

_____

Minutes:

Phonation and Registration:

_____

_____

_____

_____

_____

Vowel/Syllable:

Range and Direction:

Minutes:

Resonance:

_____

_____

_____

_____

_____

Vowel/Syllable:

Range and Direction:

Minutes:

Diction:

_____

_____

_____

_____

_____

Vowel/Syllable:

Range and Direction:

Minutes:

Expression:

_____

_____

_____

_____

_____

Vowel/Syllable:

Range and Direction:

Minutes:

Range Expansion and Agility:

_____

_____

_____

_____

_____

Vowel/Syllable:

Range and Direction:

Minutes:

Articulation:

_____

_____

_____

_____

_____

Vowel/Syllable:

Range and Direction:

Minutes:

Intonation:

_____

_____

_____

_____

_____

Vowel/Syllable:

Range and Direction:

Minutes:

References

Alldahl, Per-Gunnar (2008). *Choral Intonation*. Stockholm, Sweden: Gehrmans Musikförlag.

Archibeque, Charlene (1987). Choral Conducting Workshop, San Jose State University.

Austin, Stephen F. (February, 2008). Building Strong Voices: Twelve Different Ways! (Part II). *Choral Journal, 49*(1), 59–73.

Copley, Edith A. (Spring/Summer, 2012). Concepts of Choral Singing. *ICDA Notations*, 9.

Cottrell, Duane (2015). Building Vocal Strength with Sustained Tone Warm-Ups. *Choral Journal, 56*(3), 73–79.

Ehmann, Wilhelm and Haasemann, Frauke (1981). *Voice Building for Choirs*. Chapel Hill, NC: Hinshaw.

Ekholm, Elizabeth (2000). The Effect of Singing Mode and Seating Arrangement on Choral Blend and Overall Choral Sound. *Journal of Research in Music Education, 48*(2), 123–135.

Emmons, Shirlee and Chase, Constance (2006). *Prescriptions for Choral Excellence*. New York: Oxford University Press.

Jordan, James (2005). *The Choral Warm-Up: Method, Procedures, Planning, and Core Vocal Exercises*. Chicago, IL: GIA.

Leck, Henry (2009). *Creating Artistry Through Choral Excellence*. Milwaukee, WI: Hal Leonard.

Miller, Richard (1996). *The Structure of Singing: System and Art in Vocal Technique*. Belmont, CA: Wadsworth.

Phillips, Kenneth H. (1992). *Teaching Kids to Sing*. New York: Schirmer.

Smith, Brenda and Sataloff, Robert T. (2006). *Choral Pedagogy*, 2nd edition. San Diego, CA: Plural Publishing.

Swan, Howard (1988). The Development of a Choral Instrument, in Harold A. Decker and Julius Herford (ed.), *Choral Conducting Symposium*. Englewood Cliffs, NJ: Prentice Hall.

Walders, Patrick Michael (2005). Vocal Pedagogy and Applications for Conductors Not Trained in Singing. DMA Doctoral Dissertation, University of Maryland.

8

REPERTOIRE FOR HIGH SCHOOL CHOIRS

Effective choral teachers need to know *where* to find high quality choral music and *how* to select appropriate music for their choirs (Reames, 2001). While attendance at high school choral concerts and choral reading sessions, listening to choral recordings, and perusing choral libraries are all valuable ways to find new music, the choral director should also make use of published repertory resource guides. The search for outstanding repertoire is a lifelong pursuit, and so it is beyond the scope of this book to provide a comprehensive list of choral repertoire for secondary school choirs, but a wide selection of resources is provided here.

As with middle school choirs, some essential considerations for the selection of music for high school ensembles include:

- appropriate vocal ranges and tessituras
- vocal development objectives
- musical learning objectives
- appropriate texts
- "quality" music.

A grading system for vocal, tonal, and rhythmic challenges is a useful aid for music selection, and can be found in *Teaching Music Through Performance in Choir* (Buchanan and Mehaffey, 2005).

Levels 1 and 2 were previously discussed with regard to middle school singers, and now levels 3 and 4 will be presented for high school singers.

Level 3 literature contains *some* emphasis on:

- advanced vocal technique
- challenging tessituras
- extended breath control
- wide dynamic ranges
- numerous languages
- modal tonality, modulations, extended harmonies
- counterpoint
- difficult rhythms
- simple mixed meters.

Level 4 pieces present *extremes* in:

- breath control
- range
- dynamics
- expressivity
- alternative vocal techniques
- refined diction
- non-diatonic harmony
- frequent chromaticism
- challenging rhythms
- mixed meters.

MIXED CHOIR MUSIC

SATB pieces that meet but do not exceed Buchanan and Mehaffey's level 3 criteria include:

- Fauré's *Cantique de Jean Racine*
- Haydn's *Gloria*
- Handel's *Hallelujah, Amen* and *Let Their Celestial Concerts All Unite*
- Ives' *Circus Band*
- Mozart's *Ave Verum Corpus*
- Palestrina's *Sicut Cervus*
- Schumann's *Zigeunerleben*

- Ernani Aguiar's *Salmo 150*
- Samuel Barber's *Sure on This Shining Night*
- Adrian Batten's *O Sing Joyfully*
- Benjamin Britten's *Jubilate Deo in C*
- Javier Busto's *Ave Maria*
- Gerlad Custer's *Innisfree*
- David Dickau's *If Music Be the Food of Love*
- Gabriel Fauré's *Messe Basse*
- Daniel Gawthrop's *Sing Me to Heaven*
- Orlando Gibbons' *The Silver Swan*
- Hans Leo Hassler's *Verbum Caro Factum Est*
- Libby Larsen's *Alleluia*
- Kirke Mechem's *Love and Pizen*
- James Mulholland's *Heart We Will Forget Him*
- Donald Patriquin's *Innoria*
- Lloyd Pfautsch's *Musick's Empire*
- Jan Pieterszoon Sweelinck's *Venite Exultemus Domino*
- Randall Thompson's *The Last Words of David*
- Eric Whitacre's *Five Hebrew Love Songs*
- Bob Childcott's arrangement of *Buffalo Gals*
- Moses Hogan's arrangement of *Wade in the Water*
- Boniface Mganaga's arrangement of *Vamuvamba*
- Alice Parker's arrangement of *Hark, I Hear the Harps Eternal*
- Alice Parker and Robert Shaw's arrangement of *Johnny Has Gone for a Soldier.*

Level 4 SATB pieces include:

- Bach's *Sicut Locutus Est*
- Beethoven's *Kyrie*
- Rachmaninoff's *Bogoroditse Devo*
- Sweelinck's *Psalm 96*
- Béla Bartók's *Four Slovak Folk Songs*
- Samuel Barber's *Let Down the Bars, O Death*
- Johannes Brahms' *Geistliches Lied*
- William Byrd's *Ave Verum Corpus*
- Stephen Catman's *An Elizabethan Spring*
- René Clausen's *Three Whitman Settings*
- Aaron Copland's *Sing Ye Praises to Our King*

- Cecil Effinger's *Four Pastorales*
- Gustav Holst's *I Love My Love*
- Pierre Passereau's *Il est Bel et Bon*
- Gerald Finzi's *My Spirit Sang All Day*
- Morten Lauridsen's *O Magnum Mysterium*
- Stephen Leek's *Ngana*
- Alberto Favero's *Te Quiero*
- Claudio Monteverdi's *Sfogava con le Stele*
- Steven Sametz's *I Have Had Singing*
- Heinrich Schütz's *Die mit Tränen Säen*
- Charles Stanford's *The Blue Bird*
- Z. Randall Stroope's *Amor de Mi Alma*
- Frank Ticheli's *There Will Be Rest*
- John Tavener's *Two Hymns to the Mother of God*
- Ralph Vaughan Williams' *A Choral Flourish*
- Paul Caldwell and Sean Ivory's arrangement of *John the Revelator*.

The three comprehensive volumes by Buchanan and Mehaffey (2005, 2007, 2011) provide detailed information about the composer, the composition's historical, technical, stylistic, musical, and formal considerations, the text and translation, and suggested representative recordings of outstanding performances of each piece, as well as companion CDs.

Another resource for high quality choral literature is *Music Performed at American Choral Directors Association Conventions 1960–2000* (Schmidt, 2002). Twelve different types of choirs performed at ACDA conventions during the 40-year period, ranging from children's choirs to adult professional choirs. Relevant to high school directors are the listings for male chorus, women's chorus, senior high school choir, vocal jazz ensemble, and show choir. The book can be searched by composer, title, type of choir, and convention. Those individual pieces that have been performed numerous times over the years by high school choirs give a good indication of excellent music that *works* and a few of those titles follow:

- René Clausen's *All That Hath Life and Breath*
- Norman Dello Joio's *A Jubilant Song*
- Maurice Duruflé's *Ubi Caritas*

- Jack Halloran's arrangement of *Witness*
- Charles Ives' *The Sixty-Seventh Psalm*
- Felix Mendelssohn's *Die Nachtigall*
- Claudio Monteverdi's *Ecco Mormorar L'onde*
- Kurt Nystedt's *Cry Out and Shout*
- Brent Pierce's *Hosanna*
- Alessandro Scarlatti's *Exultate Deo*
- Robert Schumann's *Zigeunerleben*
- John Rutter's *Five Childhood Lyrics*.

The 100 most-performed pieces by high school all-state choirs from all 50 states between 1995 and 2000 were identified as part of a doctoral dissertation (Spillane, 2004). Handel was the most-performed composer, followed by Brahms, Mendelssohn, Mulholland, Mozart, Clausen, Thomas, Hogan, Thompson, Parker and Shaw, Bach, Haydn, Lauridsen, Rutter, Wilberg, and Copland. The most-programmed pieces were the following, in this order:

- Lauridsen's *Dirait-on*
- Hogan's *Battle of Jericho*
- Basler's *Missa Kenya (Gloria)*
- Frackenpohl's/Brahms' *The May Night*
- Busto's *Ave Maria*
- Martin's *The Awakening*.

Other favorites for high school mixed choir include:

- René Clausen's *Set Me as a Seal*
- Aaron Copland's *Long Time Ago*
- Emma Lou Diemer's *Three Madrigals*
- Sarah Hopkins' *Past Life Melodies*
- Morten Lauridsen's *O Magnum Mysterium* and *Sure on This Shining Night*
- John Leavitt's *Festival Sanctus*
- John Rutter's *For the Beauty of the Earth*
- Z. Randall Stroope's *Caritas et Amor*
- Randall Thompson's *Alleluia*
- Eric Whitacre's *Hope, Faith, Life, Love*.

An Annotated Inventory of Distinctive Choral Literature for Performance at the High School Level (Hawkins, 1976) provides accurate descriptions, historical perspectives, musical challenges, levels of difficulty, voicings, instrumental needs, performance times, and publishers of 100 choral masterworks that have been performed by high school mixed choirs. Other resources include *Sacred Choral Music in Print* (Eslinger, 1985) and *Secular Choral Music in Print* (Daugherty, 1987) and their later supplements and indexes; *Twentieth-Century Choral Music: An Annotated Bibliography of Music Suitable for Use by High School Choirs* (White, 1991); and for strictly American choral music, a special issue of the *Choral Journal* (March 2003) lists over 100 accessible SATB pieces.

TREBLE CHOIR MUSIC

For high school treble choir, *Teaching Music Through Performance in Choir* (Buchanan and Mehaffey, 2005) presents analyses, composer information, and model recordings of the following choral works:

- *God's Bottles* by Randall Thompson (Level 3)
- *He's Gone Away*, arr. Ron Nelson (Level 3)
- *Ave Maria* by Johannes Brahms (Level 4)
- *Heaven-Haven* by Samuel Barber (Level 4)
- *Las Amarillas* by Stephen Hatfield (Level 4)
- *O Aula Nobilis* by William Mathias (Level 4)
- *Salut au Chevalier Printemps* by Camille Saint-Saens (Level 4)
- *Rise up, My Love, My Fair One* by Imant Raminsh (Level 4).

Monica Hubbard (1998), who initiated the ACDA archive of music for women's chorus, stated that the following literature should be in the library of every women's choir director:

- *Carols for Choirs, Book 4*, arr. David Willcocks and John Rutter
- *A Girl's Garden* from *Frostiana* by Randall Thompson
- *Laudamus te* from *Gloria* by Antonio Vivaldi
- *Messe Basses pour Voix de Femmes* by Gabriel Fauré
- *Nigra Sum* by Pablo Casals
- *O Music* by Lowell Mason
- *Six Traditional Carols, Sets 1, 2, 3* by Imogen Holst
- *Three Mountain Ballads*, arr. Ron Nelson

- *Velvet Shoes* by Randall Thompson
- *The Water Is Wide*, adapted by Luigi Zaninelli.

For treble choir music written by 20th century composers, the following pieces are suggested (Guelker-Cone, 1992; White, 1991):

- *Ain't No Grave Can Hold My Body Down*, arr. Paul Caldwell and Sean Ivory
- *And Back Again* by Dede Duson
- *Autumn Fires* by Marian McLaughlin
- *Ave Maria* by Lois Land
- *Away, Melancholy* and *Gabriel's Message* by Alice Parker
- *Carol* and *High Flight* by Nancy Telfer
- *Celebration* by Louise Talma
- *Ching-a-Ring Chaw* by Aaron Copland, arr. Fine
- *Dancing Song* by Zoltán Kodály
- *Four Russian Peasant Songs* by Igor Stravinsky
- *Fragments from the Mass* by Emma Lou Diemer
- *Here Comes the Avant-Garde* by Brock McElheran
- *The Heavenly Aeroplane* by John Rutter
- *In Paradisum* by Ernst Krenek
- *In the Summer* by Lajos Bardos
- *Loch Lomond*, arr. Vijay Singh
- *Missa Brevis* by Ramona Luengen
- *The Night Will Never Stay* by Elinor Remick Warren
- *Nouns to Nouns* by Vincent Persichetti
- *O Lady Moon* by Alan Hovhaness
- *O Sacrum Convivium* by Robert Bell
- *Refuge* by Libby Larsen
- *Rose Trilogy* by Eleanor Daley
- *Songs of the Nativity* by Ruth Watson Henderson.

BASS–TENOR CHOIR MUSIC

Level 3 music for bass–tenor choirs includes (Buchanan and Mehaffey, 2005):

- *An die Frauen* by Haydn, arr. Gregory Vancil
- *Brothers, Sing On!* by Grieg, arr. Howard D. McKinney
- *I'm a-Rollin'*, arr. Paul Rardin
- *Soon Ah Will Be Done*, arr. William Dawson

- *What Shall We Do with the Drunken Sailor?*, arr. Alice Parker and Robert Shaw.

Level 4 bass–tenor choir pieces include:

- *Absalon, fili mi* by Josquin Desprez
- *Ave Maria* by Franz Biebl
- *Ballad of Jericho* by Moses Hogan
- *Manly Men* by Kurt Knecht
- *Sehnsucht* by Franz Schubert
- *Shall I Compare Thee* by Stephen Paulus.

Other high-energy pieces recommended for high school BT choirs include the following, many with varied and interesting accompaniments (Palant, 2007; Parr, 1997):

- *A-Rovin'*, arr. Norman Luboff
- *Betelehemu*, arr. Wendell Whalum
- *Come Let Us Sing unto the Lord* by Emma Lou Diemer
- *Do You Hear the People Sing?* arr. Ed Lojeski
- *Hold On!*, arr. Eugene Simpson
- *Nkosi Sikelel' iAfrika*, arr. Gabriel Larentz-Jones
- *Old Dan Tucker*, arr. Douglas Ipson or Michael Levi
- *Poor Man Lazrus*, arr. Jester Hairston
- *Prayer of the Children* by Kurt Bestor, arr. Klouse
- *Rainbow 'Round My Shoulder*, arr. Robert DeCormier
- *Steal Away*, arr. Brazeal Dennard
- *Susannah!*, arr. Jonathan Crutchfield
- *Swing Down Chariot* by André Thomas
- *Vive l'Amour*, arr. Robert Shaw and Alice Parker
- *We Shall Walk Through the Valley in Peace*, adapted by William Appling
- *Western Songs*, arr. Roger Wagner
- *Whup! Jamboree*, arr. Robert Shaw and Alice Parker.

Additional 20th century choral works for high school low voices (White, 1991) include:

- *The Tabernacle of God Is with Men* by Edwin Fissinger
- *Here Comes the Avant-Garde* by Brock McElheran

- *Dance of the One-Legged Sailor* by Brent Pierce
- *All This Night Shrill Chanticleer* by Halsey Stevens
- *Four Russian Peasant Songs* by Igor Stravinsky.

NON-HETERONORMATIVE AND NON-MISOGYNISTIC MUSIC

Many, if not most, of the recommended choral works identified in this chapter are non-heteronormative (heteronormativity is the belief that people fall into two distinct genders) and non-misogynistic (misogyny is the contempt for, or prejudice against, women or girls). However, for the choral conductor specifically seeking such repertoire, a list is provided here for bass clef choirs (created by Joshua Palkki, 2015) and for mixed and treble choirs (collected at the Transgender Singing Voice Conference, Earlham College, Richmond, Indiana, 2017).

Bass Clef Choirs

- *If You Can Walk You Can Dance* by Elizabeth Alexander
- *Mainacht* by Brahms, arr. Stroope
- *I Hate Flowers* by Judith Cloud
- *Can You Hear the Bells?* by Roger Emerson
- *Rain Music* by Laura Farnell
- *Rest Not* by Laura Farnell
- *Come Travel with Me* by Scott Farthing
- *Two Tongue Twisters* by Noel Goemanne
- *Walk a Mile* by Choplin and Pepper, arr. Hayes
- *America, the Beautiful,* arr. Kevin Memley
- *Think on Me* by James Mulholland
- *We All Have a Right* by Jim Papoulis
- *J'entends le Moulin,* arr. Donald Patriquin
- *Cover Me with the Night* by Andrew Ramsey
- *The Roof* by Andrea Ramsey
- *Loch Lomond,* arr. Earlene Rentz
- *High Flight* by Karen Robinson
- *Dereva Ni Mungo* by Jake Runestad
- *Dulcis Amor* by Steven Sametz
- *O Mister Moon* by Joshua Shank
- *Remember Me* by Halsey Stevens

- *Dies Irae* by Z. Randall Stroope
- *Paper Cranes* by Timothy Takach
- *It Is Not the Fact That I Will Die That I Mind* by Timothy Takach
- *Empty* by Timothy Takach
- *Crossing* by Mari Esabel Valverde

Treble and Mixed Choirs

- *Look Down, Fair Moon* by Mari Esabel Valverde (SA)
- *When I Was a Boy* by Evyn Surrency (SSAA)
- *Five-Year-Old Jacob* by Sandi Hammond (3-part)
- *Would You Harbor Me?* by Ysaye M. Barnwell (SATB)
- *When Thunder Comes* by Mari Esabel Valverde (SATB)
- *Best Wishes* by Mari Esabel Valverde (SATB)
- *Sing We and Chant It* by Thomas Morley, arr. William Sauerland (6-part)

SACRED MUSIC IN THE PUBLIC SCHOOLS

The question often arises regarding the legality and appropriateness of singing sacred music in public schools. Because choral music with sacred text comprises a substantial portion of the masterworks of music history, both NAfME and ACDA have published comprehensive statements to assist choral directors in their decisions regarding music from various religious and cultural traditions.

NAfME provides the following position statement on its website:

> It is the position of the National Association for Music Education that the study and performance of religious music within an educational context is a vital and appropriate part of a comprehensive music education. The omission of sacred music from the school curriculum would result in an incomplete educational experience.

Choral music directors must take steps to ensure that the performance of sacred music in any public school is "religiously neutral" in that the music is selected based on musical, educational, and artistic value, rather than to promote religious views. Questions raised in 1971 in *Lemon* v. *Kurtzman* should still be asked today at each school performance to avoid violation of the First Amendment:

- Is the purpose of the performance secular (educational) in nature?
- Does the performance *enhance* or *inhibit* religion, confuse the students, or create objections by the students' families?
- Is there "entanglement" with a religious group, as in financial support? (Performing in a church may be considered "entanglement," particularly if the church does not charge for use of the facility. One choral director avoids any question of entanglement by performing only non-sacred music when performing in a church (Drummond, 2014).)

If the answer to the first question is "yes," and the answer to the remaining questions is "no," then the Lemon Test is passed.

Other recommendations when considering the performance of sacred music (Drummond, 2014) include the following:

- Know your school's policies, and follow them.
- Know your community's traditions and expectations.
- Have a firm educational reason for all repertoire choices.
- Educate your students and your audience about the educational reasons for repertoire choices.
- "Respect and embrace diversity" (p. 31).

ACDA elegantly stated that:

> any work of art studied or performed should be selected for its inherent beauty of structure and form. Its purpose in study should be learning for the sake of developing artistic understanding and responsiveness. Often artworks are related to a specific religious/cultural tradition. The study of such works of art can enhance one's understanding and appreciation of a cultural product which a particular tradition has fostered.
>
> (www.nyacda.org/resources/study-of-music-from-a-sacred-tradition)

For NAfME's and ACDA's comprehensive position statements on the topic of the study of sacred music in the public schools, see:

www.nafme.org/about/position-statements/sacred-music-in-schools-position-statement/sacred-music-in-schools and www.nyacda.org/resources/study-of-music-from-a-sacred-tradition, as well as cautionary articles by Brown (2016) and Drummond (2014), found in the references at the end of this chapter.

SCORE ANALYSIS

A conductor's professional life revolves around score study. It is time consuming and requires discipline. No matter how young or old the conductor is, there will always be new choral compositions and arrangements to explore. Eventually, every conductor will find his or her preferred approach to score study. But whatever that approach is, the following aspects of the score need to be analyzed and deeply understood before the first rehearsal:

- range and tessituras of each voice part
- key
- tempo
- style
- texture
- language
- harmonic structure
- form
- phrases and breaths
- the composer's intent for the piece
- the performance practice of the genre or style
- conducting challenges
- musical challenges
- vocal challenges
- "teachable moments."

Approaches to realizing the music are often gained by:

- singing through all vocal parts, circling in pencil any melodic or rhythmic errors that you make (your students will make those too)
- conducting the piece in front of a mirror, practicing challenging gestures (preparatory beats, cues, expressive markings, etc.)

- playing the vocal parts on the piano, as well as the accompaniment
- listening to various recordings of the piece by various artists
- memorizing so that your head will be out of the score and the score will be in your head!

While all of the above points were made in Chapter 4, there are two additional effective strategies for score analysis and marking that will be introduced here. The first is called "Seven Trips Through the Score" with different colored pencils for realizing different aspects of the music. For example, the following color code may be used:

1. Mark formal analysis with yellow.
2. Mark important harmonic structural aspects with orange.
3. Mark important melodic features with green.
4. Mark phrases and breaths with pink.
5. Mark important dynamics, tempo, and rhythms with blue.
6. Mark important vocal line issues with red.
7. Mark important text issues with a normal lead pencil.

Then listen to a recording of the piece or play it on the piano and complete a historical analysis. You may find that this approach to score study, as practiced at the Paris Conservatory, focuses both the eyes and the ears on the most important musical characteristics of the piece.

Another well-known approach to score study is the creation of an analytical graph, sometimes called a "Structural Memorization Chart" (see Table 8.1) because of its effectiveness in deep understanding and memorization of the music. The graph is a vertical approach to analysis which presents the main structural points, beginning in measure 1 and continuing through the piece (Decker and Herford, 1988). What follows in Table 8.1 is a modified analysis of the first 35 measures of J.S. Bach's *Kyrie II* from the *Mass in B Minor* for illustrative purposes.

Words are what make choral music special. Their meaning needs to be communicated to the audience through attention to vowels, consonants, and syllable stress. The choral conductor has the responsibility to prepare the textual understanding and delivery in the following ways:

- Write out a literal translation if the piece is not in English. Enormously valuable are the four volumes of *Translations and*

Table 8.1   Structural Memorization Chart

• Form	Section I						
• Measures	1	–	18	19	–	35	
• Phrasing	1–8		9–18	19–24		25–35	
• Melodic motives	5+3		5+4	4+2		6+4	
• Meter	4/2						
• Tempo	moderato						
• Dynamics	mf		mf< f	mp <<		f>	
• Text	Kyrie eleison			Kyrie eleison			
• Voices	B	T	A S	A B		BTAS	
• Accompaniment	organ						
• Texture	polyphonic						
• Harmonic structure	f#: bII		V/VI	A: V7/V		V I	

Annotations of Choral Repertoire (Jeffers, 1988–2009). English translations, both literal and poetic, are provided for most choral masterworks originally in Latin, German, French, Italian, and Hebrew.

• Write out the IPA (International Phonetic Alphabet) symbols for all words, particularly the vowels (see Appendix C).

• Mark all primary ("1"), secondary ("2"), and tertiary ("3") syllable stresses (see Appendix C) based on a combination of natural syllable stress within a word, metric stress, and larger phrase considerations (Lamb, 1988.) Other systems may be used, including numbering as many as six levels of stress (Neuen, 1992) or marking a tenuto for stressed syllables.

PERFORMANCE PRACTICE

Authenticity is a timely topic in musical performance. It refers to the conductor's attempts to re-create a performance in the tradition from which the composition was originally conceived and performed. The aspects of a performance that may be interpreted as authentic can range from the size of the choir and its tone quality to the type of accompaniment. Knowledge of authentic approaches requires study of the music and its history, but some general interpretive guidelines will be presented here for the conductor to consider (Garretson, 1993):

Renaissance (example: Palestrina's *Sicut Cervus*)

- Meter: Music of this period was unmetered and sung with natural word stress. Although bar lines are now often added to Renaissance music, the conductor must beware of destroying the natural flow of the words. Tempo and dynamics were also determined by the natural flow of the text.
- Tone quality: Light and clear with minimal vibrato, to simulate the Renaissance boys' voices and men's falsetto voices.
- Ornamentation: Expected in Renaissance music and the interested choral director may study appropriate embellishments to the melodic line (see Madura's *Getting Started with Vocal Improvisation*).
- Expressiveness: Occurs through word painting.
- Crisp text and rhythmic interplay should be emphasized.

Baroque (example: Handel's *Hallelujah, Amen*)

- Meter: Definite and precise beat.
- Tempo: Extremes are avoided; a fermata is merely the end of a phrase and not an indication to extend the length of the pitch.
- Dynamics: Only slight changes occur between terraced dynamics levels.
- Tone quality: Pure, light, brilliant, florid; some vibrato.
- Articulation: Pulsed on rapid melismatic scale passages; *leggiero* (light) in lively passages with slight accents or separations on each note; *portato* (halfway between legato and staccato) in slower non-legato passages.
- Balance: Bass and soprano predominate.
- Expression: Determined by harmonic tension and repose.

Classical (example: Mozart's *Ave Verum Corpus*)

- Meter: Steady but with a lighter beat than Baroque; first beat of new sections emphasized.
- Tempo: Moderate, without extremes.
- Dynamics: Crescendo and decrescendo from one dynamic level to the next; no extremes.
- Tone color: Warmer tone color and more vibrato than previously, but not overdone; inner vocal parts stronger than in the Baroque.

- Articulation: Pulsed on rapid melismatic scale passages; *leggiero* in lively passages; *portato* in slower, non-legato passages.

Romantic (example: Brahms' *Geistliches Lied, Op. 30*)

- Tempos: Extremely fast or slow; rubato used.
- Dynamics: Extremes from *fff* to *ppp*, crescendo and decrescendo, *sfz, sf*.
- Tone color: Rich, dark, with vibrato.
- Articulation: Legato (elision of one word to the next).
- Expression: Free and individual expression emphasized.

20th Century

There were many different styles of music composed during the 20th century, including Impressionist, Expressionist, Neo-classical, Neo-romantic, Nationalistic, 12-Tone, and Aleatoric, so there is no short list of appropriate performance practices. The conductor, then, will need to research the composer's intent and make decisions regarding interpretation.

Many choral scores from the second half of the 20th century call for aleatoric improvisation, which leaves some elements of the musical structure open to the singer's choice (Madura, 1999). This might include freedom with words, sound effects, or given pitches and rhythms. Some aleatoric pieces are written in traditional notation and others use graphic notation. Such pieces that the choir director may choose to explore with a high school choir include:

- *All That Hath Life and Breath* by René Clausen
- *Cantate Domino* by Rupert Lang
- *Epitaph for Moonlight* and *Minimusic* by R. Murray Schafer
- *Exultet Coelum Laudibus* by John Paynter
- *Oh Ha Ha* by Pauline Oliveros
- *Psalm 98* by John Grant
- *Sanctus* by Ron Jeffers
- *Sounds Patterns* by Bernard Rands.

BRAINTEASER 8-1: ANALYZING AND MARKING THE CHORAL SCORE

Select at least one piece for a high school choir from your current field experience, or chosen by your instructor. Complete the score analysis, markings, and preparation as indicated. Submit your analysis with a copy of the score attached. Be prepared to conduct your choral methods class for practice (provide scores).

BRAINTEASER 8-2: ATTENDING A HIGH SCHOOL CHORAL CONCERT

Attend a conference reading session of high school choral music or a high school choral concert and review the repertoire suitability and programming effectiveness. Identify the title, composer/arranger, and voicing of each piece.

BRAINTEASER 8-3: COLLECTING AND ANNOTATING CHORAL SCORES

Using the various resources identified in this chapter, collect and annotate at least ten pieces for high school choir. Include some for beginning and advanced levels, and some for treble and low voices.

BRAINTEASER 8-4: CREATING A PERFORMANCE PRACTICE CHART

Compare and contrast the performance practices of the different eras of music, and apply the criteria of one period to a piece you are currently studying. Submit your paper and/or marked score.

References

Brown, Emily Pence (2016). Sacred Music in the School: A Guide for Beginning Music Teachers. *Music Educators Journal, 103*(1), 14–15.

Buchanan, Heather J. and Mehaffey, Matthew W. (2005). *Teaching Music Through Performance in Choir, Volume 1*. Chicago, IL: GIA.

Buchanan, Heather J. and Mehaffey, Matthew W. (2007). *Teaching Music Through Performance in Choir, Volume 2*. Chicago, IL: GIA.

Buchanan, Heather J. and Mehaffey, Matthew W. (2011). *Teaching Music Through Performance in Choir, Volume 3*. Chicago, IL: GIA.

Daugherty, F. Mark (1987). *Secular Choral Music in Print*. Philadelphia: Musicdata.

Decker, Harold and Herford, Julius (1988). *A Choral Conducting Symposium*. Englewood Cliffs, NJ: Prentice Hall.

Drummond, Tim (2014). Singing over the Wall: Legal and Ethical Considerations for Sacred Music in the Public Schools. *Music Educators Journal, 101*(2), 27–31.

Eslinger, Gary S. (1985). *Sacred Choral Music in Print*. Philadelphia, PA: Musicdata.

Garretson, Robert L. (1993). *Choral Music: History, Style and Performance Practice*. Englewood Cliffs, NJ: Prentice Hall.

Guelker-Cone, Leslie (May, 1992). Music for Women's Voices by Contemporary Women Composers of the United States and Canada. *Choral Journal,* 31–40.

Hawkins, Margaret B. (1976). *An Annotated Inventory of Distinctive Choral Literature for Performance at the High School Level*. Lawton, OK: American Choral Directors Association Monograph No. 2.

Hubbard, Monica (December, 1998). Women's Choirs: Repertoire, Standards, and Chestnuts. *Choral Journal, 39*(5), 59–62.

Jeffers, Ron (1988). *Translations and Annotation of Choral Repertoire*, Volumes 1–4 (1988–2009): V. 1 *Sacred Latin Texts* (Jeffers, 1988), V. 2 *German Texts* (Jeffers and Paine, Gordon, 2000), V. 3 *French and Italian Texts* (Paine, 2007), V. 4 *Hebrew Texts* (Nash, Ethan and Jacobson, Joshua, 2009). Corvallis, OR: earthsongs.

Lamb, Gordon (1988). *Choral Techniques*. Dubuque, IA: Wm. C. Brown.

Madura, Patrice D. (1999). *Getting Started with Vocal Improvisation*. Lanham, MD: R&L Education/NAfME.

Neuen, Donald (1992). Making a Statement. *Choral Journal, 33*(1), 16–17.

Palant, Jonathan (June, 2007). High School Boys: Relish the Rowdiness with Repertoire. *Choral Journal, 37*(12), 53–55.

Palkki, Joshua (2015). Gender Trouble: Males, Adolescence, and Masculinity in the Choral Context. *Choral Journal, 56*(4), 24–35.

Parr, Clayton (February, 1997). Male Choir Literature for Mixed Choir Programs. *Choral Journal, 37*(7), 28–29.

Reames, Rebecca R. (2001). High School Choral Directors' Description of Appropriate Literature for Beginning High School Choirs. *Journal of Research in Music Education, 49*(2), 122–135.

Schmidt, Sandefur (2002). *Music Performed at American Choral Directors Association Conventions 1960–2000*. Lawton, OK: ACDA, Monograph 12.

Spillane, James D. (2004). All-State Choral Music: A Comprehensive Study of the Music Selected for the High School All-State Choirs of the Fifty States from 1995–2000. Doctoral Dissertation, University of Arizona, AAT 3158159.

White, J. Perry (1991). *Twentieth-Century Choral Music: An Annotated Bibliography of Music Suitable for Use by High School Choirs*. Metuchen, NJ: Scarecrow Press.

EFFECTIVE HIGH SCHOOL CHORAL MUSIC TEACHING

Good literature and good rehearsals are two sides of the choral curriculum coin. One without the other minimizes the impact of the choral experience. National and state standards have been developed to encourage a comprehensive music ensemble curriculum, and to provide overall curricular goals and program expectations. While choral music teachers are required to follow their states' standards, they often have substantial freedom in selecting materials, sequencing learning experiences, and organizing rehearsals. The task of organizing a choral curriculum is large, and new teachers can greatly benefit from the advice of experienced conductors, the writings of esteemed researchers, and the leadership of our professional organizations.

OPPORTUNITY-TO-LEARN STANDARDS

NAfME recommends that at least two, but preferably three, choirs be offered at the high school level, differentiated by experience/age or by voice type (treble voices, low voices, or mixed). In addition, at least one alternative ensemble, such as vocal jazz, show choir, and madrigal singers, should be offered per every 450 students enrolled in the school (http://nafme.org/wp-content/files/2014/11/Opportunity-to-Learn-Standards_May2015.pdf). Alternative ensembles provide important diverse musical experiences and are major motivators for many students and will be presented in detail in the next chapter.

Other NAfME recommendations for the choral curriculum and scheduling include the following "basic" and "quality" standards (http://nafme.org/wp-content/files/2014/11/Opportunity-to-Learn-Standards_May2015.pdf):

Scheduling:

- Basic: Chorus classes should meet during the school day and their duration should be equal to that of other core courses; regular performances are expected for parents, peers, and community, but not to the extent that they interfere with music learning objectives.
- Quality: Each choral ensemble should perform at least once a year at a major venue.

Staffing:

- Basic: Instruction is provided by a certified choral music teacher, and an accompanist is provided for each ensemble of more than 50 students.
- Quality: An accompanist is provided for ensembles of 16 or more students.

Equipment:

- Basic: A set of portable choral risers is provided, as well as music stands, music folders, and appropriate chairs.
- Quality: A vocal jazz ensemble will be provided with individual dynamic handheld microphones for all singers, with a sufficient sound system.

Content:

- Basic: A library of music should consist of all original music and no materials in violation of copyright laws. At least 75 titles should be available for each type of ensemble, with at least five titles for each group added per year. An annual budget is provided for other special media or equipment supplies.

Technology:

- Basic: Computers and music software are provided, as well as technology for student assessment.
- Quality: At least one electronic instrument is available, as well as interactive boards and projectors.

Facilities:

- Basic: Choral rehearsal rooms should have at least 1200 square feet of space with a ceiling at least 14 feet high and a double-entry door, at least one practice room for every 40 students in the ensembles, and office space for each choral music teacher.
- Quality: Choral rehearsal rooms should have at least 1800 square feet of floor space with a ceiling at least 16 feet high, and at least one practice room per every 20 students enrolled in the choral ensembles.

Knowing these *Opportunity-to-Learn Standards*, published by NAfME, the leading professional music educators' organization, will enable new teachers to effectively communicate with administrators about their curriculum and scheduling needs both during the job interview process and after being hired into a choral teaching position.

NATIONAL MUSIC STANDARDS

The National Core Arts Standards (2014, www.nationalartsstandards.org/content/conceptual-framework) as well as the earlier *National Standards for Arts Education* (1994) recommend areas of achievement for music students. (The NCCAS are identical for middle school and high school ensembles, and can be found in Chapter 5). Although national standards are voluntary, individual states often develop required music standards based on them. For example, Indiana has combined both sets of national standards for high school choral ensembles (www.doe.in.gov), and these may serve as a general guide for structuring curriculum.

Performing Music

- Singing alone and with others: Students sing repertoire representing various styles and culture. They sing accurately and expressively from a score and from memory, and use proper vocal technique. They sing independently and in large and small ensembles, and they respond to the cues of a conductor.
- Playing an instrument alone and with others: Students echo and perform rhythmic, melodic, and harmonic patterns on keyboard, percussion, or original instruments, independently or

in ensembles. They maintain a steady tempo and play accurate pitches. They create simple rhythmic or melodic accompaniments to enhance vocal performance.

Creating Music

- Improvising melodies, variations, and accompaniments: Students improvise warm-ups, melodies, harmonies, and variations in the context of the choral rehearsal.
- Composing and arranging music within specified guidelines: Students create vocal warm-ups and accompaniments to enhance performance.

Responding to Music

- Reading, notating, and interpreting music: Students read and interpret vocal scores. They sight-read music using a consistent method.
- Listening to, analyzing, and describing music: Students listen to recordings of choral repertoire, and analyze and discuss elements of the composition and interpretation. They analyze choral works being rehearsed and compositional elements that affect performance.
- Evaluating music and music performances: Students establish criteria for evaluating choral repertoire and performances, and demonstrate performance behaviors appropriate to various concert venues.
- Understanding relationships between music, the other arts, and disciplines outside the arts: Students explore the relationship of music and text, and utilize writing and other art forms to enhance understanding and performance of choral repertoire. They understand physical properties related to singing.
- Understanding music in relation to history and culture: Students investigate and write about the background of the music studied, and perform repertoire in a manner that reflects cultural and historical traditions. They understand the suitability of various choral works and vocal styles for given situations. They are aware of opportunities for further study and potential careers in vocal music.

NAfME has developed sample Model Cornerstone Assessments (MCAs) that can help the teacher measure student achievement in the National Core Arts Standards. Detailed Ensemble Cornerstone Assessments can be found at www.nafme.org.

REHEARSAL PLANNING

Choral rehearsals begin with vocal warm-ups. Many choral teachers follow warm-ups with musicianship exercises, such as sight-reading or creative activities (improvising or composing). Then follows the rehearsal of literature, which should be designed like a good concert (Barrow, 1994). The first piece should be an attention-getter, followed by pieces that contrast in terms of tempo, tonality, style, texture, text, language, accompaniment, or composer. The most complex or difficult piece(s) should be placed near the middle of the rehearsal, and a memorable and moving piece placed at the end, leaving the singers with a favorite piece still echoing in their ears as they depart class. Rehearsal pacing should be quick to keep students on their toes, but not rushed or tense, with some breaks to rest the voice and relax while announcements or other business matters can be quickly relayed.

Literature-Based Warm-Ups

Vocal warm-ups have been discussed in detail in Chapters 3 and 7. Another effective approach to creating warm-ups is to derive them directly from the repertoire being studied. For example, warm-ups may be created that focus on difficult rhythms, intervals, or articulations found in the pieces to be rehearsed that day. This approach is an efficient use of time because when the music is rehearsed, many potential musical problems have already been resolved due to the warm-up (Coker, 1984).

Sight-Singing

Effective teaching of sight-singing skills must include both daily group practice and regular individual assessment. While this might seem to be standard operating procedure, a study of large-group adjudicated festivals in all 50 states revealed that only 25 states required sight-singing as part of the adjudication for high school choirs. Perhaps if more festivals required sight-singing competence, choir directors would devote more instructional time to practice and assessment of this skill (Norris, 2004).

Indiana State School Music Association (ISSMA, 2016) contests adjudicate high school choirs on the following sight-reading criteria, depending on the level of choir. This list of criteria provides a helpful outline of important content to be covered in daily sight-singing practice, through exercises that are one to two levels easier than the typical literature the ensemble performs (*National Standards*, 1994).

Beginning Level:

- Meter: 4/4, 2/4, 3/4
- Key: C, F, G, B-flat major
- Rhythm: Whole, half, quarter, eighth, dotted-quarter, dotted-half notes and rests
- Voicing: Unison and two-part, unaccompanied

Intermediate Level:

- Meter: 4/4, 2/4, 3/4
- Key: C, F, G, B-flat; *add B, E, D, A* major
- Rhythm: Whole, half, quarter, eighth, dotted-quarter, dotted-half notes and rests; *add sixteenth notes, triplets*
- Voicing: Unison and two-part; *add three/four-parts*, unaccompanied

Advanced Level:

- Meter: 4/4, 2/4, 3/4; *add 6/8*
- Key: C, F, B, E, G, D, A, B-flat
- Rhythm: Whole, half, quarter, eighth, dotted-eighth, dotted-half notes and rests, sixteenth notes, triplets; *add dotted-eighth and syncopation*
- Voicing: Unison, two-part, and three/four-part, unaccompanied.

Building Choral Excellence by Steven Demorest (2001) is a landmark resource for understanding effective ways to teach sight-singing in the choral rehearsal. He reported that the following musical experiences predict success at sight-singing:

- at least six years of piano study
- additional instrumental experience

- regular group practice of sight-singing
- individual testing of sight-singing
- specific feedback regarding sight-singing attempts.

In his book, Demorest reviews 21 different methods for teaching sight-singing, and concludes that there is no one best way to teach it, other than consistently. Many conductors were trained using the number system for scale degrees and so prefer to teach with that; others prefer moveable *do* solfege because its syllables are conducive to singing beautiful vowel sounds; and others trained in fixed *do* solfege believe in that system.

Regarding rhythm reading, many teach students to clap a notated rhythm (such as two eighths, two eighths, four sixteenths, quarter note) while counting aloud the beat subdivisions (e.g., "1-and, 2-and, 3-ee-and-a, 4"), while others prefer the syllable system used in Zoltán Kodály's (e.g., "ti-ti, ti-ti, ti-ri-ti-ri, ta") or Edwin Gordon's (e.g., "du-de, du-de, du-ta-de-ta, du") approach. The Takadimi system (e.g., "ta-di, ta-di, ta-ka-di-mi, ta") is also very popular (see Musical Example 9.1). The point to be taken is that while no one system has been found to be the best, any one of them can be effective if the teacher knows it well, uses it consistently, and structures instruction sequentially.

Musical Example 9.1   Sight-Reading Rhythm Systems

A suggested sight-singing sequence (Demorest, 2001) is to begin with the rhythm of an exercise or piece and have the singers

1. identify the time signature and starting beat
2. scan the example for rhythmic repetitions or similarities

3. set a tempo and chant the rhythm (on counts or syllables)
4. note any errors, and repeat to correct.

Then focus on the pitches and have the singers

5. identify the key signature, tonality, and starting pitch
6. scan for melodic patterns that are repetitive or similar
7. sing the tonic chord and starting pitch (the teacher may play the scale of the exercise, the I–IV–V–I progression, and the starting pitch; ISSMA, 2016)
8. set a tempo and sing
9. note errors, and repeat to correct.

Students who are poor sight-singers will benefit from practice using these additional strategies (Henry, 2008):

- Use Curwen hand signs (particularly for kinesthetic learners) (McClung, 2008).
- Sing out loud during practice.
- Keep the steady beat in the body without stopping.
- Get through the whole melody without stopping.
- Keep eyes on the music.
- Skip the easy parts.

The great choral conductor Robert Shaw began the rehearsal of every piece by combining the pitches with count-singing (e.g., "one and two and tee [sic] and four and") before adding any lyrics or diction complexities. This technique solidifies the pulse and rhythms.

Improvising

While many aspects of the national standards seem realistic, some are known to be challenging, specifically the creative activities of improvising and composing (Madura Ward-Steinman, 2007). Teachers often are inadequately prepared to teach these skills (Song, 2014) and also feel that there simply is not enough time to make these standards a priority when there are performances to prepare. Yet it is important to remember the philosophy behind the standards, which is that students can become more complete musicians through creative music-making.

Improvising is usually associated with "scat-singing," as performed by vocal jazz ensembles or solo jazz artists. However, vocal improvisation has had a long history in classical music, even before notation existed. It was common for singers to improvise ornaments and embellishments throughout the medieval, Renaissance, Baroque and Classical periods. Choral singers were often skilled in improvisatory techniques, using diminution, augmentation, and ornaments such as the trillo, gruppo, tremolo, minuta, and appoggiatura. Vocal improvisation skill began to die out in the 19th century when highly virtuosic cadenzas required notation. Beginning again in the 20th century, though, improvisation became expected of choral performers of "chance" music, where various spontaneously created sound effects were integral to the music. Examples of choral improvisation in traditional choral styles can be found in *Getting Started with Vocal Improvisation* (Madura, 1999), while popular music improvisation will be addressed in the next chapter.

Singers can practice improvising freely at first, then impose some musical structure on that freedom, and over time learn the "language" of a particular style of music, such as jazz, early music, raga, or gospel. *Vocal Improvisation Games for Singers and Choral Groups* (Agrell and Madura Ward-Steinman, 2014) provides easy and enjoyable ways to begin improvising in the choral ensemble. While singers may feel some trepidation at first, they soon take ownership in and feel exhilarated by their improvisation experiences. Try some of these "games":

- *Warm-Up Game: Group Chord.* 4–100 singers. On cue, every member of the choir sings a note, any note, and holds it. This will create a large, dissonant chord. Everyone stops on cue. Repeat the exercise several times. For each repetition, each member of the group must adjust/alter his or her note so that it becomes more consonant and fits within the overall chord. Keep repeating the exercise until the choir has collectively agreed on a consonant chord (p. 2).
- *Rhythm Game: Sound Wall.* 4–20 singers. The singers select or create and memorize a short musical phrase. Each individual sings the melodic phrase, but at any tempo and in any rhythm. They cannot deviate from the pitches or the order of the pitches. They can only speed up or slow down the phrase or individual pitches within the phrase. This will create a giant "wall of sound" (p. 6).

- *Melody Game: Holiday Ornaments.* 3+ singers. The teacher demonstrates simple melodic ornaments as tools for vocal improvisation, such as upper neighbor tones, lower neighbor tones, anticipations, appoggiaturas, and passing tones on an age-appropriate well-known holiday melody, such as *Dona Nobis Pacem* or *Carol of the Bells.* After the demonstration, each singer sings one phrase while adding one ornament. Afterward, discuss the types of ornaments used (p. 12).
- *Harmony Game: Harmonic Community.* 4–100 singers. Start with a familiar song, such as a spiritual, and repeat for at least ten minutes, allowing everyone to experiment and contribute to the overall harmony (p. 16).
- *Depiction Game: Picture This.* 3–16 singers. The leader or the group chooses something to depict as a "soundscape" with voices, such as a beach scene, a crowded freeway, a forest, or an artwork. One singer enters at a time. Record the result; the students listen, learn, and evaluate the improvisation, and generate ideas for the next improvisation. Students may use bodily percussion, mouth noises, or "found sounds" (p. 19).
- *Miscellaneous Game: Circle Song I.* 6–16 singers. Stand in a circle, eyes closed. Anyone may start by improvising a simple ostinato pattern. Anyone may join in at any time, but added voices must fit what's there. Vocal sounds may include nonsense syllables, humming, sound effects, poetry quotes, or lyrics made up on the spot (p. 43).

Composing

Composing in Choir (Kerchner and Strand, 2016) is another important resource for high school choir directors. Complete lesson plans from multiple contributors are provided for composition projects in the choir. For example, Mary Kennedy contributed an assignment for the choir to compose a round, after the choir has learned and sung several in choir class. Students are instructed to write both the lyrics and the melody for a round, and to decide on the mode, meter, key, vocal range, and mood. The teacher gives lessons on word stress and its relationship to rhythmic feel, on the importance of balancing repetition and variety, and on the placement of consonance versus dissonance within a phrase. A small group of students performs the round for the other choir members, followed by class feedback and discussion regarding further refinement of the choir's composition.

Composing countermelodies to a simple pentatonic song is another accessible approach for choir members. Sandra Babb and Janice Smith provided a lesson on arranging a folk song that is based on the pentatonic scale, such as *Cindy*. The melody's notation is projected on a screen. Students begin by composing a melodic ostinato to accompany the melody; then they create a descant to include in the arrangement. Countermelodies are then created. The choir members practice singing the parts after they are created to identify what works and what doesn't. Finally, the choir is divided into four groups, with each group singing one of the four vocal parts: melody, ostinato, descant, and countermelody. This class performance is recorded so that the singers can listen and assess their new arrangement for its strengths and areas to improve.

Rehearsing the Literature

Score Study Applications

Score study sets up the conductor for efficient rehearsals. An overall analysis of the form, texture, and unifying element(s) of the piece is a useful starting point in planning consecutive rehearsals (Demorest, 1996). By knowing its form, the conductor can plan to teach the music in sections or blocks. This approach is satisfying for several important reasons: Singers can learn a manageable part of the whole form within a rehearsal, they will feel a sense of accomplishment for having learned a complete section, and they will find memorization to come more easily than without attention to the structure of the piece.

Texture analysis will help the conductor prioritize the learning of vocal parts. For example, if the piece is homophonic, having everyone sing the melody wherever it appears in the piece is a good way to start. Then having everyone sing each of the harmonizing parts keeps them all engaged in music-learning, and also makes them aware of the role of those parts in supporting the melody, but not overpowering it. If the piece is polyphonic, highlighting and rehearsing the imitative parts make the learning of interweaving vocal lines more understandable and accessible.

The unifying element of a piece should be pointed out to the singers, whether it is a repeated melodic or rhythmic motive, an unusual harmonic progression or meter, a particular text setting, or an improvisatory climax of the piece. Clearly, the structural approach to learning a composition (its form, texture, and unifying element) is more conducive to the singers' comprehensive understanding of the music than always starting from the beginning of the work and "drilling notes."

Teaching a New Piece

- When introducing a new piece, the conductor should say a few words about the piece and/or the composer.
- It is beneficial to get the singers involved in the music as soon as possible by playing a good recording or playing through it on the piano.
- On the second hearing the singers may hum or sing along.
- Any of the sight-reading systems identified in this chapter may be applied to learning a new piece.
- Always aim for rehearsing at least two vocal parts at a time for efficiency.
- Rehearse with as little piano support as possible in order to develop independent musicians.
- Once the singers know the rhythm, they may lightly speak the text in rhythm (the speaking should never become heavy or unmusical).
- If the text is not in English, the students may sing on a neutral syllable.
- Often the learning of a new piece requires that it be taken at a slow, steady tempo for optimal concentration on all the musical aspects.
- Isolate difficult sections and correct mistakes or they will become harder to unlearn.
- Correcting trouble spots requires repetition of the correction, followed by working into it from several measures earlier to ensure the correction is secure.
- Finally, make sure that every rehearsal, including the first one, has at least one shared sublimely beautiful musical experience.

A fine high school choir works in every rehearsal to achieve the qualities of beautiful singing: good diction, precision of rhythm and pitches, tempo, dynamics, intonation, tone control, balance, blend, phrasing, and interpretation (Cooksey, 1977; ISSMA, 2016). It can be overwhelming, though, to consider and organize everything that your choir members should learn during their high school years. The following publications can assist in planning a comprehensive and sequential choral music curriculum at the high school level.

Choral Curriculum Resources for High School

Buchanan, Heather J. and Mehaffey, Matthew W. (2005, 2007, 2011). *Teaching Music Through Performance in Choir, Volume 1, 2, 3.* Chicago, IL: GIA Publications.

Demorest, Steven M. (2001). *Building Choral Excellence: Teaching Sight-Singing in the Choral Rehearsal.* New York: Oxford University Press.

Experiencing Choral Music (2008). New York: Glencoe/McGraw-Hill.

Teaching Choral Music: A Course of Study (2006). Lanham, MD: Rowman & Littlefield/NAfME.

Telfer, Nancy (2006). *Successful Performing.* San Diego, CA: Kjos.

EFFECTIVE TEACHING STRATEGIES

Specific teaching strategies have been researched and found to significantly improve ensemble members' attentiveness and achievement. The new choir teacher who practices and masters the following three strategies will find them to be very useful teaching tools.

The Complete Teaching Cycle

On a micro-level, a rehearsal is made up of dozens of teaching "cycles" which can be designed to maximize student achievement and attitude. The "complete teaching cycle" consists of three parts:

1. the teacher's demonstration or clear instructions for the singers to perform a particular musical task
2. the singers' performance of or response to the task
3. specific teacher feedback regarding the accuracy of students' performance or response (Price, 1983, 1992).

An example of the three-step complete cycle is this:

1. The director models and gives clear verbal instructions to the choir to stand with proper singing posture.
2. The singers respond with their singing posture.
3. The director gives immediate specific feedback regarding the singers' resulting posture.

Another example is this:

1. The teacher asks the singers to imitate a vowel sound she models.
2. The singers imitate the vowel sound.
3. The teacher provides immediate feedback regarding the accuracy of the sound.

The feedback may, in turn, lead to a new instruction, followed by student response, and then more feedback. Studies have found that this three-part cycle is effective for achievement and attitude in a rehearsal.

Although the cycle may sound simplistic, consider situations where you have observed choral directors disregarding one of the three steps. Is step one ever left out—the presentation by the director of what is expected of the singers? Do directors ever eliminate step two by stating what needs to be fixed but not giving singers the opportunity to fix it? Is step three, feedback, ever missing? Give examples.

Conductor Magnitude

The intensity ("magnitude") of a conductor is a motivating factor in a rehearsal. Conductors should not be self-conscious about showing their passion and enthusiasm for the music, because this engages the choir. Facial expressions, body movement, speaking volume, speech speed, eye contact, vocal inflections, pacing, and positive reinforcement can all be used to make your rehearsal an interesting one (Yarbrough, 1975; Yarbrough and Madsen, 1998). Learning to vary these expressions is an important tool for teachers. It is easy to "tune out" the teacher whose voice is always loud and fast—switching to a hushed tone can get everyone's attention quickly! Vary your body movement by sometimes moving around and sometimes staying behind the music stand; vary your pacing from very quick to pausing for a few moments to relax. It creates the dramatic effect to keep students attentive. In fact, high conductor magnitude is so influential that secondary students have rated a teacher's "effectiveness" as excellent even when the information being taught was inaccurate (Madsen, 2003)!

Teacher Talk

Most new teachers talk too much. The students are there to sing, not to listen to the teacher talk longer than necessary. The danger of too much "teacher talk" is that students often become off-task because they are not actively learning, resulting in behavior problems and lack of motivation. The teacher would do well to limit most instruction to "seven words or less" because more than that is difficult to recall. Remember the "7 plus or minus 2" rule, which pertains to the human capacity to keep only five to nine bits of information in our active short-term memory (Miller, 1956). Keeping students' attention is paramount, and while many teachers master the "seven words or less" rule relatively easily, some really struggle without concentrated discipline applied. Certainly, there are times when the teacher needs to give longer instructions than seven words, but when it is not necessary, refrain from doing so. Remember students' capacity for remembering your points, and let the students sing, which is why they enrolled in your choir!

There are many more pointers for creating an inspiring rehearsal environment. Take these to heart:

- Always show enthusiasm for teaching and music.
- Be encouraging; 80% approvals and 20% disapprovals were found to result in significant gains in performance and attitude (Freer, 1992).
- Be assertive in giving instruction; don't *ask*.
- Always give a reason for repeating something.
- Tell singers *how* to fix an error, not just that they made one.
- When playing a recording, tell the students to listen for something in particular (Apfelstadt, 2015).
- Music must move; human beings must move.
- Never work just for notes.

- Do not rehearse music that is not problematic.
- Rehearse the last part of the piece first to ensure a solid ending.
- Force your students to watch you. Make them memorize the first two choral measures of the piece.
- Do not sing with your choir in rehearsal or performance; you can't hear them.
- Do not mouth the words with your choir in performance, unless it is intermittent in a memorized piece.
- Let half the choir critique the other half.
- Build relationships.
- Understand your singers' point of view (Archibeque, 1997).
- Begin on time.
- Always demand proper posture.
- Rehearse in a circle or in different places in the room.
- Have the rehearsal order written on the board.
- Alternate standing and sitting.
- Play the piano softly; ask your accompanist to play softly.
- Don't undertake too much (Rogers, 1999).
- Admit your mistakes, but don't make a habit of apologizing.
- Make every rehearsal a creating session, not a correcting session.
- Have high expectations; don't ever settle for less.
- Cultivate your sense of humor.
- Be inspiring every minute of every rehearsal.
- Be yourself.

ASSESSMENT AND EVALUATION

Assessment and evaluation are fundamentally connected to teaching. To clarify the fuzzy difference between the two terms, *assessment* is usually thought of as the *formative* and minute-by-minute reflections about student progress toward objectives during the rehearsal, while *evaluation* is often considered the *summative* judgment of what has been learned (Straight, 2002). Teachers need to be skilled in both. They need to be able to teach and assess the singing simultaneously in order to give continual feedback that shapes the music being rehearsed. They also need to spend time evaluating learning in order to provide feedback to students and their parents about their achievement in choral music, usually through letter grades. These both become easier with practice.

The following 12 criteria were used for evaluation and grading by high school choral teachers who were members of the Ohio Music Education Association (OMEA) (Kotora, 2001). They are listed in order from most to least used in assigning grades:

1. concert performance
2. student participation
3. student attendance
4. singing tests
5. written tests
6. student attitude
7. audio recordings
8. individual performances
9. video-recordings
10. independent study/written projects
11. check sheets/rating scales/rubrics
12. student portfolios.

Although these teachers rated concert attendance and class participation as more important for determining a student's grade than actual music skills, they also expressed frustration at not being able to find the time to accurately assess those skills. They reported several obstacles to measuring musical skills as a basis for grades:

- time limitations due to large classes, short class periods, and full class schedules
- difficulty in keeping accurate records
- difficulty in assessing in a large ensemble setting
- philosophical differences between students and parents regarding assessment in music class
- lack of administrative support for music assessment
- lack of teacher training in methods of music assessment.

CLASSROOM MANAGEMENT

According to a review of 11,000 research studies over 50 years, the most important factor that influences student learning is effective classroom management (Wang, Haertel, and Walberg, 1993/1994). The choral director who has selected appropriate music for the choirs, has prepared the music and an effective rehearsal, shows great conductor magnitude and enthusiasm, focuses on the positive, and has developed a reputation of success for the choral program will have few classroom management problems. This level of teacher accomplishment may take a couple of years to establish though, and so here are a few practical guidelines for effective management:

- Regularly attend workshops offered by NAfME on classroom management techniques.
- Read every classroom management resource you can, such as

  o *Responsible Classroom Management for Teachers* by J. Allen Queen and colleagues (1997), which explains the different principles, goals, strategies, and problems associated with five main discipline models, ranging from highly student-centered to highly teacher-centered models

  o *The First Days of School: How to Be an Effective Teacher* by Harry and Rosemary Wong (1998), which includes a powerful set of teacher materials for ensuring a positive class environment

  o *Tips: Discipline in the Music Classroom* (Rossman, 1989), which provides brief and practical ideas to take immediately into the classroom such as:

    ▪ Take a photo on the first day of class and learn students' names overnight.
    ▪ Never lose your temper. Teachers may "act" angry, but not lose control of their emotions.
    ▪ Have a signal for expecting quiet, rather than making a habit of shouting over the students' voices.
    ▪ Create behavior contracts that are signed by the teacher and the students, and sometimes the parents.
    ▪ When a student misbehaves, continue teaching the class while moving toward the disruptive student. Often simple proximity will cause the problem to stop.
    ▪ Never make threats you can't or shouldn't carry out.
    ▪ Develop a student leadership system within the ensemble; include as many students as practical in discussions about ensemble policy.

- Observe many master teachers and experiment with different classroom management strategies to find which ones work for your personality and disposition.
- Know the school's rules and policies, and enforce them from day one.
- Be firm, fair, and consistent with rehearsal rules and consequences.

Finally, be certain to re-read "Classroom Management and Discipline" in Chapter 2, which provides a comprehensive review of essential classroom management strategies that are also applicable to high school choir.

BRAINTEASER 9-1: OBSERVING ROBERT SHAW'S COUNT-SINGING APPROACH

View one of the *Robert Shaw: Preparing a Masterpiece* video-recordings listed in the resources for this chapter, and write a two-page paper describing his method of "count-singing" and other effective rehearsal techniques observed.

BRAINTEASER 9-2: CREATING A SIGHT-SINGING LESSON PLAN

Create a ten-minute sight-singing lesson plan, using Demorest's nine steps, to teach a section of the piece you analyzed in the last chapter, or another moderately easy piece for high school choir (see Table 9.1). Consider adding the additional teaching strategies that have been found to help poor sight-readers.

BRAINTEASER 9-3: DEVELOPING A CURRICULUM UNIT PLAN

Using the national standards, and the improvisation and composition resources cited, develop a four- to eight-week unit plan for including ten minutes of the creative activities of improvising and/or composing in every high school choir rehearsal.

Table 9.1 Sight-Singing Lesson Plan

Name of ensemble:

Material (including title, composer/arranger, voicing, etc.):

National and/or state standard addressed:

Instructional objective:

Procedure (minutes):

1.

2.

3.

4.

5.

6.

7.

8.

9.

10.

Summative assessment:

BRAINTEASER 9-4: COMPARING AND CONTRASTING CHORAL CURRICULUM GUIDES

In peer groups, compare and contrast the choral curriculum resources recommended in this chapter. Then, individually, write three consecutive 15-minute lesson plans for one choral piece, beginning with the introduction to the piece. Review the topic of lesson planning in Chapter 5 and use the format provided in Table 5.3.

BRAINTEASER 9-5: PRACTICING THE COMPLETE TEACHING CYCLE

Practice the Complete Teaching Cycle while teaching your sight-singing lesson plan, or other lesson plan of your choice, to your peers. Have your peers comment on your use of it. After practicing the cycle a few times, video-record yourself teaching the cycle in your field experience, and analyze the technique in a self-report.

BRAINTEASER 9-6: PRACTICING CONDUCTOR MAGNITUDE

Teach your sight-singing lesson plan, or other mini-lesson, to your peers, exploring the use of varied facial expressions, body movement, speaking volume, speech speed, eye contact, vocal inflections, quick pacing, and positive reinforcement. After practicing with your peers, incorporate conductor magnitude in your field experience while video-recording yourself, and self-evaluate the recording. This attention-getting strategy can be a lifesaver in a blasé rehearsal!

BRAINTEASER 9-7: PRACTICING "7 WORDS OR LESS"

Practice teaching your sight-singing lesson plan, or other mini-lesson, to your peers, allowing yourself to say "7 plus or minus 2" words each time you stop the group to say something. Choose your words carefully. Perhaps plan them ahead if you have a tendency to get tongue-tied or ramble; for example, "Everyone sing *loo* please;" "Turn to page 3, system 2, measure 11;" "Let's try that again with a better breath;" "Watch me!" and "Thanks for your great effort today, Singers!" After practicing with your peers, try it in your field experience while video-recording yourself and self-evaluate the recording.

BRAINTEASER 9-8: DEVELOPING EVALUATION CRITERIA

Discuss the pros and cons of the 12 criteria for grading, as well as the obstacles to evaluation, as described in this chapter. Then, individually, decide on the criteria for grading your future students, assign percentages for grading each criterion, and submit to your instructor.

References

Agrell, Jeffrey and Madura Ward-Steinman, Patrice (2014). *Vocal Improvisation Games for Singers and Choral Groups.* Chicago, IL: GIA.

Apfelstadt, Hilary (2015). The How of Rehearsing. *Choral Journal, 56*(1), 73–75.

Archibeque, Charlene (August, 1997). A Choral Director's Rehearsal Checkup. *Choral Journal, 38*(1), 33–34.

Barrow, Lee G. (1994). Programming Rehearsals for Student Success. *Music Educators Journal, September 1994,* 24, 27–28.

Buchanan, Heather J. and Mehaffey, Matthew W. (2005). *Teaching Music Through Performance in Choir, Volume 1.* Chicago, IL: GIA.

Buchanan, Heather J. and Mehaffey, Matthew W. (2007). *Teaching Music Through Performance in Choir, Volume 2.* Chicago, IL: GIA.

Buchanan, Heather J. and Mehaffey, Matthew W. (2011). *Teaching Music Through Performance in Choir, Volume 3.* Chicago, IL: GIA.

Coker, Timothy Columbus (1984). Choral Warm-Up Exercises as a Key to Teaching Music Literature and Vocal Technique. PhD Doctoral Dissertation, University of Southern Mississippi, AAT 8518316.

Cooksey, John M. (1977). A Facet-Factorial Approach to Rating High School Choral Music Performance. *Journal of Research in Music Education, 25*(2), 100–114.

Demorest, Steven M. (January, 1996). Structuring a Musical Choral Rehearsal. *Music Educators Journal, 82*(4), 25–30.

Demorest, Steven M. (2001). *Building Choral Excellence: Teaching Sight-Singing in the Choral Rehearsal.* New York: Oxford University Press.

Experiencing Choral Music (2008). New York: Glencoe/McGraw-Hill.

Freer, Patrick K. (December, 1992). Education Research: Practical Implications for the Rehearsal. *Choral Journal, 33,* 28–34.

Henry, Michele L. (2008). The Use of Specific Practice and Performance Strategies in Sight-Singing Instruction. *UPDATE: Applications of Research in Music Education, 26*(2), 11–16.

Indiana State School Music Association (2016). *Music Festivals Manual: 2016–2017 School Year*. Indianapolis: ISSMA.

Kerchner, Jody L. and Strand, Katherine, eds. (2016). *Musicianship: Composing in the Choir*. Chicago, IL: GIA.

Kotora, E. James (2001). Assessment Practices in the Choral Music Classroom: A Survey of Ohio High School Choral Music Teachers and College Choral Methods Teachers. Doctoral Dissertation, AAT 3036343.

McClung, Alan C. (2008). Sight-Singing Scores of High School Choristers with Extensive Training in Movable Solfege Syllables and Curwen Hand Signs. *Journal of Research in Music Education, 56*(3), 255–266.

Madsen, Katia (2003). The Effect of Accuracy of Instruction, Teacher Delivery, and Student Attentiveness on Musician's Evaluation of Teacher Effectiveness. *Journal of Research in Music Education, 51*(1), 38–50.

Madura, Patrice D. (1999). *Getting Started with Vocal Improvisation*. Lanham, MD: Rowman & Littlefield/NAfME.

Madura Ward-Steinman, Patrice (Spring, 2007). Confidence in Teaching Improvisation According to the K-12 Achievement Standards: Surveys of Vocal Jazz Workshop Participants and Undergraduates. *Bulletin of the Council for Research in Music Education, 172,* 25–40.

Miller, George A. (March, 1956). The Magical Number Seven, Plus or Minus Two: Some Limits on Our Capacity for Processing Information. *Psychological Review, 63,* 81–97.

National Standards for Arts Education (1994). Lanham, MD: Rowman & Littlefield/NAfME.

Norris, Charles E. (Spring, 2004). A Nationwide Overview of Sight-Singing Requirements of Large-Group Choral Festivals. *Journal of Research in Music Education, 52*(1), 16–28.

*Opportunity-to-Learn Standards for Music Instruction: Grades PreK-12 (*1994). Lanham, MD: Rowman & Littlefield/NAfME.

Price, Harry E. (1983). The Effect of Conductor Academic Task Presentation, Conductor Reinforcement, and Ensemble Practice on Performers' Musical Achievement, Attentiveness, and Attitude. *Journal of Research in Music Education, 31*(4), 245–257.

Price, Harry E. (1992). Sequential Patterns of Music Instruction and Learning to Use Them. *Journal of Research in Music Education, 40*(1), 14–29.

Queen, J. Allen, Blackwelder, B.B. and Mallen, L.P. (1997). *Responsible Classroom Management for Teachers and Students*. Upper Saddle River, NJ: Prentice Hall.

Robert Shaw: Preparing a Masterpiece, Vol. 1 (1991, video). *A Choral Workshop on Brahms' A German Requiem*. New York: Carnegie Hall.

Robert Shaw: Preparing a Masterpiece, Vol. 2 (1992, video). *A Choral Workshop on Beethoven's Missa Solemnis*. New York: Carnegie Hall.

Robert Shaw: Preparing a Masterpiece, Vol. 3 (1992, video). *A Choral Workshop on Berlioz's Requiem*. New York: Carnegie Hall.

Rogers, Bruce (March 27, 1999). *Choral Rehearsal Techniques*. Educational Session at CMEA, Ontario, CA.

Rossman, R. Louis (1989). *Tips: Discipline in the Music Classroom*. Lanham, MD: Rowman & Littlefield/NAfME.

Song, Anna (2014). Music Improvisation in Higher Education. *College Music Symposium, 53.* www.music.org/pdf/pubs/symposium/symposium53.pdf.

Straight, H. Steven (2002). *The Difference between Assessment and Evaluation.* Retrieved on January 10, 2009 from assessment.binghamton.edu/documents/assessment_evaluation_straight.ppt.

Teaching Choral Music: A Course of Study (2006). Lanham, MD: Rowman & Littlefield/NAfME.

Telfer, Nancy (2006). *Successful Performing.* San Diego, CA: Kjos.

Wang, M.C., Haertel, G.D., and Walberg, H.J. (December/January, 1993/1994). Synthesis of Research: What Helps Students Learn? *Educational Leadership, 51*(4), 74–79.

Wong, Harry K. and Wong, Rosemary T. (1998). *The First Days of School: How to Be An Effective Teacher.* Mountain View, CA: Harry K. Wong Publications.

Yarbrough, Cornelia (1975). Effect of Magnitude of Conductor Behavior on Students in Selected Mixed Choruses. *Journal of Research in Music Education, 23*(2), 134–146.

Yarbrough, Cornelia and Madsen, Katia (1998). The Evaluation of Teaching in Choral Rehearsals. *Journal of Research in Music Education, 46*(4), 469–481.

10

DIRECTING VOCAL JAZZ, CONTEMPORARY A CAPPELLA, SHOW CHOIR, MUSICAL THEATER, MADRIGAL DINNERS, GOSPEL CHOIRS, AND MULTICULTURAL ENSEMBLES

Successful high school choral teachers were asked to make recommendations for college coursework in choral literature, and they consistently expressed the need for instruction in a wider variety of styles beyond the five major classical periods, as well as more exposure to small ensembles and madrigal literature (Bolt, 1983). Likewise, the *Opportunity-to-Learn*

Figure 10.1   Vocal Jazz Ensemble

Standards (1994) state that at the high school level there should be at least one alternative ensemble offered, such as vocal jazz or contemporary a cappella, for every 450 students enrolled in the school. These alternative ensembles can provide learning opportunities in improvising, arranging, and composing music, world music, popular singing styles, microphone technique, and integrating dancing and acting with singing. In addition, the experience of singing in a small ensemble develops keen listening and ear-training skills, musical independence, and leadership (Zorn, 1973). Therefore, this chapter will focus on the skills and knowledge needed to direct vocal jazz ensembles, contemporary a cappella groups, show choirs, gospel choirs, multicultural choirs, madrigal dinners, and musical theater productions.

VOCAL JAZZ ENSEMBLES

Vocal jazz is an art form that brings together choral singing, improvisation, American popular and instrumental jazz repertoire, chamber music experience, and microphone vocal technique. For these reasons, it broadens the core choral experience with a new style of music and new approaches to singing. It provides the extra challenges that come with small ensemble singing, including close harmonies that require fine intonation, and therefore is a perfect fit for your extra-motivated and/or gifted students.

Roots

Vocal jazz is a relatively recent phenomenon in the big picture of choral music. The first professional vocal jazz groups that influenced our concepts of vocal jazz today became active in the 1950s and 1960s and include:

- Lambert, Hendricks and Ross
- The Swingle Singers
- The Four Freshmen, and
- The Hi-Lo's.

By the 1970s the Manhattan Transfer had burst on the scene, and college and high school vocal jazz ensembles began to spring up around the country, starting in the Pacific Northwest where vocal jazz continues to be a stronghold. Since the 1980s the influence of vocal jazz has spread around the nation and the world, with outstanding groups such as:

- the Real Group from Sweden
- the Idea of North from Australia, and
- the New York Voices.

It is important to listen to recordings of these influential ensembles to develop a historically authentic aural concept of vocal jazz.

Arrangers

The following list of vocal jazz arrangers includes the original grand masters of the genre as well as newer arrangers who have been influencing the ongoing development of vocal jazz:

- Dave Barduhn
- Jennifer Barnes
- Randy Crenshaw
- Dave Cross
- Rosana Eckert
- Anders Edenroth
- Jeremy Fox
- Greg Jasperse
- Cathy Jensen-Hole
- Anita Kerr
- Ken Kraintz
- Kirk Marcy
- Kerry Marsh
- Phil Mattson
- Darmon Meader
- Gene Puerling
- Paris Rutherford
- Kirby Shaw
- Vijay Singh
- Ward Swingle
- Roger Treece
- Michele Weir
- Steve Zegree.

Arrangements

The following list of selected SATB vocal jazz arrangements includes easy to moderately difficult pieces that are appropriate for secondary school choirs. While SATB arrangements are listed here, there is no shortage of vocal jazz for SAB, treble, and men's groups. In fact, several of the tunes listed below are available in other voicings.

- *Alice in Wonderland* by Paris Rutherford
- *Amazing Grace* by Jeremy Fox
- *America the Beautiful* by Kirk Marcy
- *Anthropology* by Paris Rutherford
- *Baby Won't You Please Come Home* by Jacques Rizzo
- *Begin the Beguine* by Greg Jasperse
- *Blue Skies* by Steve Zegree
- *Blues Down to My Shoes* by Kirby Shaw
- *Bourée* by Ward Swingle
- *Bridge over Troubled Water* by Kirby Shaw
- *Café* by Jeremy Fox
- *Chile Con Carne* by Anders Edenroth
- *Cottontail* by Darmon Meader
- *Desafinado* by Phil Mattson
- *Doctor Jazz* by Kirby Shaw
- *Down at Smokey Joe's* by Ken Kraintz
- *Down St. Thomas Way* by Dave Cazier
- *Fever* (SSA) by Kirby Shaw
- *Fly Away Birdie* by Matt Falker
- *Fly Me to the Moon* (SSA) by Rosana Eckert
- *For All We Know* by Dave Barduhn
- *Georgia on My Mind* by Gene Puerling
- *God Bless the Child* (SSA) by Steve Zegree
- *Happiness Is a Thing Called Joe* by Anita Kerr
- *He Bop-N-Re Bop* by Vijay Singh
- *Holiday Blues* by Roger Treece
- *How Deep Is the Ocean* by Rosana Eckert
- *I'll Be Seeing You* by Phil Mattson
- *I'm Old Fashioned* by Jennifer Barnes
- *In My Life* by Steve Zegree
- *I've Got You under My Skin* by Phil Mattson

- *Love Walked In* by Steve Zegree
- *Lovely Ride* by Rosana Eckert
- *Loves Me Like a Rock* by Darmon Meader
- *More I Cannot Wish You* by Phil Mattson
- *The Most Wonderful Time of the Year* by Jamie Dyer
- *Muddy Water* by Michele Weir
- *My Country 'Tis of Thee* by Kirby Shaw
- *My Romance* by Gene Puerling
- *Nature Boy* by Kerry Marsh
- *New York Afternoon* by Michele Weir
- *Night and Day* (TTB) by Kerry Marsh
- *A Nightingale Sang in Berkeley Square* by Gene Puerling
- *One Note Samba* by Roger Emerson
- *Oo-Pop-Dah* by Dave Barduhn
- *Operator* by Kirby Shaw
- *Orange Colored Sky* by Leighton Tiffault
- *Over the Rainbow* by Teena Chinn
- *Route 66* by Dick Averre
- *Scat Blues in C* by Randy Crenshaw
- *Shortnin' Bread* by Dave Cross
- *Sing, Sing, Sing* by Darmon Meader
- *Singin' in the Rain* by April Arabian
- *Smack Dab in the Middle* by Darmon Meader
- *South of the Border* by Sharon Broadley
- *Straighten up and Fly Right* by Kirby Shaw
- *Ticket to Ride* by Michele Weir
- *Walkin'* by Bob Stoloff
- *Walkin' My Baby Back Home* (TTB) by Tim Buchholz
- *What a Wonderful World* by Phil Mattson
- *Words* by Anders Edenroth
- *You Must Believe in Spring* by Phil Mattson

More ideas for repertoire can be gathered from vocal jazz reading sessions, especially at ACDA and JEN (Jazz Education Network) conferences; state-approved festival lists for vocal jazz; and websites of vocal jazz publishers, especially the University of Northern Colorado Jazz Press (www.uncjazzpress.com), Sound Music Publications (www.smpjazz.com), and Singers.Com (www.singers.com/jazz).

Performance Practice

Swing

Although vocal jazz arrangements come in a variety of rhythmic styles, such as Latin, rock, or ballad, the fundamental rhythmic style of jazz is swing, and as Duke Ellington said, "It don't mean a thing if it ain't got that swing!" While Latin, rock, and ballad jazz arrangements interpret eighth notes as written, it is now common knowledge that, in swing music, eighth notes must be "swung" in a triplet feel, as seen in Musical Example 10.1. There should also be a slight emphasis on the off-beats (2 and 4) to enhance the swing feel.

Musical Example 10.1   Swing Rhythm

Swing is visceral and must be internally felt. Accomplished jazz singers have identified the following artists who have strongly influenced their own feel for swing: singers Sarah Vaughan, Ella Fitzgerald, and Nat King Cole, and instrumentalists Miles Davis, Sonny Rollins, and Clifford Brown (Madura Ward-Steinman, 2014).

Improvisation

Many vocal jazz choral arrangements provide space for improvisation, which is considered the essence of jazz. But choral directors often lack training in improvisation, and while they have a strong interest in improvisation, they don't feel that they can teach it. It is all too common practice for directors to allow any and all volunteers to perform scat solos, and those volunteers often have little to no knowledge of jazz or guidance from their teacher. The traditions of jazz deserve more attention than that. Choir directors need to be aware of the following basic jazz experiences that will assist their students in developing improvisation skills (Madura, 1996, Madura Ward-Steinman, 2007, 2008):

- Listen to live and recorded jazz extensively, both vocal and instrumental.

- Practice imitating and transcribing jazz rhythms and solos.
- Learn the harmonic structure underlying any improvisation by singing the chord roots.
- Shape the improvised solo as the telling of a story, with a beginning, a climax, and an end.
- Listen to and musically interact with the other singers and instrumentalists.

Scat-Singing

Scatting is the act of improvising using syllables. To use scat syllables that sound authentic, note the following suggestions:

- Listen to and imitate (or transcribe) scat syllables heard on recordings by such masters as Ella Fitzgerald, Darmon Meader, and Kurt Elling.
- Listen to instrumental jazz, particularly horns (such as Charlie Parker, Louis Armstrong, and Lee Morgan), and try to imitate their sounds, creating syllables that come close to their articulations.
- Study Bob Stoloff's book *Scat!* (1996) for an encyclopedia of scat syllables that work with various rhythms, melodies, vocal bass lines, and vocal percussion.

The Blues

A standard chord progression for beginning scat-singing is the 12-bar blues. The beginning improviser should first become familiar with the chord structure by singing the roots of the chords on the syllable *doo*, holding each for four beats.

```
4/4   I7   /   I7   /   I7   /   I7   /
      IV7  /   IV7  /   I7   /   I7   /
      V7   /   IV7  /   I7   /   I7   //
```

Next, arpeggiate the chords by singing a chord tone on each beat, as seen in Musical Example 10.2. For example, in the 12-bar blues in the key of C, the I7 chord is C-E-G-Bb, the IV7 chord is F-A-C-Eb, and the V7 chord is G-B-D-F.

After gaining familiarity with this basic 12-bar blues chord structure (there are more advanced versions with many chord substitutions

Musical Example 10.2   Arpeggiated 12-Bar Blues

possible), the singer can experiment with notes from the blues scale (*do me fa fi so te do*) for improvising. The blues scale degrees are:

1   flat 3   4   sharp 4   5   flat 7   1

Notate the blues scale in the key of C:

_____
_____
_____
_____

Practice the blues scale both ascending and descending in your chosen key of the 12-bar blues. The great jazz pedagogue David Baker called the blues scale a "horizontal scale" because it can be used to improvise over all of the chords in the 12-bar blues. For example, if the 12-bar blues is in the key of C, notes from the C blues scale can be used to improvise over the whole piece even when the chords change. While this is simple in theory, the challenges are many for the novice improviser:

- fear of improvising
- the dissonance of the flat third in the blues scale against the major third in the I7 chord (aim to make it "hurt so good")

- pitch accuracy of the chromatic notes, especially in the descending form of the scale
- the decision of which notes and rhythms to choose when improvising.

The simplest way to avoid these problems is to put many limitations on what the singers may choose, making improvisation attempts "safe." Limitations for beginning improvisers might include the following:

- At first, instruct the singers to use only scale degree 1 (*do*) of the blues scale, on the syllable *doo*, but to make sure it swings;
- add the aspect of story-telling by creating tension and release with dynamics or rhythms but still only singing the first scale degree; and
- limit the number of measures students may improvise to two or four measures.
- When students are comfortable, gradually add other pitches from the blues scale, other scat syllables, and more measures.

By limiting the allowable pitches of the blues scale for improvising in the early attempts, singers don't have to worry about "wrong notes," which reduces the fear of failure and enhances the spirit of play. Students may also be encouraged to compose short motives made up of some of the notes of the blues scale, and repeat them several times for effect (this repeated pattern is called a "riff").

The blues scale can be used to improvise to any 12-bar blues vocal jazz arrangement such as *Dr. Blues, Oo-Pop-Dah, Scat Blues in C, Things Ain't What They Used to Be, Doodlin', Route 66, Centerpiece,* and *Tenor Madness.* Students can "trade fours" (improvise a solo for four measures each) or scat-sing a 12-bar chorus.

When one tires of the blues scale, other scales can be gleaned from each chord type. Because each chord in the 12-bar blues is a dominant seventh chord, its Mixolydian mode (a major scale with a lowered seventh degree) is implied. Thus, any of the notes of the C Mixolydian scale may be used to improvise over the C7 chord; any notes of the F Mixolydian scale may be used over the F7 chord; and so forth, for all dominant chords.

An 11-minute video of me teaching the 12-bar blues lesson above, titled *Unraveling the Mystery of Improvisation: Scat-Singing,* can be found through the following links: www.musicedseries.org and www. youtube.com/watch?v=AQOrAy MkUHM. My lesson is the last one on each page.

The 12-bar blues is one way to start improvising with a familiar chord structure in vocal jazz, but there are countless others. The understanding of chord/scale relationships is important to the authentic language of jazz, just as the imitating and transcribing of other musicians' solos is common practice among jazz musicians. Important resources for learning to improvise jazz vocally can be found below. A special vocal jazz issue of the *Choral Journal* can be accessed by ACDA members through this link: http://acda.org/ccj.asp?ID=1708 (Madura Ward-Steinman, 2015).

Accompaniment

Many vocal jazz arrangements are a cappella, but much of the repertoire is arranged for the traditional jazz "rhythm section" of piano, bass, and drums. The rhythm section is an authentic characteristic of jazz, and choral directors often use an experienced rhythm section from the high school's instrumental jazz ensemble to rehearse and perform with the vocal jazz group. These instrumentalists play jazz because they enjoy improvising, and therefore the vocal jazz ensemble director needs to give them plenty of opportunities to do so. They may take solos in the vocal jazz arrangements and/or perform instrumental-only (or with a solo jazz singer) pieces in concert.

Vocal Jazz Sound

Vocal jazz is traditionally performed with a relatively small ensemble, ranging anywhere from 4 to 16 voices. Typically a sound system is used for close micing technique, with one to two singers per microphone. Although there are commonalities with classical singing, there are also significant differences. In vocal jazz choral singing, vibrato is minimized due to the careful tuning required for the close voicings and complexity of the jazz chords. A relatively bright sound is also desirable which can be achieved with an inner smile and a more shallow jaw. Consonant diction can also be relaxed because the microphone reduces the need for stressed consonants, and lyrics are usually sung in the vernacular. For example, the opening text from *Centerpiece*,

"The more I'm with you, pretty baby," should be pronounced "priddy," as one would speak it. These and other differences, such as note-bending, jazz inflections, and breath-to-tone ratios, are carefully explained and illustrated through the use of spectrographs in Diana Spradling's indispensable book *Jazz Singing: Developing Artistry and Authenticity* (2007).

While the sound equipment is an added burden and often an unknown area for choral directors, there are usually students in the high school who have a strong interest and experience in running sound systems, and they can enroll in your ensemble as the sound engineer. The standard microphone for vocal jazz is the Shure SM 58, and complete specifications for a desirable sound system can be found in Zegree's *The Complete Guide to Teaching Vocal Jazz* (2002).

Certainly vocal jazz may be performed without an elaborate sound system (mics, stands, cables, mixer, amplifier, equalizer, and speakers), particularly if the group is a large one, but it should be kept in mind that close micing is a technique that produces that ideal sound of vocal jazz, modeled by such groups as the New York Voices, the Real Group and the Manhattan Transfer. One caveat, however, is that close micing amplifies *both* right and wrong notes, and therefore should be added to the rehearsal process only after the music is well-learned. It is an outstanding and thrilling learning experience to sing in a small ensemble with close micing for those students who can rise to the level of musicianship needed for that type of performance.

Vocal Jazz Resources

Amerind, Gregory (2015). The Collegiate Vocal Jazz Ensemble: A Foundational History. *Choral Journal*, *55*(11), 18–27.

Emerson, Roger (2015). Starting a Vocal Jazz Ensemble. *Choral Journal*, *55*(11), 53–59.

Meader, Darmon (2016). *Vocal Jazz Improvisation: An Instrumental Approach*. Maplewood, NJ: Darmon Meader Music.

Spradling, Diana R. and Binek, Justin (2015). Pedagogy for the Jazz Singer. *Choral Journal*, *55*(11), 6–17.

Weir, Michele (2015). The Scat Singing Dialect: An Introduction to Vocal Improvisation. *Choral Journal*, *55*(11), 28–42.

Weir, Michele (2015). *ScatAbility* phone app. www.michmusic.com.

BRAINTEASER 10-1: ATTEND A VOCAL JAZZ ENSEMBLE CONCERT

Attend a high school, collegiate, or professional vocal jazz ensemble concert or rehearsal. Identify the ensemble, the literature, and characteristics as emphasized in this chapter. Share your findings with your choral methods class and submit a three-page paper to your instructor, along with the concert program.

CONTEMPORARY A CAPPELLA

Roots

Barbershop and Sweet Adelines

A purely American choral art form is Barbershop music. While this type of music invokes images of white males singing vaudeville songs in straw hats, the Society for the Preservation and Encouragement of Barber Shop Quartet Singing in America (SPEBSQSA) is working to break down cultural barriers, preserve lost history, and reach out internationally. Barbershop singing originated in the African-American barbershops in Nashville, Memphis, and New Orleans as early as 1843, and by 1880 it was heard in minstrel shows all over North America (Ayling, 2004). Sweet Adelines director Mo Field explained that it became "gentrified and codified by a largely white and exclusive group . . . and is largely America-centric, often Christian expressive, white, hetero, and cis-normative. Music education is needed in the area" (Sharon, 2016, p. 185.)

Barbershop harmonies consist of a melody sung by the lead, a tenor harmonizing above and a baritone harmonizing below the melody, and the bass singing the roots and fifths. These voice parts are also used in the female equivalent of Barbershop, Sweet Adelines, rather than "soprano/alto" labels. Barbershop is an accessible style of music for many adolescents because there is often a voice part that fits the various stages of the changing voice. Although the traditional group is a quartet of individual voices, it can be expanded to any number of singers. The SPEBSQSA (www.barbershop.org) and Sweet Adelines International (www.sweetadelinesintl.org) are major resources for musical scores, media, educational workshops, and concert programs.

Collegiate A Cappella

Collegiate a cappella ensembles began in 1909 with Cole Porter as a member of the Yale University Whiffenpoofs, followed by other Ivy League groups (Rapkin, 2008). But it wasn't until the 1980s that the number of a cappella groups began a dramatic surge to about 250 ensembles, and then doubled every decade to approximately 2000 in existence today. Deke Sharon, widely known as "the Father of Contemporary A Cappella," founded the Contemporary A Cappella Society of America (CASA) when he was a college student, and is largely responsible for the enormous growth and popularity of the genre. He is a prolific arranger, with more than 2000 to his credit. He produced the shows *The Sing-Off*, *Pitch Perfect*, and *Pitch Perfect 2*, is responsible for the Contemporary A Cappella Recording Awards (CARA), the International Championship of Collegiate A Cappella (ICC), Best of College A Cappella (BOCA) compilations, and much more.

High School A Cappella

CASA includes a high school web link (www.casa.org/hs) which contains helpful articles and blogs for choir directors. Although contemporary a cappella is primarily known for being collegiate or professional, there is a strong high school presence. And while many contemporary a cappella groups are student-directed and/or extra-curricular, some are part of the high school choral curriculum. For example, Brody McDonald, who is at the forefront of the a cappella movement, began developing his well-known conference-performing group Eleventh Hour during his first year of teaching at Kettering Fairmont High School in Ohio (McDonald, 2012). Similarly, Lisa Forkish created the group Vocal Rush at Oakland (CA) School for the Arts, and they won the International Championship of High School A Cappella (ICHSA) in 2012, 2013, 2015, and 2017 (Sharon, Spalding and McDonald, 2015). Other consistent competition winners include Ben Spalding's group Forte from Centerville H.S. (OH), Travis Erickson's group Enharmonic Fusion from DeKalb H.S. (IL), Tom Paster's group Highlands Voices from Northern Highlands Regional H.S. (NJ), and Dennis Gephart's group Limited Edition from Port Washington H.S. (WI). Many of these groups have recorded CDs and received CARA nominations and awards in the following high school categories: Best High School Album, Best High School Arrangement, Best High School Solo, and Best High School Song.

"There is no better time than the present to start a contemporary a cappella group at your high school," says Ben Spalding. Spalding, McDonald, and Michael Meyer, all experienced high school a cappella directors, identified some of the unique benefits of offering a contemporary a cappella (CAC) ensemble (www.casa.org/hs):

- Shows like *Glee, The Sing-Off,* and *American Idol* have increased the number of students interested in and enrolling in choir.
- Students want to perform popular music; some students don't want to perform classical music.
- Pop music can be of high quality, pedagogically sound, educationally viable, interesting for the audience, and exciting and engaging for students.
- Many good published arrangements are available.
- Many CAC festivals and competitions are available for feedback and encouragement.
- It has become easier and more affordable to record a CD, which provides a significant learning experience for students.
- Participation in CAC groups teaches skills such as collaboration, improvisation, evaluation, emulation, independence, tuning, keeping time, and visual presentation.
- Vocal percussion has a "coolness factor" that attracts students.
- CAC participation can provide opportunities for singers to create a performable arrangement.
- CAC groups are more easily transportable than show choirs or larger choirs.
- CAC groups can exist for virtually any level, size, and gender.

Michael Meyer started "Lunchtime Music Groups" at Durham Academy (NC) and by the third year over 100 students were participating in the contemporary a cappella group! He allowed anyone in who was interested, and felt that the greatest motivators for students to join were having a collegiate CAC ensemble perform for them, and having very easy arrangements that they could learn a part of at each lunchtime rehearsal. He also formed a more advanced second group of 16 singers.

Starting a High School CAC Group (McDonald, 2012):

- Elect 4–16 singers for individual micing, or 17–32 without amplification.
- Select the greatest lead soloist you can.
- Select a low and powerful bass.
- Define your group's intended image.
- Know the audience to whom you most want to appeal.
- Decide if you want to buy published arrangements, hire an arranger, or arrange the music yourself.

Rehearsing a High School CAC Group:

- Balance director-led rehearsals with student-led rehearsals without the director present.
- Create rhythmic sight-reading exercises that use vocal percussion.
- Create melodic sight-reading exercises using pitches from pop tunes for singers to discover.
- Create bass line and harmony warm-ups based on a pop tune, such as *Billy Jean* by Michael Jackson; or use *Loop Songs* (Gröger, 2009) for warm-ups; transpose up and down.
- Rehearse similar rhythmic layers together before adding contrasting layers.
- Rehearse the vocal bass and vocal percussion together.
- Experiment with syllables to sound as much like the intended instruments as possible.
- Have the singers practice looking at the audience, at the soloist, or at each other, but nowhere else.
- Practice in a double arc which works well for tight performance spaces; change the group's formation for different tunes; determine body movements that don't detract from the soloist.

Arrangements

Some published CAC arrangements (www.acdacal.com/repertoire-resources/a_cappella):

- *A Dream Is a Wish Your Heart Makes*, arr. Rochefort/Minshall (SSAA)
- *At Last*, arr. Kerry Marsh (SSSAAA)
- *Bella's Finale*, arr. Deke Sharon (SSSAA)

- *Girls Just Want to Have Fun*, arr. Deke Sharon (SSAA or SSA)
- *In My Life*, arr. Steve Zegree (SSAA)
- *Just the Way You Are/Just a Dream*, arr. Deke Sharon (SSSAAA)
- *Stitches*, arr. Brandy Kay Riha (SSA)
- *White Winter Hymnal*, arr. Alan Billingsly (SSAA)
- *Come Fly with Me*, arr. Kevin Keller (TTBB)
- *For the Longest Time*, arr. Roger Emerson (TTBB)
- *Lazy Day*, arr. David Wright (TTBB)
- *Signed Sealed Delivered (I'm Yours)*, arr. Deke Sharon (TTBB)
- *Stand by Me*, arr. Raugh/Sharon (TTBB)
- *To Make You Feel My Love*, arr. Aaron Dale (TTBB)
- *Africa*, arr. Bryan Sharpe (SATTB)
- *Dynamite*, arr. Alex Phan (SATTB)
- *Firework*, arr. Ben Bram (SSATTB)
- *Good Time*, arr. Robert Dietz (SSAATB)
- *I Need Your Love*, arr. Ben Bram (SSATB)
- *I've Got the Music in Me*, arr. Deke Sharon (SSAATTBB)
- *Jar of Hearts*, arr. J.D. Frizzell (SSATB)
- *Run to You*, arr. Kirby Shaw (SSATB)
- *Stars and Stripes Forever*, arr. David Wright (SATB)
- *Sing*, arr. Wayne Grimmer (SATB)
- Free Deke Sharon arrangements (all voicings) at www.deke sharon.com/deke-sharon-free-arrangements.html

Writing CAC Arrangements (Sharon, Spalding, and McDonald, 2015):

- Choose a song that showcases your soloist.
- Listen to the original recording repeatedly.
- Purchase the sheet music (to save time transcribing from the recording).
- Decide on a form; keep it to 90 seconds to leave people wanting more.
- Write out the solo line from beginning to end.
- Write out or outline a low bass line.
- Identify and mark the chord structure.
- Write out the harmonic upper voices clustered as a unit at least an octave above the bass line, considering rhythmic variety, syllables, voice leading, texture, arpeggiation, and instrumental sounds.

- Note where singers will breathe.
- Alternatively, singers may use this process to learn and arrange by ear.

Performance Practice

Vocal Percussion

- Closed Hi-Hat Cymbal ("t" or "tik")
- Open Hi-Hat Cymbal ("tss")
- Closing the Hi-Hat ("tss-ut")
- Rim Shot ("k")
- Bass Drum ("b")
- Snare Drum ("poo" or "kih")
- Crash Cymbal ("ksh")
- Tom-Toms and Fill ("toom" or "doom")
- Brushes ("ff-tf")
- Use very close micing (regularly clean the mic heads).

Vocal Bass Line

- Experiment with the best imitative sound.
- Examples: "dm," "duhm," "dome," "doh," "thm," "thum," "thawm."
- Use close micing.
- Balance all other voices to the bass.

Singing Solo/Lead

- Be yourself. You will never sound exactly like the original.
- Learn the original exactly, and then embellish it a little.
- Embellishments may include runs, changing range, changing rhythm, and simple improvisation.

Sound Technology

As in vocal jazz, a high quality sound system and technician are an essential part of a contemporary a cappella group's performance. While the specifics regarding the complexity of sound reproduction, effects, and recording technology are beyond this chapter, resources are provided with all the necessary information about microphones, amps, speakers, mixing console, EQ, reverb, loopers, and effects pedals.

Vocal Health

Contemporary a cappella singers must take the same precautions as all singers do to protect their voices. Abusing the voice through screaming at public events, talking over loud noises, singing anything that hurts, and singing too much can all do harm to the vocal instrument. Specific to vocal percussion and beatboxing, researchers did examine whether these techniques would be risk factors for vocal cord damage. Interestingly, they found that because these techniques utilize various areas of the vocal tract, they may actually protect against glottal injury (Glodich, 2015).

Contemporary A Cappella Resources

McDonald, Brody (2012). *A Cappella Pop: A Complete Guide to Contemporary A Cappella Singing.* Van Nuys, CA: Alfred.

Madura Ward-Steinman, Patrice (2017). Choral Pedagogy Responds to the Media: American Idol, Glee, The Voice, The Sing-Off, and . . ., in Abrahams, F. and Head, P.D. (ed.), *The Oxford Handbook of Choral Pedagogy.* New York: Oxford University Press.

Sharon, Deke (2016*). The Heart of Vocal Harmony: Emotional Expression in Group Singing.* Milwaukee, WI: Hal Leonard.

Sharon, D., Spalding, B., and McDonald, B. (2015). *A Cappella.* Van Nuys, CA: Alfred.

BRAINTEASER 10-2: ATTEND A CONTEMPORARY A CAPPELLA CONCERT

Attend a contemporary a cappella concert or rehearsal (high school, collegiate, or professional), and reflect upon the points made in this chapter. Submit a three-page paper, along with the concert program.

BRAINTEASER 10-3: ARRANGE A CONTEMPORARY A CAPPELLA PIECE

With your choral methods class peers, arrange a contemporary a cappella piece according to the guidelines presented in this chapter, and rehearse it until it "works." Reflect on the experience.

SHOW CHOIR

Roots

The first high school show choirs were called "swing choirs" in the 1940s. At first the term referred simply to choirs that performed popular music, but in the 1950s they began to add choreography, and by the 1960s rhythm section accompaniment. It was at the Reno Jazz Festival in 1971 that a distinction between Show-Pop and Vocal Jazz groups was made by having separate competitions for each genre (Spradling, 2001). Then in 1975 the Bishop Luers High School Swing Choir Contest in Fort Wayne, Indiana, started the competition craze that continues to this day.

Today, show choir is defined as "a mash-up between a standard choir, a dance team, and a drama club, which competes with similar groups throughout the country" (Weaver and Hart, 2011, p. ix). The size and mobility of the shows often require a very large budget to cover the expenses of choreographers, transportation to festivals and contests, festival registration, costuming, props, band, music, and additional staff. Fundraising and parent organizations are critically important to the success of the show choir. There are more than 1000 show choirs in high schools throughout the United States and Canada, and they are listed in the richly illustrated book *Sweat, Tears, and Jazz Hands: The Official History of Show Choir from Vaudeville to Glee* (Weaver and Hart, 2011).

National Standards

National Standards of Excellence for Show Choirs were developed by ACDA (www.acda.org) to recognize the value of show choir as an enhancement of the core choral program. They also emphasize the responsibility of choral directors to maintain musical excellence and integrity in singing, movement/dance, instrumental accompaniment, integrating art forms, reading and notating music, stylistic awareness, performance practice, individual creativity, entertainment as art, and the treatment of history and pop culture. The rigors and complex demands of combining music, dance, and theater into a single artistic performance are recognized.

Competitions

Three show choir expert teachers shared their knowledge with choral methods students at Indiana University: Brad Gardner from Franklin

Central High School in Indianapolis, Patricia Wiehe from North Central High School in Indianapolis, and Ly Wilder from the IU Singing Hoosiers and Show Choir Camps of America. Their combined experience directing the most highly competitive and successful show choirs informs the points below.

Merits of Competitive Show Choir

- Competition promotes excellence
- Improves the overall stage presence and facial expressions of the concert choir when students are involved in both (show choir season is January–April, so students should be in concert choir during the fall semester)
- Develops physical conditioning and breath support
- Develops teamwork, peer leadership, and community building
- Teaches students to perform well under pressure, to take responsibility for their performance, respect judges' feedback, appreciate the efforts of other choirs, and develop a personal standard of excellence
- Provides a tangible measure of achievement
- Creates networks with other schools
- Attracts males to the choral program

Downsides of Competitive Show Choir

- It requires a lot of time and money.
- The focus on competition can detract from the art of music-making.
- Competition is intimidating, and may cause a loss of focus on what's important in life.
- Competition can "create a monster": first place results in a trophy and feelings of success; second place results in the feeling that it wasn't a good year.
- Education suffers when the entire focus is on winning (e.g., there is little time left to work on sight-reading and other music skills).
- The music can be trite, such as style mashing or stylistic separation.
- Teachers make personal sacrifices and may feel burnout and stress.
- Singers exhibit poor singing techniques, including vocal tension during competitions.

The show choir sound is usually bright, and belting is common (the use of the chest voice in the higher range) (Alder, 2012). This is one of the most pervasive controversies regarding vocal technique and vocal health in show choirs. *The Vocal Athlete* (LeBorgne and Rosenberg, 2014) presents an overview of 30 years' worth of historical and pedagogical approaches to belting, and is well worth reading. Healthy belting theories are espoused by the following contemporary singing pedagogues: Jo Estill, Jan Sullivan, Larra Henderson, Jeannette LoVetri, Robert Edwin, Seth Riggs, Lisa Popeil, Mary Saunders-Barton, and Randy Buescher.

Adjudication

A show choir's technique, artistry, and repertoire effect are judged in the three categories of vocal, visual, and instrumental elements (ISSMA, 2016):

- Vocal: Breath Support and Control, Intonation, Tone Quality and Blend, Diction and Enunciation, Rhythmic and Pitch Accuracy, Interpretation and Style, Dynamics, Phrasing and Expression, Variety and Pacing of Repertoire, and Balance between Voices and Accompaniment
- Visual: Alignment and Spacing, Muscle Control, Precision and Control of Props, Movement Uniformity and Control, Complete Control of Dance Fundamentals, Facial Expression, Professionalism, Transitions, Variety, Pacing, Costuming, Staging, and Balance of Visual and Musical Elements
- Instrumental: Balance, Intonation, Pitch and Rhythmic Accuracy, Dynamics and Expressive Phrasing, Professionalism, and Overall Effect
    - o   The band is comprised of a rhythm section and horns, including two trumpets, alto sax, tenor sax, and trombone.
    - o   The band must never be louder than the singers.

Arrangements and Arrangers

Two types of arrangements are commonly used by show choirs: stock arrangements and custom arrangements.

- Stock arrangement characteristics: inexpensive, fast access, great for starter groups, simple instant legal rights, but lack competitive aspects; can be found at www.jwpepper.com or www.custom arrangements.net. Renowned arrangers include Alan Billingsley, Mark Brymer, Roger Emerson, Mac Huff, Greg Jasperse, Ed Lojeski, Kirby Shaw, and Steve Zegree.
- Custom chart characteristics: expensive ($150–1000 per chart), time consuming, but custom-made for your group's competition; must acquire legal rights, which can be secured by going to halleonard.com, contacting the composer, or using a service such as Tresona.com for a fee. In-demand arrangers include Erik Van Cleve, Jeff Bowen, Dave Fehr, Josh Greene, Jeremy Landig, Linda McEachran Southard, and Ly Wilder.
- Usually five arrangements are needed per show:

    o Opener: establishes the story; shows off strengths; hooks the audience; needs a great band
    o Second Number: contrasts musically and visually with opener and ballad; simple props can help; can be a novelty number and/or humorous
    o Ballad: showcases great choral singing, not much movement
    o Fourth Number: contrasts with ballad and closer; must create excitement for the closer
    o Closer: most exciting number with the best dancing; fast and driving.

Choreography and Choreographers

- A choreographer is needed for two to six hours per song.
- Choreographer fees range from nothing (student choreographers) or $300 per song (for beginning choreographers), to $2500 per song plus travel expenses for pros. Some charge $20K per show.
- Watch other groups to see what you like, and ask around to find out who you can afford; book a year in advance for the pros.
- "Cleaning" ensures that everyone knows and is executing choreography correctly; use mirrors with curtains for practice and use student dance captains; usually hired out.
- In-demand choreographers include Jarad Voss, Damon Brown, Marty De Mott, Shawn Eck, Heith Gemar, April James, Dwight Jordan, Ron Morgan, Randy Sage, Linda McEachran Southard, Stephen Todd, Michael Weaver, and Brennan Wilder.

Budget

Expenses

In addition to the fees for the services named above (arrangers and choreographers), other show choir production expenses include:

- fees for staff, clinicians, and hired musicians
- legal acquisition of the rights to arrange, sheet music, folders/binders, band charts, and rehearsal CDs
- costumes, including cleaning and repairs
- makeup, including lipstick, blush, eye shadow, eyeliner, mascara, foundation, primer, and false lashes
- staging equipment, risers, stairs, carts, clothing racks, hangers, organization tubs, props, and set pieces
- competition entry fees
- bus fees (mileage and hourly pay); other transportation fees (equipment truck, gas, mileage)
- meals while traveling
- sound equipment.

Support and Income

Because of the enormous expense of running a show choir program, parents' help in offsetting costs is vital. Common roles of the Booster Club officers include co-presidents (one in training), two costume moms, secretary, treasurer, spirit chair, publicity chair, recruitment chair, reception chair, car wash helpers, fruit sale helpers, photographers, and program chairs. Parents contribute greatly to the impact of the program on the community and in overall public relations (Wiehe, 2008). A word of caution, though, from long-time show choir director Randi Carp (1999), in her workshop "The Care and Feeding of Parents," who stressed that there are some topics that should be off limits to parents; namely, music selection, grades, curriculum, and how to spend school funds.

Other sources of income include:

- each show choir member's annual fee of $300 to $500 to cover expenses
- concert admission
- school funding

- hosting show choir competitions
- fundraising events, such as the Cow Patty Drop, Ball Drop, Festival for Funds, Food Fundraiser (candy, fruit, pies), Cookie Walk, Cutting the Costs, Duck Races, Haunted Mansion, Dinner Show, Regionalized-Community Fundraisers (Oktoberfest, Apple Dumpling Sale, Bridgestone Invitational Valet Parking), and America Sings (see Weaver and Hart, 2011).

Despite the complex nature of directing a show choir program, Kirby Shaw claimed that the show choir experience can make a "positive, even life-changing impact . . . for performers and audiences" (Thomas, 2005, p. 107).

Resources

Choir teachers are strongly encouraged to attend the Show Choir Camps of America (www.showchoircamps.com) which is one of the mostly highly respected camps of its kind. The week-long Teacher's Program covers the following topics specific to show choir: reading sessions, rehearsal strategies, vocal health care, bridging classical and pop choral sound, implementing technology, producing a show on a limited budget, starting a show choir, developing a show, organizing a retreat, costuming, and the opportunity to participate in an optional teachers' show choir. Although rather expensive (approximately $700 for registration, room, and board), teachers have claimed that it was the best $700 they had ever spent, the best week of their summer, and should be attended by every new teacher and any teacher who will be directing a show choir. Other resources are indicated below.

Show Choir Resources

LeBorgne, Wendy D. and Rosenberg, Marci (2014). *The Vocal Athlete*. San Diego, CA: Plural.

Weaver, Mike and Hart, Colleen (2011). *Sweat, Tears, and Jazz Hands: The Official History of Show Choir from Vaudeville to Glee*. Milwaukee, WI: Hal Leonard.

Zegree, Steve (2010). *The WOW Factor: How to Create It, Inspire It, and Achieve It*. Milwaukee, WI: Hal Leonard.

BRAINTEASER 10-4: ATTEND A SHOW CHOIR CONCERT

Attend a show choir concert and write a three-page report on the repertoire, accompaniment, vocal tone quality, costumes, dancing, and staging.

MUSICAL THEATER

Musical theater direction comes with most high school music choral teaching positions. Usually the drama teacher handles all of the non-musical issues, while the choral director takes charge of making sure that a show is chosen that is musically accessible to the actors, and of auditioning and coaching the singers. If the instrumental music teacher does not participate in the musical production, the choral director may also have the responsibility of auditioning the instrumentalists and directing the pit orchestra/band (Bruenger, 2005).

Figure 10.2 Musical Theater

Vocal Health

Many of the benefits of the show choir experience are the same for participating in a musical theater production. Likewise, many of the same concerns, particularly with regard to vocal belting and singing while dancing, require special attention. One study (cited in LeBorgne and Rosenberg, 2014) found that 85% of musical theater majors in college had vocal cord trauma, and so the high school musical director must teach the singers to use their voices in a healthy way. Plenty of hydration and vocal rest should be advised during the rehearsals leading to performance. And while belting is common in musical theater productions, the director needs to take these precautions in rehearsals (McDonald, 2012):

- Warn the students that if they feel any discomfort in the voice, they should avoid it and let the musical director know.
- Properly warm up the entire range of the voices.
- Teach the singers to use resonance rather than tension to project a full sound.
- Be sure the actors are singing in the comfortable part of the range most of the time.
- Become informed about healthy belting techniques (as described in *The Vocal Athlete*).

Vocal Expression

The musical director also needs to teach the student actors how to communicate the meaning of the lyrics they sing. The singer has to connect emotionally and truthfully to the solo, which is commonly referred to as Method Acting. Suggestions for helping singers develop this personal and compelling approach to singing are provided by Brunetti (2006) in *Acting Songs*:

- First, write out the lyrics and read them naturally (no "acting"); decide what the lyrics emotionally mean to you, not someone else. Imagine scenarios regarding the lyrics.
- Then speak the lyrics to the exact rhythm of the song.
- Add the melody, allowing yourself to be expressive. "Live out loud" (p. 53). Imagine and express a scenario.

- While choirs need to over-pronounce, soloists should sing the way they speak.
- Gesture should come naturally if the singer is fully immersed in the imaginary world of the song.
- Be emotionally engaged as soon as the introduction starts.
- Don't just sing well. Think about what you're saying, to whom, and what you hope to accomplish in your imaginary world by saying it. Let your defenses down and the audience will be moved.

Selecting the Musical

Larry Mitchell's book (2012) *A Practical Handbook for Musical Theater*, 5th ed., has been called "the standard of the industry" and is a lifesaver for choosing musicals, auditioning and casting for musicals, selecting the production staff, and outlining the production timeline. Mitchell lists 120 musicals for high school performers, and provides a summary of each one with regard to cast, chorus, songs, choreography, and technical needs.

He also categorizes them by their requirements, such as an ensemble cast (e.g., *big, Brigadoon, Camelot, Carousel,* and *Cats*); a strong male lead (e.g., *Beauty and the Beast, Crazy for You, The Fantasticks, Godspell,* and *Happy Days*); a strong female lead (e.g., *Anything Goes, Mame, Once upon a Mattress, Thoroughly Modern Millie,* and *Wonderful Town*); and both a strong male and female lead (e.g., *Annie Get Your Gun, Evita, The King and I, Phantom of the Opera,* and *South Pacific*). Other categories include Excellent Musicals for the Chorus (e.g., *Fiddler on the Roof, Footloose, 42nd Street, Hairspray,* and *High School Musical*); highly choreographed musicals (e.g., *Guys and Dolls, Pippin, Singin' in the Rain, West Side Story,* and *The Wiz*); and small cast musicals (*Cleopatra and the Slave Girls of Venus, Cotton Patch Gospel, Joseph and the Amazing Technicolor Dreamcoat,* and *Little Shop of Horrors*).

Scheduling Auditions and Rehearsals

Audition and Casting Schedule (Mitchell, 2012):

- Day 1: The show is introduced
- Day 2: A sign-up list of the principal singing and acting roles is posted
- Day 3: Preliminary dialogue auditions for the principal roles begin
- Days 4–5: Auditions continue

- Days 6–7: Music auditions for the singing roles
- Days 8–9: Callbacks for the major roles
- Day 10: Announcement of the principal cast

Timeline for Production Committees:

- Scenery and Set Construction: Allow 7–8 weeks
- Scenery and Set Painting: Allow 5–6 weeks
- Costumes: Allow 6–7 weeks
- Properties: Allow 4–5 weeks
- Program: Allow 4–5 weeks
- Publicity: Continually
- Tickets: 3 weeks before opening
- Stage Crew: 2 weeks before opening
- Lighting and Sound Crew: 2 weeks before opening
- Makeup: 1½ weeks before opening
- First Dress Rehearsal: Include costumes and props
- Second Dress Rehearsal: Include costumes, props, and makeup
- Third Dress Rehearsal: Complete, non-stop run-through of show

Staffing the Musical (Mitchell, 2012)

Adults (may occupy more than one position)

- General Director (usually the drama teacher)
- Stage Director
- Costumer
- Musical Director (you, the choral director)
- Choreographer
- Technical Director
- Scenic and Lighting Designer
- Set Painting Supervisor
- Publicity Manager
- Box Office Manager
- House Manager

Students

- Makeup Designer
- Properties Manager

- Lighting Technician
- Sound Manager
- Publicity Chair
- Program Chair
- Stage Manager

Budget

Like show choir productions, musical theater productions are expensive and can cost as much as $20,000 in high schools that have a tradition of putting on elaborate shows (Upchurch, 2013). The expenses and a rough estimate for a major production include acquiring rights from New York to produce the show ($2000–$6000), pit orchestra if hiring pros ($4000), advertising ($2000), props and set design ($2000), costuming ($1000), lighting and sound ($1500), choreography ($600–$1500), backdrop ($1000), plus miscellaneous expenses such as hired help, gifts, concessions, transportation, and student t-shirts. The majority of the costs are covered by the previous year's proceeds from ticket sales, and the remaining from selling ads for the program and fundraising. Certainly the costs could be reduced with student and parent help.

The musical is considered to be extra work for the choral director, with rehearsals and performances taking place outside of the school day, and often into the late hours of the evening as the performance dates approach. The choral teacher can expect to receive an extra financial stipend for this activity. For the music teacher who must direct the show without the aid of a drama teacher, the task is immense. However, the list of Musical Theater Resources below, which includes web addresses of rental agencies for musicals, provides a solid foundation.

Musical Theater Resources

Brunetti, David (2006). *Acting Songs.* North Charleston, SC: BookSurge.
Mitchell, Larry (2012). *A Practical Handbook for Musical Theater*, 5th ed. Cedar Rapids, IA: Dominion.
Dramatic Publishing Co. (www.dramaticpublishing.com)
Heuer Publishing LLC (www.heuerpub.com)

Music Theatre International (www.mtishows.com)
Pioneer Drama Service (www.pioneerdrama.com)
Rodgers and Hammerstein Theatre Library (www.rnh.com)
Samuel French, Inc. (www.samuelfrench.com)
Tams-Witmark Music Library, Inc. (www.tams-witmark.com)
Theatrical Rights Worldwide (www.theatricalrights.com)

BRAINTEASER 10-5: ATTEND A MUSICAL THEATER PRODUCTION

Attend a high school musical theatre production and notice the role that the choral music director plays in the production. If possible, attend rehearsals for the show and volunteer to assist. Write and submit a three-page reflection paper.

MADRIGAL ENSEMBLES

A madrigal group is a small "chamber" ensemble that, like vocal jazz ensembles and contemporary a cappella groups, challenges your students to achieve higher levels of musical independence and higher standards for accuracy in aural skills, intonation, blend, diction, dynamics, and more. The term madrigal usually refers to unaccompanied English or Italian songs of the late 16th and early 17th century, in a free style strongly influenced by the text (Apel, 1972).

The following pieces are recommended for the high school madrigal ensemble, and can be found as separate octavos or through madrigal collections, such as *The Oxford Book of English Madrigals*, *The Oxford Book of Italian Madrigals*, and *Carols for Choirs* (Thomas, 1995):

- *Adieu, Sweet Amarillis* by John Wilbye
- *The Agincourt Carol*, Anonymous
- *April Is in My Mistress' Face* by Thomas Morley
- *Audite Nova!* by Orlandus Lassus
- *Come Again, Sweet Love* by John Dowland
- *El Grillo* by Josquin Desprez
- *Fa Una Canzone* by Orazio Vecchi
- *Fair Phyllis I Saw* by John Farmer
- *Hark All Ye Lovely Saints* by Thomas Weelkes
- *Il Bianco e Dolce Cigno* by Jacques Arcadelt

- *Il Est Bel et Bon* by Pierre Passereau
- *Late in My Rash Accounting* by Thomas Weelkes
- *Now Is the Month of Maying* by Thomas Morley
- *Riu, Riu, Chiu*, Anonymous
- *The Silver Swan* by Orlando Gibbons
- *Sing We and Chant It* by Thomas Morley
- *So Well I Know Who's Happy* by Orazio Vecchi
- *Though Amaryllis Dance* by William Byrd
- *Weep, O Mine Eyes* by John Bennett.

Madrigal Dinners

The Madrigal Dinner is a theatrical (and often comedic) re-creation of an Elizabethan Renaissance feast, complete with singers, instrumentalists, actors, menu, music, script, costumes, makeup, and sets, and is usually presented during the Christmas holiday season or in early spring. Each student has an acting role, even if a minor one, such as a food server who can speak in an Olde English dialect.

Scott Buchanan, Director of Choral Activities at Indiana State University, shared these components for producing the annual madrigal dinner. Essential components: a castle concept, dinner script, dinner music, a formal processional, a toast with wassail and the *Wassail Song*, the *Boar's Head Carol*, a narrator/jester who keeps the flow going with instructions and jokes, a blessing before dinner for health and prosperity, and dismissal with a receiving line. Optional components: brass for pre-dinner music and processional fanfares; other instruments from the period; a 15-minute play (usually a parody of a familiar tale); audience participation carols; and a holiday concert after dinner. Any special talents of your singers, such as juggling, dancing, or acrobatics, could also be a featured part of the event.

Script

A good script is key to a successful madrigal dinner and it is advisable to purchase, rent, or borrow a published one. Scripts are available from many sources including Madrigal Scripts from Madrigal Traditions (www.madrigalscripts.com), Knight-Shtick Press (www.madrigaldinner. com), and Jest Scripts (www.madrigaldinners.com). They provide suggestions for all theatrical aspects of the madrigal dinner.

Menu

Printed menus are usually placed on the tables, and they are created with archaic spellings and fonts. Most authentic madrigal dinners offer several courses, including barley soup, wassail (hot spiced cider), wild rice, meat or fowl, baked fish, roasted vegetables, hearty bread, fruits and puddings, such as the traditional white figgy pudding made with figs or spiced pumpkin, or other sweet baked breads. Madrigal dinners can vary from two courses to seven or more, and can be served banquet style on large tables that seat eight, or one course at a time delivered by servers who act and speak in a manner that suits the Renaissance mood. All food is budgeted with the caterer into a per plate cost. A useful resource is *Fabulous Feasts: Medieval Cookery and Ceremony* by M.P. Cosman.

Costumes, Makeup, and Sets

Everyone involved in the entertainment should be in costume and makeup, including the director and accompanist. Costumes for men include boots, pants, shirt, vest, and hat; and costumes for women include shoes, layered skirts, bodice, shirt, hat, and scarf. Long hair should be braided (see the Tudor Shoppe at www.tudorshoppe.com and Historical Clothing Realm at www.historicalclothingrealm.com.)

Simple sets can include a raised head table for the actors, painted façade pieces to look like stone walls, shields with coats of arms, and tablecloths with centerpieces of branches and berries. It is wise to take advantage of willing drama teachers or parents to help provide inexpensive costumes and decorations.

Music

Any madrigal that fits the theme of the Elizabethan Renaissance madrigal dinner may be sung, and fortunately many madrigals are available free of charge on the Choral Public Domain Library (www.cpdl.org). In addition to the madrigals listed earlier in this chapter, the following accessible choral works may also be featured during a madrigal dinner.

Two- and Three-Part

- *As Fair as Morn* by John Wilbye, arr. Russell Robinson
- *Canzonette a tre voci* by Claudio Monteverdi

- *Fire, Fire* by Thomas Morley, arr. Russell Robinson
- *Greensleeves* by R. Vaughn Williams
- *Old Fox Wassail* by Stephen Hatfield
- *Tomorrow Shall Be My Dancing Day* by John Rutter

SAB

- *A Celtic Christmas* by Audrey Snyder
- *Masters in This Hall* by Catherine Bennett
- *Nowell, Nowell: The Boar's Head* by Theron Kirk
- *Wassail! Wassail!* by Mac Huff

SATB

- *Auld Lang Syne* by Lee Kesselman
- *Banquet Fugue* by John Rutter
- *Boar's Head Carol* by Stephen Hatfield
- *Deck the Halls* (in 7/8), arr. James McKelvy
- *Functional Music for Christmas Madrigal Dinners* by John V. Mochnick
- *Here We Come A-Wassailing* by John Rutter
- *I Saw Three Ships*, arr. Alice Parker and Robert Shaw
- *Occhi, Manza Mia* by Orlando di Lasso
- *Psallite* by Michael Praetorius
- *Wexford Carol* by Dale Warland.

It is better to keep a madrigal dinner short and simple during the first few years of teaching, saving more elaborate productions for a few years down the road. Take all costs into consideration (venue, publicity, food service, costumes, decorations, scripts, music) and determine the ticket price to cover all expenses with at least some profit. It is advisable to keep the ticket price reasonable for your first year or two, which may run from $15 to $35. Eventually, the madrigal dinner can become an excellent fundraiser for the choral program.

BRAINTEASER 10-6: ATTEND A MADRIGAL DINNER

Attend a madrigal dinner with members of your choral methods class. Discuss your experience, and submit a three-page reflective paper along with the madrigal dinner program. If possible, go to dress rehearsals and volunteer to help.

GOSPEL CHOIR

Students enjoy singing gospel music because of its positive message and high energy. As educators' awareness of the importance of teaching and reaching diverse cultures grows, so does the number of high school gospel choirs. Yet it is a style of music that many choral directors have little familiarity with. As with learning any unfamiliar style, it helps to bring experienced gospel singers into the high school rehearsal to demonstrate authentic performance practice. It is recommended, however, that the choir director review the NAfME and ACDA guidelines for rehearsing and performing sacred music in the public schools as clarified in Chapter 8. An extra-curricular student-led gospel choir is an option that can be a powerful motivator for some students' participation. For example, one study showed that African-American choral students from six urban high schools liked Black gospel music significantly more than their White, Hispanic, and Asian peers did, and also more than their African-American and White choral teachers did (Murdock, 2016). Student-led gospel choirs may fill a gaping hole in our inclusive philosophy of choral music education.

Figure 10.3 Gospel Choir

Performance Practice

Gospel choirs often learn their music by ear, which improves the students' aural skills. Considerations for learning by ear include the following:

- Listen to a recording of a piece to learn the music and lyrics.
- If the original arrangement is voiced for SAB, a tenor part may need to be added.
- Key centers may need to be changed to accommodate the high school voice.
- Transcription of the parts involves notating the characteristic vocal techniques, such as slides, dynamics, and other stylings, as well as instrumental accompaniment. Although gospel vocal technique often includes belting, the choral director is always responsible for teaching healthy vocal tone (Turner, 2008).

Not only does gospel music teach a historically important American art form and culture, it trains the musicians to hear and imitate melodies, harmonies, rhythms, and forms in a way not taught in the traditional choral rehearsal. In addition, it encourages freedom of expression for the conductor, who may choose to repeat certain sections of the music, and for the singers, who may choose from a whole host of stylistically authentic embellishments of melody and rhythm, that can transfer from one gospel song to another (Madura, 1999). These embellishments include:

- blue notes
- upper and lower neighbor tones
- anticipations
- octave displacements
- *portamento*
- rhythmically "worrying the note" (subdividing or repeating in a rapid manner)
- syncopation
- altering the meter from simple duple to a swinging 12/8
- delaying the end of the phrase to include passing tone ornamentation
- growls
- hums
- cries.

Recording Artists

Gospel music can enrich our students' musical experience, and there is no substitute for listening to internalize authentic style. Many of the following gospel artists, choral works, and resources were recommended by Raymond Wise, Director of the African American Choral Ensemble at Indiana University. Artists for listening include: Yolanda Adams, Vanessa Bell Armstrong, Anthony Brown and Group Therapy, Milton Brunson and the Thompson Community Choir (The Tommies), Shirley Caesar, James Cleveland, Darrel Coley, Sam Cooke, Andrae Crouch, Ricky Dillard and New Generation, Fisk Jubilee Singers, Aretha Franklin, Kirk Franklin, JJ Hairston and Youthful Praise, Edwin Hawkins, Mahalia Jackson, Kurt Karr, Donald Lawrence, Patrick Lundy and Ministers of Music, Donnie McClurkin, Sanctified Singers, Marvin Sapp, Don Shirley, Richard Smallwood, Rosetta Tharpe, Tye Tribett, Hezekiah Walker, Clara Ward, Thomas Whitfield and Company, and Raymond Wise and Raise Choir.

Published Music

The following choral works are highly recommended for the SATB gospel choir:

- *Ain't-A That Good News* by Rollo Dilworth
- *Amazing Grace*, arr. Jack Schrader
- *Anthem of Praise* by Richard Smallwood, arr. Keith Hampton
- *Blessed Assurance*, arr. Keith Hampton
- *Freedom Train* by Rollo Dilworth
- *Gloria* by André Thomas
- *Go Tell It on the Mountain*, arr. Greg Jasperse
- *Gospel Mass* by Robert Ray
- *He Is Marvelous* by Rosephanye Powell
- *He's Counting on You* by Raymond Wise
- *He's Never Failed Me Yet* by Robert Ray
- *I Just Want to Say Thanks* by Raymond Wise
- *In the Sanctuary* by Kurt Karr, arr. Victor Johnson
- *It Is Good to Give Thanks* by Stan Pethel and John Parker
- *It Won't Be Long* by Andrae Crouch, arr. Rouse
- *I've Got a Robe* by Raymond Wise

- *Just Jesus*, arr. Robert Morris
- *Lord I Love You Yes I Do* by Raymond Wise
- *Lord Send Your Spirit* by Raymond Wise
- *Make a Joyful Noise* by Raymond Wise
- *Michael, Row that Gospel Boat!* by Greg Gilpin
- *My God Is Real* by Kenneth Morris, arr. Steve Potts
- *O Happy Day* by Edwin Hawkins, arr. Kirby Shaw
- *Oh What a Beautiful City* by Jeffrey Webb
- *Praise His Holy Name* by Keith Hampton
- *Psalm 117* by James Glover
- *Ride the Gospel Train* by Glenda Franklin
- *Rise up Shepherd and Follow*, arr. Martin Ellis
- *Shine the Light* by Raymond Wise
- *Take Me to the Water* by Rollo Dilworth
- *This Little Light of Mine*, arr. Neil Johnson
- *Total Praise* by Richard Smallwood, arr. Doreen Rao
- *True Light* by Keith Hampton
- *Walk On* by Raymond Wise
- *Worthy to Be Praised* by Byron Smith.

Publishers

- Raise Publishing: www.raiseonline.com/sheet-music
- NTIMEMUSIC.com, Inc.: www.ntimemusic.com/Scripts/default.asp
- GIA Publications: www.giamusic.com/sacred_music/african_american.cfm

---

Resources for Gospel Music

The Gospel Music Workshop of America, www.gmwanational.net

National Convention of Gospel Choirs and Choruses, www.ncgccinc.com/wp

Hampton University Ministers' Conference (Choir Directors' and Organists' Guild), minconf.hamptonu.edu/pages/closed/

BRAINTEASER 10-7: ATTEND A GOSPEL CHOIR PERFORMANCE

Attend a gospel choir performance or invite a gospel choir director to your choral methods class to teach you a piece. Discuss the experience, and write and submit a three-page reflective paper.

MULTICULTURAL CHORAL ENSEMBLES

Since 1979 ACDA has created goals to increase diversity and inclusion in both its membership and its conference choral performances. The National Committee on Ethnic Music and Minority Concerns was formed, and increases in both minority participation at conferences and in publications to raise awareness of racist texts in choral music were evident. African-American ensembles and clinicians were noticeably increased in the 1980s. In 1992 the committee was re-named the National Committee on Ethnic and Multicultural Perspectives, reflected in the first special focus issue of the *Choral Journal*. Intergenerational multicultural honor choirs and world music reading sessions became regular features at national ACDA conferences. Today the committee recognizes "the multifaceted and multi-ethnic realm of world music through identifying and encouraging the performance of repertoire of diverse cultures, and developing projects that enhance the choral art" (www.acda.org).

Standards

Seven standards were developed by the ACDA Ethnic and Multicultural Perspectives committee for the purpose of encouraging choral directors to become informed, sensitive, open-minded, and proactive regarding:

- Repertoire
- Choral/Vocal Production
- Rehearsal Techniques and Instruction
- Professional Growth and Development
- Recruitment and Retention
- Performance
- Advocacy.

Repertoire

The following multicultural choral works are highly recommended:

SATB

- *Ahrirang,* arr. Robert DeCormier
- *Bo Ree Baht,* arr. Dale Jergenson
- *Chi Chi Cha* by Judith Tucker
- *Chinese Folk Songs,* vol. 2, by Chen Yi
- *Denko* by Nitanju Bolade Casel
- *Desh,* arr. Ethan Sperry
- *El Besu,* arr. Vicente Chavarria
- *El Mambi,* arr. Carlos Abril
- *Erev Shel Shoshanim,* arr. Jack Klebanow
- *Fiesta* by Cristian Grases
- *Gamelan* by R. Murray Schafer
- *Gate, Gate* by Brian Tate
- *Iraqi Peace Song,* arr. Reiersrud and Tennenhouse
- *Kalinda* by Sydney Guillaume
- *Kodesh Heim* by Nick Page
- *Kua Rongo Mai Koe,* arr. Eddie Quaid
- *La Llorona* by Vicente Chavarria
- *Morning Song,* arr. James E. Green
- *Mouth Music* by Dolores Kean and John Faulkner
- *Native American Ambiances* by Jackson Berkey
- *Ose Ayo,* arr. Brian Tate
- *Prairie Love Song,* arr. Dale Jergenson
- *Sarkandaila Roze Auga,* arr. Andrejs Jansons
- *Sililiza,* arr. Jim Papoulis
- *Songs of Ecuador* by Robert Greenlee
- *Suliram,* arr. Robert deCormier
- *This We Know* by Ron Jeffers
- *Tzur Mishelo Acheinu* by Charles Davidson
- *Umi Sono Ai,* arr. Rachel Stenson
- *Vamudara,* arr. Dumisani Maraire
- *Wonfa Nyem* by Abraham K. Adzenyah
- *Yal Asmar Ellon* by Edward Torikian
- *Zahucali Chladne Vjetry v Doline,* arr. Ivan Hrusovsky

Treble Voices

- *A Zing-a-Za* by Mary Goetze
- *Chiu, Chiu, Chiu* by Jill Gallina
- *Cinz Chansons Folklorique d'Haiti* by Electo Silva
- *Da Hai a Gu Xiang*, arr. Yang Hong-Nian
- *El Rio*, arr. Diana Saez
- *Hotaru Koi* by Ro Ogura
- *Lammaa Badaa Yatathanna*, arr. Joy Ondra Hirokawa
- *Reel a'Bouche* by Malcolm Daglish
- *Sililiza*, arr. Jim Papoulis
- *Silmala Triceja Dancojot* by Jekabs Graubins
- *Shlof, Mayn Fegele* arr. Lee R. Kesselman

Low Voices

- *Desh*, arr. Ethan Sperry
- *Two Latvian Carols* by Andrejs Jansons.

Publishers

Choral scores from all over the world have become widely available for purchase, particularly through the following publishers' websites. If not immediately visible on the websites, simple select "choir" and "multicultural/world" for a wealth of repertoire from which to choose.

- www.earthsongschoralmusic.com
- www.worldmusicpress.com
- www.alliancemusic.com
- www.sbmp.com
- www.singers.com/index.html
- www.jwpepper.com
- www.halleonard.com
- www.alfred.com
- www.shawneepress.com

Performance Practice

The challenge for choral music educators is to present this music in authentic ways. Occasionally we hear performances of "world music" where the only connection to the actual culture is the title of the piece; or perhaps only snippets of another culture's folk songs may be incorporated into a westernized choral score (Volk, 1998). Mary Goetze (2000), founder of the International Vocal Ensemble at Indiana University, emphasized the importance of transmitting the music with integrity by utilizing published music carefully and studying aural and video resources for learning unfamiliar languages and singing styles. Judith Cook Tucker of World Music Press presents a checklist for evaluating multicultural materials (1990). Questions to ask include:

- Was a "culture bearer" involved in the music preparation?
- Is the cultural context of the piece presented?
- Is specific geographical information included?
- Is the original language included, with appropriate translation?
- Are illustrations or photographs included?
- Is there an authentic recording with the actual sounds of the voices and instruments within context?
- Are sacred pieces excluded? (They *should* be out of respect for the culture.)

It is essential for the choral director of multicultural music to study and listen to authentic recordings in preparation for teaching their choirs. This chapter will not cover the multitude of resources for study and listening, because they can be found on the ACDA website under *Repertoire and Resources*, then *Repertoire Specific*, and finally *Ethnic Music*, as well as in the growing range of library and online resources on multicultural music.

BRAINTEASER 10-8: LEARNING WORLD MUSIC

Bring in a world music "informant" to your choral methods class to teach a song. Discuss the experience and submit a three-page reflective paper.

References

Alder, A.L. (2012). Successful High School Show Choir Directors: Their Perceptions About Their Teaching and Administrative Practices. Doctoral Dissertation, Ball State University, ProQuest Dissertations and Theses 382 (1035153102).

Amerind, Gregory (2015). The Collegiate Vocal Jazz Ensemble: A Foundational History. *Choral Journal, 55*(11), 18–27.

Apel, Willi (1972). *Harvard Dictionary of Music*, 2nd ed. Cambridge, MA: Belknap Press of Harvard University.

Ayling, Benjamin C. (2004). A Historical View of Barbershop Music and the Sight-Reading Methodology and Learning Practices of Championship Barbershop Quartet Singers, 1939–1963. *International Journal of Research in Choral Singing, 2*(1), 53–59.

Bolt, Gerald R. (1983). Choral Repertoire Selection Competency Development in Undergraduate Music Education Curricula. Doctoral Dissertation, Arizona State University, ATT 8315795.

Bruenger, Susan (September, 2005). Preparing a Broadway Musical: Instrumental Considerations. *Choral Journal, 46*(3), 50–57.

Brunetti, David (2006). *Acting Songs*. North Charleston, SC: BookSurge.

Carp, Randi (1999). The Care and Feeding of Parents. CMEA Conference Session, March 27, 1999.

Cosman, Madeleine Pelner (1976). *Fabulous Feasts: Medieval Cookery and Ceremony*. New York: George Braziller.

Emerson, Roger (2015). Starting a Vocal Jazz Ensemble. *Choral Journal, 55*(11), 53–59.

Glodich, Justin (2015). Vocal Percussion in Contemporary Choral Music. *Choral Journal, 56*(5), 73–79.

Goetze, Mary (2000). The Challenges of Performing Choral Music of the World. In *Performing with Understanding: The Challenges of the National Standards for Music Education*. Lanham, MD: Rowman & Littlefield/NAfME.

Gröger, Bertrand (2009). *Loop Songs: 44 Warm-Up and Performance Studies for Jazz, Pop and Gospel Choirs*. New York: Schott.

ISSMA (2016). *Music Festivals Manual: 2016–2017 School Year*. Indianapolis: ISSMA.

LeBorgne, Wendy D. and Rosenberg, Marci (2014). *The Vocal Athlete*. San Diego, CA: Plural.

McDonald, Brody (2012). *A Cappella Pop: A Complete Guide to Contemporary A Cappella Singing*. Van Nuys, CA: Alfred.

Madura, Patrice D. (1996). Relationships among Vocal Jazz Improvisation Achievement, Jazz Theory Knowledge, Imitative Ability, Musical Experience, Creativity, and Gender. *Journal of Research in Music Education, 44*(3), 252–267.

Madura, Patrice D. (1999). *Getting Started with Vocal Improvisation*. Lanham, MD: Rowman & Littlefield/NAfME.

Madura Ward-Steinman, Patrice (Spring, 2007). Confidence in Teaching Improvisation according to the K-12 Achievement Standards: Surveys of Vocal Jazz Workshop Participants and Undergraduates. *Bulletin of the Council for Research in Music Education, 172*, 25–40.

Madura Ward-Steinman, Patrice (Summer, 2008). Vocal Improvisation by Australian and American University Jazz Singers: Case Studies of Outliers' Musical Influences. *Bulletin of the Council for Research in Music Education, 177*, 29–43.

Madura Ward-Steinman, Patrice (2014). The Vocal Improviser-Educator: An Analysis of Selected American and Australian Educators' Influences and Pedagogical Views. *International Journal of Music Education, 32*(3), 346–359.

Madura Ward-Steinman, Patrice, ed. (2015). Special Focus Issue: Vocal Jazz. *Choral Journal, 55*(11).

Madura Ward-Steinman, Patrice (2017). Choral Pedagogy Responds to the Media: American Idol, Glee, The Voice, The Sing-Off, and . . ., in Abrahams, F. and Head, P.D. (ed.), *The Oxford Handbook of Choral Pedagogy.* New York: Oxford University Press.

Meader, Darmon (2016). *Vocal Jazz Improvisation: An Instrumental Approach.* Maplewood, NJ: Darmon Meader Music.

Mitchell, Larry (2012). *A Practical Handbook for Musical Theater*, 5th ed. Cedar Rapids, IA: Dominion.

Murdock, Jeffrey A. (2016). Where Preference Meets Praxis: Exploring the Choral Musical Preferences of Urban High School Students and Their Teachers. ProQuest Dissertations and Theses Global (1725215618), Order No. 3728597.

Opportunity-to-Lean Standards for Music Instruction (1994). Lanham, MD: R&L Education/National Association for Music Education (NAfME).

Rapkin, Mickey (2008). *Pitch Perfect: The Quest for Collegiate A Cappella Glory.* New York: Gotham.

Sharon, Deke (2016). *The Heart of Vocal Harmony: Emotional Expression in Group Singing.* Milwaukee, WI: Hal Leonard.

Sharon, D., Spalding, B., and McDonald, B. (2015). *A Cappella.* Van Nuys, CA: Alfred.

Spradling, Diana R. (December, 2001). National Standards of Excellence for Show Choirs. *Choral Journal, 42*(5), 61–62.

Spradling, Diana R. (2007). *Jazz Singing: Developing Artistry and Authenticity.* Edmonds, WA: Sound Music.

Spradling, Diana R. and Binek, Justin (2015). Pedagogy for the Jazz Singer. *Choral Journal, 55*(11), 6–17.

Stoloff, Bob (1996). *Scat!* Brooklyn, NY: Gerard & Sarzin.

Thomas, Janice (October, 1995). Revisiting the Madrigal Ensemble. *Teaching Music, 3*(2), 34–35.

Thomas, Ken (2005). Competitive Show Choirs Festivals: What Are the Benefits? An Interview with Kirby Shaw. *Choral Journal, 45*(7), 107–109.

Tucker, Judith Cook (1990). *A Checklist for Evaluating Multicultural Materials.* Danbury, CT: World Music Press.

Turner, Patrice E. (December 2008). Getting Gospel Going. *Music Educators Journal, 95*(2), 62–68.

Upchurch, Gwen Witten (January, 2013). Lecture on Producing a High School Musical, Indiana University, Bloomington.

Volk, Terese (1998). *Music, Education and Multiculturalism.* New York: Oxford University Press.

Weaver, Mike and Hart, Colleen (2011). *Sweat, Tears, and Jazz Hands: The Official History of Show Choir from Vaudeville to Glee.* Milwaukee, WI: Hal Leonard.

Weir, Michele (2015). The Scat Singing Dialect: An Introduction to Vocal Improvisation. *Choral Journal, 55*(11), 28–42.

Weir, Michele (2015). *ScatAbility* phone app. www.michmusic.com.

Wiehe, Pat (Spring, 2008). The Functions and Value of a Show Choir Parent Organization. *Resound, 31*(3), 9–10.

Zegree, Stephen (2002). *The Complete Guide to Teaching Vocal Jazz.* Dayton, OH: Heritage Music.

Zegree, Steve (2010). *The WOW Factor: How to Create It, Inspire It, and Achieve It.* Milwaukee, WI: Hal Leonard.

Zorn, Jay D. (Spring, 1973). Effectiveness of Chamber Music Ensemble Experience. *Journal of Research in Music Education, 21*(1), 40–47.

11

CHECKLISTS FOR PRACTICAL MATTERS: CONCERTS, FESTIVALS, TRAVEL, TECHNOLOGY, AND THE FIRST YEAR OF TEACHING

Graduates of music education programs are generally well prepared with the musical skills they will need as choral music teachers, but they often find that it is the practical, organizational, and business aspects of the new teaching position for which they feel unprepared. This chapter provides several guidelines for success in the practical matters of concert and festival preparation, travel, technology, and other challenges of the first year of teaching.

CONCERT PROGRAMMING AND PLANNING

Programming Principles

When planning for concerts, choose choral repertoire based on these four criteria:

- high quality
- appropriateness for the age and level of the students
- educational merit
- audience appeal.

After the music has been selected, organize the concert order based on the following guidelines:

- Begin the concert with a piece that will grab the audience's attention.
- Lead to a high point two-thirds of the way through the concert.
- End with something so beautiful that the audience wants to hear more.
- Keep the concert short enough so that the audience leaves wanting more.
- Plan an intermission if the concert is more than one hour, and use the time for major equipment changes.
- Minimize time during choir changes.
- Prepare program notes for the audience that inform them about the music and the educational goals of the choral program.
- From the first to the last piece in the concert, carefully plan where there should be variety and where there should be continuity. Group pieces together with continuity, but keep audience attention through variety. Balance variety and continuity in the following aspects of the music:

  o ensemble order
  o difficulty level
  o tonal centers
  o modes
  o sacred versus secular
  o serious versus light
  o text relationships (language)
  o texture
  o accompaniments
  o voicings
  o tempo
  o meter
  o cultures
  o history
  o movement
  o antiphonal effects.

Long-Term Concert Planning

Once the repertoire has been selected, concert planning involves careful consideration of the time it will take for the singers to learn the music well. One sure-fire way to allow enough preparation time is the following meticulous but successful strategy. For each choir:

• Count the number of measures in all of the pieces.
• Count the total minutes of rehearsals before the concert in which to prepare the pieces.
• Then divide the number of measures by the number of minutes of rehearsals.
• On the calendar, note which measures of each piece need to be covered at each rehearsal in order to be prepared for the performance. Build in extra time for memorization of the music and unexpected interruptions to the rehearsal schedule.

This long-range planning exercise will give a very realistic understanding of how much music needs to be learned per rehearsal, assuring a steady progression to the goal, and avoiding the stress of ill-prepared music at concert time. This schedule can also be used to provide the singers with your expectations for their daily preparedness.

Short-Term Concert Planning

In preparation for the concert, simulate performance characteristics as closely and as many times as possible to reduce anxiety. This can be done by:

• rehearsing in the performance space as many times as feasible, where the aural and visual differences can be distracting
• running the entire concert set without stopping
• practicing quiet and quick concert stage entry and exit
• practicing proper stage presence (no talking between pieces, no touching one's hair or face, no scratching, etc.).

The Final Warm-Up

The final warm-up before the performance should be a familiar one to the singers, with the director focusing on:

• deep breathing
• relaxed but proper posture

- confidence through positive comments
- encouragement to enjoy the performance (Robinson and Althouse, 1995).

With adequate preparation, plenty of simulated performances, and a positive attitude by the director, the choral performance will be a peak experience for the singers and a musical gift to the audience.

SPECIAL CHORAL PERFORMANCES

There are many advantages to having students participate in honor choirs, choir festivals, and choir tours. Choirs often reach their highest levels of achievement in preparation for these events, and individuals will remember their choir trips for a lifetime. There are many guidelines that will assure that festivals and tours provide optimal educational benefits and run smoothly.

Honor Choirs

Honor choirs are made up of individual students from numerous schools selected through an anonymous recorded audition to perform at a state, regional, or national conference of professional music organizations, such as NAfME and ACDA. If selected, students are sent several pieces of music in advance, and are expected to have it prepared in time for a few days of intense rehearsals at the conference site with a well-known honor choir conductor. Conferences often feature a range of honor choirs, which may include children's, middle school, high school, TTB, treble, vocal jazz, and collegiate honor choirs. These experiences offer outstanding growth opportunities for students, and the honor of being chosen for these ensembles is unforgettable.

Festivals, Contests, Competitions, and Clinics

There are many opportunities for secondary school choirs to perform alongside other school choirs in both competitive and non-competitive venues, both at one's home school site and through travel to nearby schools. Each type of performance has the educational value of providing assessment of a choir's strengths and weaknesses, and so choir directors should strive to provide a balance of opportunities for their singers.

- Festivals:

    o   are usually non-competitive
    o   are adjudicated by a panel of experienced choral teachers who provide written scores and recorded comments regarding various aspects of the choral performance
    o   require music to be selected from a specified list
    o   are open to the other performing ensembles to hear
    o   are occasionally called "contests" despite the non-competitive nature of the event
    o   may include choirs combining for a mass number conducted by a guest conductor.

- Clinics:

    o   may be part of a festival where, after an adjudicated performance, one of the choral judges spends a concentrated amount of time working with the choir, or
    o   may include an invitation to a guest conductor to visit your school site and work with your choir (and other invited choirs if a larger event is desirable).

- Competitions:

    o   pit one choir against others to "win"
    o   award engraved trophies or plaques to the winners
    o   include a panel of expert choral judges who provide written scores and recorded comments
    o   are often referred to as "contests"
    o   raise performance standards and provide motivation, but teachers should beware of excessive pressure, time commitments, or unhealthy rivalry among choirs that may interfere with the educational benefits.

Adjudication

As the new choral director prepares the choirs for adjudicated performances, attention must be given to those criteria upon which the choir will be judged. General categories for adjudication include the following, depending on the type of choir and type of festival (ISSMA, 2008):

- Intonation
- Tone Quality
- Balance and Blend
- Breathing Technique
- Note Accuracy
- Rhythmic Accuracy
- Diction and Enunciation
- Dynamics, Phrasing, Expression
- Tempo
- Inter-relationship with the Accompaniment
- Interpretation and Musicianship
- Visual Technique
- Visual Artistry.

Travel

Choir trips provide students with enjoyable learning opportunities to perform for other schools' groups and choral directors, and to enrich the lives of those unable to attend their regular concerts, such as those in senior residencies, hospitals, and elementary schools (Gilbert, 2005). The experience of traveling and seeing new sights together is a bonding and life-broadening one for choristers, and is often the incentive for students to join the choir. Although short tours are advised during the first years of teaching, the following guidelines also apply to extended tours for the veteran music teacher (Olson, 2008):

- Make sure the music is the main reason for the trip.
- Decide on a destination six months to a year ahead of time, and include students and parents in that decision.
- Check your school's rules regarding pre-approved arrangements with companies.
- Check all possible funding opportunities, such as through the school, through grants, and through fundraising activities; expect that students will pay a portion of the costs.
- Book busses from six months to a year in advance, and use a bus company that is approved by the U.S. Department of Defense to ensure high safety standards.
- Use a professional booking agency for longer tours and get recommendations from other trusted choral directors.

- Hold several meetings with parents and students in advance of the trip to provide information and answer questions.
- Parent contact information and medical release forms must be completed and collected.
- Plan for one chaperone per four to eight students.
- Provide plenty of bottled water for everyone.
- Plan to keep students busy during downtime to avoid problems.
- Plan any sightseeing or theme park visits after your performance, if possible.
- Strict rules of conduct and dress code must be enforced, even when not performing.
- Close supervision (unannounced visits, curfew) of students in hotel rooms is essential.

Voice Care

Additional guidelines for vocal health during choir trips follow (Robinson and Althouse, 1995):

- Arrange for the singers to get enough rest the night before a performance by enforcing a "lights-out" time.
- Encourage singers to drink plenty of water, especially in dry hotel rooms.
- Instruct singers to rest their voices while traveling by watching videos, listening to recordings, or sleeping.
- Avoid over-rehearsing the voice; ask for light singing occasionally and plan rehearsal breaks.

TECHNOLOGY FOR CHORAL MUSICIANS

Technology standards state that choral music students should be able to sing using computer-assisted instruction and assessment software, and to practice choral parts using music production and practice/accompaniment software. Teachers also benefit from technology that helps them organize their busy lives. Fortunately, there are many tools and resources available for learning to use technology. Despite the fact that technology advances rapidly, some of the current tools and resources are presented here.

iPads have many uses in the choral classroom, including recording video for self-assessment, listening to a recorded rehearsal, enlarging lyrics for ease in reading, and assisting students with disabilities. They can be used for note-taking by the students and instructor, and can connect to the Internet for YouTube and listening examples in class (see Riley, 2013). They are portable, easy to use, and have a variety of available apps. Some of the useful apps for choral students include:

- PitchMe (chromatic tuner; transcribes detected pitches to notation; helpful for intonation)
- Virtuoso (piano for pitch reference)
- GarageBand (for chordal accompaniment)
- Cleartune (chromatic tuner)
- Epic Chromatic tuner
- Metronome
- Steinway metronome
- forScore (music reader)
- Pocketscore (can store, edit, transcribe, play, and export scores)
- *Do-Re-Mi* Ear Training (portable solfege practice tool)
- LaDiDa (creates accompaniment to match singing)
- Vocal Training (provides voice lessons and tips)
- Songify (turns speech into music)
- Talkapella (turns talking into a cappella harmony)
- QuickVoice Recorder (for audio and video-recording)
- Notes, Calendar, Reminder (for organization).

More information on new apps, and on grants for purchasing tablet computers, can be found on the websites for NAfME (www.nafme.org), the Association for Technology in Music Instruction (ATMI) (www.atmimusic.com) and the Technology Institute for Music Education (TI:ME) (www.ti-me.org).

Cloud-based technology also has numerous applications to the choral classroom (see Doebele, 2012). By storing and accessing music files on a remote server or network (that is, "in the cloud") we can listen to them anywhere we have Internet access, eliminating the need to transport CDs to class or have extra hard drive space to store digital recordings. Some cloud-based music resources that are convenient and cost-effective are the following:

- Amazon Cloud (www.amazon.com/clouddrive)
- Google Play (play.google.com)

- iCloud (www.apple.com/icloud)
- Pandora Radio (www.pandora.com)
- Spotify (www.spotify.com)
- YouTube (www.youtube.com).

Technology Resources for Music Teachers

Rudolf, T.E., Richmond, F., Mash, D., Webster, P., Bauer, W.I. and Walls, K. (2005). *Technology Strategies for Music Education*, 2nd ed. Wyncote, PA: TI:ME.

Williams, D.B. and Webster, P.R. (2008). *Experiencing Music Technology*, 3rd ed. Boston, MA: Schirmer Cengage Learning.

FINAL WORDS OF WISDOM

And so this book comes to a close. You are now looking forward to student teaching, to applying for an instructional license, and to landing your first choral music teaching position. There will be challenges that your college coursework could not have completely prepared you for because each teaching position, each school, and indeed each class of students is different.

Student Teaching

A successful student teaching experience predicts a successful music teaching career. The following advice for choral student teachers is worth heeding (Schneider, 2015):

- "Effective teaching is composed of 50 percent people skills and 50 percent musical skills" (p. 51). To prepare for student teaching, take advantage of opportunities to work with and manage people towards a goal.
- Be proactive and communicate with the cooperating teacher several times before the first day of student teaching; find out how much the cooperating teacher will allow you to teach.
- Respect the fact that accepting a student teacher adds to the everyday demands that the cooperating teacher faces.
- Have a goal of planning and executing a concert from start to finish, with complete control of at least one ensemble.

- Be professional at school and in public: Dress like a teacher, do not engage in social media with students, purge anything from your social media that could appear unprofessional.

The First Year of Teaching

Advice for your first year of teaching (Bumgarner, 2015) comes from choral teachers with decades of experience.

- Don't expect to be "Teacher of the Year." If you complete the first year and want to come back the next year, you've been successful!
- Master classroom management: know how to get students focused and engaged.
- Network with other teachers to call on for help when needed.
- Set high standards for repertoire, student behavior, and work ethic.
- Make sure your students know that you care about them.
- Don't be "friends" on social media with students; never be alone with a student.
- All expectations, calendar activities, and performances need to be approved (by music staff, principal, and athletic director) and posted well before the school year starts in order to avoid conflict.
- Hold choir auditions before Spring Break for the following year.
- Advocate for and actively demonstrate the importance of choral music in the school.
- Select repertoire for the realistic level of your choir to avoid frustration.
- Begin warm-ups or start a notation assignment as soon as the bell rings.
- Involve students in discussions or reflective writings about the music being studied or about other music in their lives.
- Take time to nurture yourself through your own music, your family and friends, diet, exercise, and sleep when needed, even when school planning isn't finished. It never is!
- Protect your voice by using varied pitch frequencies and dynamic levels when speaking. Also, "conductors who routinely

sing during . . . rehearsal, particularly outside their normal voice range, are more susceptible to hoarseness, vocal nodules, vocal fold hemorrhages, or permanent vocal injury" (Schwartz, 2009, p. 307).

- When a conflict with another teacher or administrator arises, try to consider their point of view, stay positive and composed, and resolve the issue face-to-face (rather than in an email) and in private.
- Find a way to regularly communicate expectations to parents, but don't overwhelm them with more than one email message per week.
- Students are often emotionally attached to the previous choral teacher. Handle that with respect, sensitivity, and care. Don't make drastic changes the first year.
- Be kind to everyone, including all school staff and parents; express gratitude.
- Admit your misunderstandings and mistakes.
- Brainstorm about ways to collaborate with teachers in other disciplines.
- At the end of each rehearsal, quickly write down what needs to be worked on at the next rehearsal.
- Remember that most students don't join choir just for the music, but especially for the music teacher.
- Find an organized way to file all paperwork and musical scores.
- Get out of your classroom regularly and greet students in the hallways; visit feeder schools and conduct warm-ups or sectionals there.

Mentoring

When you encounter challenges, you will have your university professors, fellow teachers, and administrators to call upon for solutions. In addition, many states now assign every new teacher with a certified mentor teacher, who can be enormously helpful in supporting you through some of the adjustment phases of the first year and helping you to fulfill your potential. ACDA also provides a mentor program (https://mentoring.acda.org/) for ACDA members. Seek out and sign up for a mentor who is prepared to be a motivator, a resource, a supporter, and a coach for you in the following areas (Blosser, 2016):

- Running a choral program

  o maintaining a budget
  o concert attire
  o accompanist considerations
  o communication with parents and students
  o auditions for a tiered program
  o building a performance calendar
  o programming a concert
  o tours

- Advocacy for your program

  o how to talk to administration
  o dealing with traditions
  o excellence in music

- State-required programs, such as edTPA, RESA, and SLOs
- Personal considerations

  o archiving work
  o social media and students
  o healthy work–life balance.

A few hard bumps in the teaching road are inevitable, especially in the first few years, but each one is a lesson in how to be a better teacher. As you strive to become a better choral musician and teacher through conferences, summer study, a mentor relationship, and networking, the rewards of teaching music to impressionable young singers increase exponentially, and your professional life becomes exceptionally satisfying and meaningful.

BRAINTEASER 11-1: CREATING A CHORAL CONCERT AND PROGRAM

Create an imaginary middle school and/or high school choral concert program complete with names of the school, town, concert date, repertoire, singers, accompanists, etc. You may spend up to $800 on music to be performed at a spring concert featuring all of the department's choirs. You must create at least one select/advanced choir, one non-select choir, and one treble or low voice choir. This concert should be approximately one hour in length. Be realistic in regard to the ability level of the singers you might expect or hope to have at your first position. This project is broken down into several parts:

1. Select music for your program. Complete and submit the Concert Planning Grid (see Table 11.1), which should help you realize some aspects of your selection process.
2. Submit a *music order list*. Make certain that it includes titles, composers'/arrangers' names, voicings, publishers, catalog numbers, price per copy, and total price of order.
3. Write a *press release* that would be sent to newspapers and radio and TV stations.
4. Put together the *concert program*, including a cover design. This should be a complete program with singers' names, concert selections, and other important items (e.g., it is customary to include a brief list of "thank yous," especially to district and building administrators). The program will be evaluated on neatness, creativity in design, accuracy, and readability. An example is provided in Figures 11.1 through 11.3.

Table 11.1 Concert Planning Grid

Concert Title: **Theme (if one):**

Title/Composer	Tempo	Meter	Key/Mode	Language	Voicing	Accomp.	Period/Style	Length

Willowbrook High School

presents the 18th annual

Spring Showcase Concert

Tuesday, May 19, 2020

At Seven O'clock in the Evening

Figure 11.1 Concert Program Cover

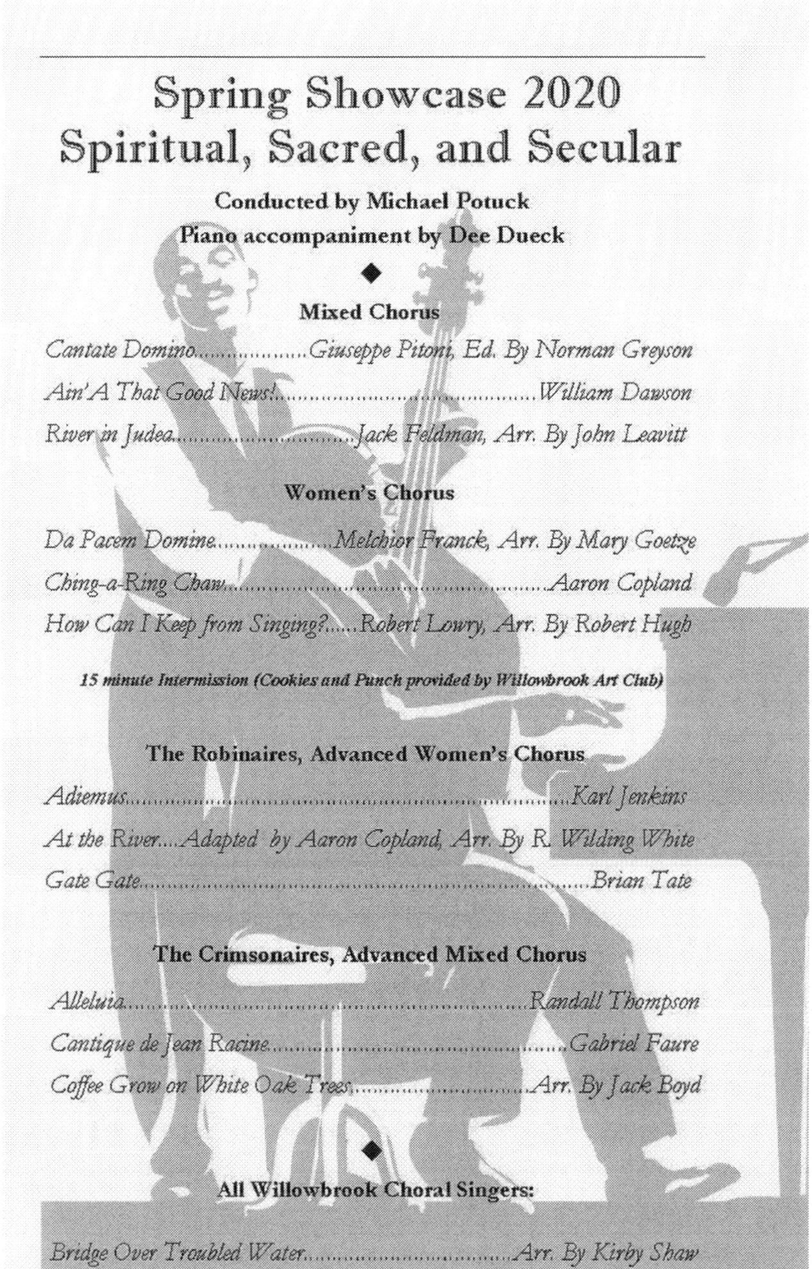

Spring Showcase 2020
Spiritual, Sacred, and Secular

Conducted by Michael Potuck
Piano accompaniment by Dee Dueck

◆

Mixed Chorus

Cantate Domino.....................*Giuseppe Pitoni, Ed. By Norman Greyson*

Ain' A That Good News!.................................*William Dawson*

River in Judea...............................*Jack Feldman, Arr. By John Leavitt*

Women's Chorus

Da Pacem Domine.....................*Melchior Franck, Arr. By Mary Goetze*

Ching-a-Ring Chaw..*Aaron Copland*

How Can I Keep from Singing?......*Robert Lowry, Arr. By Robert Hugh*

15 minute Intermission (Cookies and Punch provided by Willowbrook Art Club)

The Robinaires, Advanced Women's Chorus

Adiemus...*Karl Jenkins*

At the River....*Adapted by Aaron Copland, Arr. By R. Wilding White*

Gate Gate..*Brian Tate*

The Crimsonaires, Advanced Mixed Chorus

Alleluia...*Randall Thompson*

Cantique de Jean Racine...................................*Gabriel Faure*

Coffee Grow on White Oak Trees............................*Arr. By Jack Boyd*

◆

All Willowbrook Choral Singers:

Bridge Over Troubled Water.......................*Arr. By Kirby Shaw*

Figure 11.2 Concert Program Pages 2 to 3

Mixed Chorus

Soprano:	Alto:	Tenors:	Basse/Baritone:
Janie Aswell	Ashley Aberfelt	Sam Adams	Rick Brogan
Kim Barrington	Bekka Crenkerton	Herbie Hancock	Jimmy Brommer
Julia Kendricks	Zula Etherbert	Robert Harrison	Robbie Casters
Maria Lupos	Yolanda Gooth	Abraham Lincoln	Michael Eziks
Margaret Pedlow	Kimberly Lork	Richie Noorman	Darren Etman
Tenisha Pootant	Samantha Martinez	Gregory Potts	Kyle Falk
Carla Ramon	Rain Potren	Adam Shaff	Rob Loner
Simone Sutton	Shania Twain	Ann Simon	Mitchell Moonchild
Mary Weston		Mark Zeeger	

Women's Chorus

Soprano I:	Soprano II:	Alto I:	Alto II:
Brooke Garner	Trisha Avery	Samantha Appleseed	Megan Birdland
Jamie Hilton	Erin Barker	Brooke Brooner	Laura Comport
Sara Milton	Jessie Jokersmith	Ashley Caterson	Sarah Davies
Gretchen Numan	Meghan Lockerbee	Nancy Davers	Susie Mossport
Brittney Soreman	Nicole Pollard	Helen Hunt	Belinda Quimby
Maria Westbird	Jenny Rusters	Sara Sassman	Betsy Westman
		Sabrina Zorkin	Katinka Yorturit

Robinaires, Advanced Women's Chorus

Soprano I:	Soprano II:	Alto I:	Alto II:
Julia Asher	Ina Bass	Laura Applebee	Jenna Adams
Bethany Brewton	Kristin Kennedy	Maggie Banter	Sarah Barner
Carneron Conner	Nancy Jokers	Tina Grims	Caroline Casters
Richelle Ditoro	Brittney Jors	Anna Houser	Amy Dugger
Elisha Mountain	Penelope Mothers	Erica Janners	Susie Maniton
Sara Nanter	Michelle Poplars	Queen Latifah	Christina Sommer
Tara Rooney		Sarah Rinner	Tara Zoonker

Crimsonaires, Advanced Mixed Chorus

Soprano:	Alto:	Tenor:	Bass/Baritone:
Lisa Acur	Mandy Ashton	Jan Apers	Sam Bronter
Helen Broadway	Ashley Conner	Zack Binsworth	Heath Catz
Nicole Johnson	Hope Copeland	Ryan Blaner	Ryu Hyabusa
Amy Kidder	Grace Efferton	Blake Conners	Kevin Isthman
Jenna Moon	Kate Mossberg	Micah Dimmer	Brian Jackson
Katie Nant	Kerry Motzter	Timothy Efforts	Bryan Jockson
Kara Overt	Bethany Noting	Chris Gemmins	Smith Kackler
Sarah Ponch	Debra Potsan	Jon Jimmers	Ron Levler
Wendy Sooty	Mary Sasstrich	Gregory Locke	Barry Manilow
Lisa Turner	Kristin Wower	Mark Potron	Abe Porter
Kimmy Zork	Sara Zeen	Rerrington Steele	
	Cindy Zorter	Kevin Yorker	

Figure 11.2 continued

Special Thanks to....

Superintendent *Bob Marlow*

Principal *Ted Grogan*

Vice Principal *Janet Jackson*

Willowbrook H.S. Janitors *Peg Kelly, John Jimmers, Ron Fromer, Ken Greespon, Jane Biggs, Rick Ronson*

Sound/Lights *Michael Jackson and Wayne Jackson*

Ticket Sales *Barbara Potuck*

Thanks to our Donors!

Wal-market

Willowbrook Arts Club

Hacienda Mexican Restaurant

F.C. Soccer Club

Walt Dairy

Dan Kozlow

Crescent Doughnuts

Priceless Treasures

Choir Boosters

Linway Movie Theater

Mark and Jane Goldsmith

Dr. Patrice Madura

Julia Mercury

Randy Jackson

Figure 11.3   Concert Program Back Cover

References

Blosser, Amy Johnston (2016). *Mentoring the New Choral Conductor: Essential Tips for the First Five Years*. Presentation at the ACDA Central Division Professional Conference, Chicago, IL.

Bumgarner, Amanda (2015). Notes for Success (Part 1): Advice for the First-Year Choral Teacher. *Choral Journal, 55*(10), 8–17.

Bumgarner, Amanda (2015). Notes for Success (Part 2): Advice for the First-Year Choral Teacher. *Choral Journal, 56*(1), 28–36.

Bumgarner, Amanda (2015). Notes for Success (Part 3): Advice for the First-Year Choral Teacher. *Choral Journal, 56*(2), 32–43.

Doebele, Alexa (2012). Music in the Cloud for the Modern Choral Director. *Choral Journal, 52*(5), 91–95.

Gilbert, Nina (May 2005). Virtual Roundtable Part II: More Advice from Choir Tour Professionals. *Choral Journal, 45*(10), 37–54.

Indiana State School Music Association (ISSMA) (2008). *Music Festivals Manual*. Indianapolis, IN: ISSMA.

Olson, Catherine Applefeld (August, 2008). Music in Motion. *Teaching Music, 16*(1), 34–47.

Riley, Patricia (2013). Teaching, Learning, and Living with iPads. *Music Educators Journal, 100*(1), 81–86.

Robinson, Russell and Althouse, Jay (1995). *The Complete Choral Warm-Up Book*. Van Nuys, CA: Alfred.

Rudolf, T.E., Richmond, F., Mash, D., Webster, P., Bauer, W.I. and Walls, K. (2005). *Technology Strategies for Music Education*, 2nd ed. Wyncote, PA: TI:ME.

Schneider, Sally (2015). Preparing for Classroom Success: Advice for Choral Student Teachers. *Choral Journal, 55*(10), 51–52.

Schwartz, Sandra M. (2009). Voice Range Profiles of Middle School and High School Choral Directors. *Journal of Research in Music Education, 56*(4), 293–309.

Williams, D.B. and Webster, P.R. (2008). *Experiencing Music Technology*, 3rd ed. Boston, MA: Schirmer Cengage Learning.

APPENDIX A
SCALE AND ARPEGGIO FINGERINGS

Scales and arpeggios need to be performed with a pianistic fingering that allows for fluent execution of the exercise. The determination of what is an acceptable fingering is at the discretion of the instructor. The fingerings below are widely accepted and recommended.

MAJOR Scale			Tonic Arpeggio		Dom 7 Arpeggio	
Black-key groups						
D–flat/	RH	2312341	RH	412	RH	4123
C#	LH	3214321	LH	214	LH	4321
G–flat/	RH	2341231	RH	1 23	RH	2341
F#	LH	4321321	LH	(1)32	LH	4321
B	RH	1 231234	RH	"	RH	1 234
	LH	(1)321432	LH	"	LH	(1)432
C Major fingering						
C	RH	1 231234	RH	1 23	RH	"
	LH	(1)432132	LH	(1)42	LH	"
G	RH	"	RH	"	RH	"
	LH	"	LH	"	LH	"
D	RH	"	RH	1 23	RH	"
	LH	"	LH	(1)32	LH	"
A	RH	"	RH	"	RH	"
	LH	"	LH	"	LH	"
E	RH	"	RH	"	RH	"
	LH	"	LH	"	LH	"
A–flat	RH	3412312	RH	412	RH	4123
	LH	3214321	LH	214	LH	2143

Others

E–flat	RH 3123412	RH "	RH "
	LH 3214321	LH "	LH "
B–flat	RH 4123123	RH 412	RH 4123
	LH 3214321	LH 321	LH 3214
F	RH 1 234123	RH 1 23	RH 1234
	LH (1)432132	LH (1)42	LH 3214

HARMONIC MINOR
C major fingering

C	RH 1 231234	RH 1 23	RH 1 234
	LH (1)432132	LH (1)42	LH (1)432
D	RH "	RH "	RH "
	LH "	LH "	LH "
G	RH "	RH "	RH "
	LH "	LH "	LH "
A	RH "	RH "	RH "
	LH "	LH "	LH "
E	RH "	RH "	RH "
	LH "	LH "	LH "
G#/	RH 3412312	RH 412	RH 4123
A–flat	LH 3214321	LH 214	LH 2143
C#/	RH "	RH "	RH 4123
D–Flat	LH "	LH "	LH 4321
F#/	RH 3412312	RH "	RH 2341
G–Flat	LH 4321321	LH "	LH 4321

Black-key groups

B–flat	RH 4123123	RH 231	RH 4123
	LH 2132143	LH 321	LH 3214
E–flat/	RH 3123412	RH 1 23	RH 4123
D#	LH 2143213	LH (1)42	LH 2143

Others

F	RH 1 234123	RH "	RH 1234
	LH (1)432132	LH "	LH 3214
B	RH 1 231234	RH "	RH 1 234
	LH (1)321432	LH "	LH (1)432

The above fingerings are to be extrapolated for the appropriate number of octaves—if a (1) occurs in the LH, the student is expected to substitute the fifth finger at the beginning of the exercise, and the RH requires the use of the fifth finger at the top.

APPENDIX B

SCORE EXCERPTS FOR PRACTICE

Motet, *Ave verum corpus*

K 618, Baden, June 17 1791

Wolfgang Amadé Mozart
(1756–1791)

2

A virgin most pure

English traditional carol
arr. Charles Wood (1866 - 1926)

1. A virgin most pure, as the prophets do tell, Hath brought forth a baby, as
2. In Bethlehem Jewry a city there was, Where Joseph and Mary to-
3. But when they had entered the city so fair, A number of people so

it hath befell; To be our Redeemer from death, hell, and sin, Which Adam's trans-
gether did pass, And there to be taxed with many one mo, For Caesar com-
mighty was there, That Joseph and Mary, whose substance was small, Could find in the

gression had wrapped us in.
manded the same should be so. *Aye, and therefore be merry; Re- joice, and be you*
inn there no lodging at all.

mer- ry; Set sorrow aside; Christ Jesus our Saviour was born at this tide.

Da pacem

à trois voix égales

Ch. Gounod

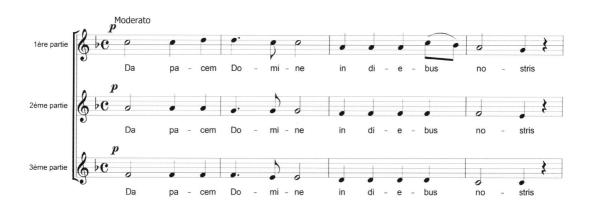

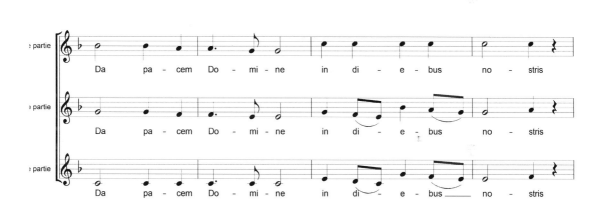

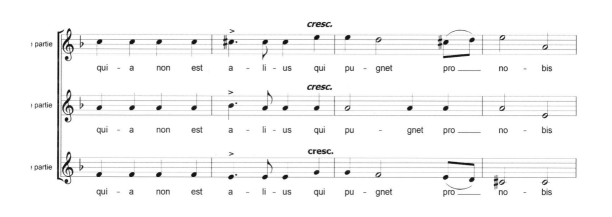

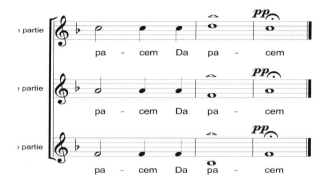

partie

pa – cem Da pa – cem

partie

pa – cem Da pa – cem

partie

pa – cem Da pa – cem

All Lust und Freud (Gagliarda)

SATB a cappella

Hans Leo Hassler
(1564-1612)

SOURCE: Lustgarten, Deutche Lieder zu vier, fünf, sechs uch acht Stimmen (1601)
(collected edition published by Breitkopf & Härtel, 1887)
NOTES: Some archaic text has been modernized. Note values have been halved.
Text underlay appears erroneous in Breitkopf edition, at m. 19 (repeat, v. 1) text begins
"mich dunckt ich ..." rather than "merck mich..."

Edited by Rafael Ornes

ed. 6/11/99

Appendix C

The International Phonetic Alphabet and Word Stress

IPA SYMBOLS FOR AMERICAN VOWEL SOUNDS

Vowel	IPA Symbol	Sound
A	[ɑ]	father
A	[æ]	cat
E	[ɛ]	bet
E	[i]	street
I	[I]	fit
O	[ɔ]	lawn
U	[^]	cut
U	[u]	boot
U	[U]	book
Unstressed schwa	[ə]	ros<u>e</u>s, the, a
Diphthongs:		
	[ai]	night
	[au]	now
	[ɛi]	stay
	[ɔi]	boy
	[ou]	go
	[iu]	few

IPA AND WORD STRESS FOR MOZART'S *AVE VERUM CORPUS*

LATIN IPA SYMBOLS FOR VOWELS

A	E	I	O	U
[ɑ]	[ɛ]	[i]	[ɔ]	[u]

```
1 2 1  3   1  3      1  3    3  2  13 1  2  3
Ave verum corpus    natum de Maria Virgine
```

```
1 2 1    3     2 3 12   3   1 2   3  1 2  3
Vere passum      immolatum in cruce pro homine
```

```
1 3  2 3  2  3 1 3  2 3  1  3 1  2 3
cujus latus perforatum unda fluxit sanguine
```

```
2  3  1 3    1  2 13
Esto nobis praegustatum
```

```
2    1 3 2 1  2 3
in mortis examine
```

1 = primary stress, 2-secondary stress, 3 = unstressed

Appendix D
The Purposes of ACDA

The purposes of ACDA as stated at https://acda.org/page.asp?page=acda_history:

- To foster and promote choral singing, which will provide artistic, cultural, and spiritual experiences for the participants.
- To foster and promote the finest types of choral music to make these experiences possible.
- To foster and encourage rehearsal procedures conducive to attaining the highest possible level of musicianship and artistic performance.
- To foster and promote the organization and development of choral groups of all types in schools and colleges.
- To foster and promote the development of choral music in the church and synagogue.
- To foster and promote the organization and development of choral societies in cities and communities.
- To foster and promote understanding of choral music as an important medium of contemporary artistic expression.
- To foster and promote significant research in the field of choral music.
- To foster and encourage choral composition of superior quality.
- To cooperate with all organizations dedicated to the development of musical culture in America.
- To foster and promote international exchange programs involving performing groups, conductors, and composers.
- To disseminate professional news and information about choral music.

APPENDIX E
NAfME MISSION, VISION, AND VALUES

The NAfME mission, vision, and values as stated at http://www.nafme.org/about/mission-and-goals/:

Mission:

To advance music education by promoting
the understanding and making of music by all

Vision:

Leading the world in music education, empowering
generations to create, perform, and respond to music

Values:

Community, Stewardship, Comprehensiveness,
Inclusion and Equity, and Innovation

Index

Page numbers in **bold** refer to Tables and page numbers in *italic* refer to Music Examples